I AM CALLED ALBAN

The Story of St Alban and His Legacy

Laurence Attewill

The Choir Press

Copyright © 2023 Laurence Attewill

All rights reserved. No part of this publication may be reproduced or transmitted in any form or by any means, electronic or mechanical including photocopying, recording or any information storage or retrieval system, without prior permission in writing from the publishers.

The right of Laurence Attewill to be identified as the author of this work has been asserted by him in accordance with the Copyright, Designs and Patents Act 1988

First published in the United Kingdom in 2023 by
The Choir Press

ISBN 978–1–78963–346–7

Disclaimer

Whilst every effort has been made to seek owner permission to use certain images this has not always been possible. The author apologises for any omissions in this respect.

For my father
Leonard John Spencer Attewill

Lay Canon and Cathedral Warden
1981–88

and for my wife
Carolyn Mary Attewill
who died shortly before the publication of this book

Contents

Preface	vii
Acknowledgements	ix
Part One: The First Millennium	1
1 Background	3
2 The Martyrdom of Alban	21
3 The Anglo-Saxon Transition	41
4 Political Consolidation, Religious Conversion	52
5 The Saxon Monastery of St Alban	60
6 The Norman Abbey	79
7 Conclusion to Part One	88
Part One Timeline	92
Part Two: The Medieval Monastery	93
8 Historical Setting	95
9 The St Albans Monastery	108
10 The Fruits of Their Labours	132
11 The End of St Albans Monastery	166
Part Two Timeline	181
Part Three: From Parish Church to Cathedral	183
12 The Parish Church of St Alban in a Period of Religious Turmoil	184
13 The Long Eighteenth Century – The Great Slumber	196
14 Rebirth	206
Part Three Timeline	231
Epilogue	233
Index	236

Preface

Why another book on St Alban?

Sometime in the third century it is widely believed that a man was executed in Britain for his faith in Christianity. Nothing is known with certainty, but the man's name may have been Alban, who was probably a Romano-British citizen resident in Verulamium. We don't know his family background or his profession or exactly when in the third century the martyrdom happened. What we do know is that this martyrdom, whether real or mythical, was fervently believed by an initially small but steadily growing body of Christians, eventually giving rise to the biggest and most illustrious medieval monastery in England and subsequently to the cathedral we have at St Albans today.

This story, sufficiently dramatic in itself, is set in the context of tectonic events that shaped the world that we still live with today: the collapse of the Roman Empire and the secession of Britain; the mass immigration of Germanic peoples leading to the birth of a new nation, England, and her language; the rise of Christianity and its contribution to the legacy of western liberalism.

In this book I have attempted to recount the whole story – starting in Roman Britain, the background to Alban's martyrdom, right up to the establishment of St Albans Cathedral in the beginning of the twentieth century. The main events of this narrative are well known: Alban's martyrdom, the flowering and eventual dissolution of the medieval monastery and the rebirth of the old abbey church as a cathedral. But it is only by exploring the less well-documented periods between these events – the century or more that elapsed between the martyrdom and the arrival of Germanus in 429, the possibility of the survival of British Christianity in Verulamium during the coming of the Saxons in the fifth and sixth centuries, the foundation of the Saxon monastery and finally the precarious survival of the abbey church in the long eighteenth century – that the case for the continuity of veneration of St Alban can be examined and supported.

While there is an extensive literature covering the history of St Albans and its abbey from Norman times to the present day, the story of Alban and his legacy in the first millennium has been poorly served since the publication of Rushbrook Williams' *A History of St Albans Abbey* in 1917. True, there is no shortage of specialist single-discipline academic papers on the relevant archaeology and early Church history, but I haven't come across a recent single-volume account, for the general reader, of the origins and martyrdom of Alban and the subsequent cult of St Alban and its survival through the Anglo-Saxon transition, the foundation of the Saxon monastery of St Albans and its final destruction and reconstruction by the Normans. Part One of this book is intended to fill this gap.

I have tried to provide a similarly broad-based account in Part Two, which carries the story on from the foundation of the Norman monastery through to its dissolution in the reign of Henry VIII. This period – the Middle Ages – of over 400 years contains as much drama as does the first millennium, and it is against this background that I have described in some detail the rise and fall of what was, at its peak, the prime monastery in England. Part Three of the book covers the events that saw the humbled abbey church, which narrowly escaped destruction, rescued by the townspeople to survive 300 years of service as a parish church. There was, however, no way that a small and not particularly prosperous town of St Albans could adequately look after its huge church, so by the beginning of the nineteenth century the Abbey, as it has always been affectionately known, faced collapse. The story ends with an account of how this disaster was averted and the abbey became the cathedral of the diocese of Hertfordshire and Bedfordshire.

As a non-academic non-historian I haven't, nor was qualified to have, written the book in a traditional academic style. Rather it is modelled, if anything, on Rushbrook Williams' *Story of St Albans Abbey*: serious and detailed where appropriate, set in a description of the broader context. I have not shrunk from either conjecture or from an occasional humorous aside, and I hope these excursions will be forgiven. Above all I have tried to impart the supreme interest of the story.

Acknowledgements

I might as well come clean at the outset that I'm neither a historian by education nor even an academic by profession, but a retired civil engineer. My only qualification for writing this book is a profound love of St Albans and a fascination with, and a belief in the centrality of, history. St Albans Abbey formed an important part of my boyhood: I was a cathedral chorister and attended the adjacent school. Although I have not lived in St Albans for many years, it still refuses to let me go – not just family connections, which are strong, but odd reminders, such as that of being assigned rooms, as an undergraduate, in the St Albans quad at Merton College Oxford. For my weekly shop in Wallingford I park the car in the St Albans carpark, close to the site of the priory, once a daughter house of St Albans. I even get a *frisson* of excitement when I see the signpost to St Albans on the M25.

As an amateur writer I am more indebted to historian friends who gave support and advice than would normally have been the case. In particular I wish to thank two Mertonian colleagues, both of whom read history, for their encouragement and support: David Ure and Sir David Madden. I also wish to acknowledge the assistance given to me by Jon Mein of the St Albans and Hertfordshire Architectural and Archaeological Society, Rob Piggot, the St Albans Cathedral archivist and Stephen de Silva, the chief cathedral guide. My cousin, the Rev'd John Tapper, former vicar of Folkestone and the Very Rev'd Keith Jones, a family friend and former sub-dean of St Albans, both kindly provided valuable ecclesiastical oversight. Colin Donnelly, then a PhD student of Professor Diarmaid MacCulloch, carried out a careful scrutiny of Parts One and Two with commendable forbearance. Lastly, my thanks to my family and in particular to my sister, Jan Fielden, for her advice and to my late wife, Caddy, for her enthusiastic support, encouragement and artistic contributions. Finally I would like to thank Miles Bailey and his team in the Choir Press for their expertise in producing this book.

The Shrine of St Alban

PART ONE

The First Millennium

1

Background

Our greatest advantage in coping with tribes so powerful is that they do not act in concert... thus while they fight singly they are all conquered.

Tacitus, writing about the British in his *Life of Agricola*

Introduction

This chapter provides a broad high-level description of the Roman occupation of Britain, which formed the backdrop to the martyrdom of Alban which is recounted in Chapter 2.

The Roman city of Verulamium, the forerunner to St Albans, situated some 20 miles north-west of London, is central to the Alban story. It was, in its prime, the second Roman city in the province of Britannia and if it had not been so important it would not have been a *municipium* – a Roman city with self-governing status – and Alban would have been tried, sentenced and executed elsewhere, probably in the capital, London, or Londinium as it then was. Verulamium was established by the Romans adjacent to or within Verlamion, a late Iron Age oppidum or township which served as the capital of the Catuvellauni tribe. By the time of the Roman invasion in AD 43, the Catuvellauni had entered into what was effectively a non-aggression pact with the Romans, which resulted, after the conquest, in relatively favourable terms for the upper-class Catuvellaunians and the consequent prosperity and long-term sustainability of Verulamium.

The Iron Age

Verlamion flourished in the late Iron Age in Britain (880 BC to the first century AD) which was a period of steadily increasing prosperity and population growth, driven primarily by technological advances associated with the use of iron and by warmer, less extreme weather[1], leading to the

---

[1] Nicholas Crane: *The Making of the British Landscape*, p. 174.

abandonment of hill fortifications in favour of lowland settlements in the south and east[2].

Climate change in the Iron Age affected all of Europe but its beneficial effect was mostly felt in north Europe, including Britain, where summers hitherto had been too short, too wet and too cool for ideal arable farming. From about 200 BC summers became warmer, longer and drier so that crop yields increased, the range of crops that could be grown widened and marginal boggy land became viable. Climate has always been changing but between 100 BC and AD 200 – a period known as the Roman Optimum – the climate not only became warmer but as important more stable, due to a combination of relatively low levels of both volcanic and solar activity[3]. This climate change was exploited through the technological advances made possible by the use of iron and especially the introduction of iron-tipped ploughshares capable of ripping through the heavy clays that characterised much of lowland Britain.

There was therefore a shift in settlement patterns, resulting in the abandonment of hill fortifications in favour of lowland settlements in the south and east. By the end of the Iron Age much of the forest cover in the south and east of Britain had been cleared and replaced with agriculture, both pastoral and arable. This change in land use made possible, by the end of the pre-Roman period, an increase in food production capable of supporting a substantial and well-established population: this led to the possibility of regional and international trade.

Tribal groupings and corresponding warrior elites evolved with increased prosperity and population growth and for the first time in our history names of tribes and their leaders emerge. With increased prosperity came increased trade and immigration from the near continent, especially the Germanic-speaking Belgic tribes of north-east Gaul[4]. The tribe that occupied the area north of the River Thames was the Catuvellauni, which grew to be one of the most powerful in Britain.

---

[2] Francis Pryor: *Britain BC*, p. 420.
[3] McCormick et al: *Climate Change During and After the Roman Empire*
[4] Stephan Oppenheimer: *The Origins of the British*, p. 318

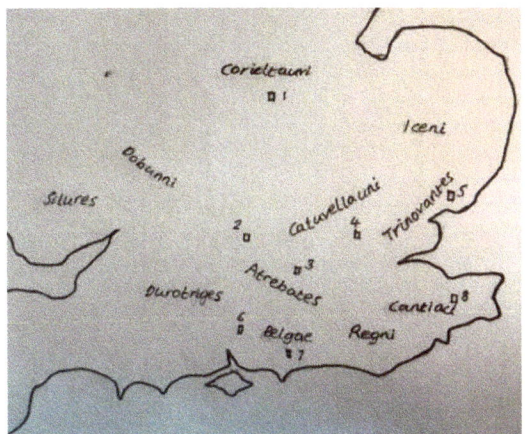

Tribes and Oppida in Southern Iron Age Britain

	Celtic/Roman name	*Modern name*
1	Ratae Corieltauvorum	Leicester
2	Dorcic	Dorchester-on-Thames
3	Calleva Arbrebatum	Silchester
4	Verlamion	St Albans
5	Camulodunum	Colchester
6	Venta Belganum	Winchester
7	Noviomagus Reginorum	Chichester
8	Durovernum Cantaicorum	Canterbury

The Catuvellauni and Julius Caesar

In the mid-first century BC Julius Caesar, a Roman consul and general, was engaged in subduing the Gallic tribes who were supported by warriors from east of the Rhine and from Britain. Once northern Gaul was pacified he turned his attention to Britain, partly to counter the threat they posed to a Roman Gaul, partly because of the possibility of tapping Britain's mineral wealth and partly to advance his political career[5]. In 55 BC he mounted an expeditionary force to the Kent coast but was beset by logistical difficulties and adverse weather, which led to his withdrawal.

He returned the following year with a much larger force – about 30,000 men – and a better planned campaign in which he penetrated southern Britain. After crossing the Thames he advanced on the Catuvellauni and the Trinovantes heartlands. The meaning of Catuvellauni was 'excelling in battle', and such was their reputation. Under their warlord Cassivellaunus they mounted a formidable

---

[5] David Mattingly: *An Imperial Possession*, p. 64.

opposition but eventually were forced to surrender and agree terms, which would have included the surrender of hostages. These, after suitable re-education in the mainland empire, may well have subsequently returned to Britain, where they would have wielded considerable pro-Roman influence.†

After the departure of Roman forces the power of the Catuvellauni expanded until their territory extended from the North Sea in the east to the Atrebates tribe, based at Silchester, in the west and from the Iceni in the north east to the Canti in the south east. During this time contacts and trade links with the Belgae of the near continent steadily increased and Cassivellaunus' successor, Tasciovanus, began to mint high-denomination coins in Verlamion as well as in the seat of his tribe at Camulodunum[6].

Coins minted at Verlamion in about 25 BC. (With permission of wildwinds.com, ex Southeby auction 1999.)

Verlamion

These trends led to the coalescence of economic activity into centres of population and industry generally known as oppida – essentially resembling townships rather than towns – in that they were organic rather than planned, and populated extensively rather than intensively. One of these oppida, Verlamion, grew to be one of the largest and most important north of the River Thames. From 25 BC it served as the capital of the Catuvellauni tribe, whose land included all of what is now Hertfordshire, Bedfordshire, Buckinghamshire, the south east of Oxfordshire and the south of Cambridgeshire[7].

Verlamion was situated at the crossroads of two ancient trackways that subsequently became known as Akeman Street, an east–west track from Cirencester to Colchester, and Watling Street connecting Canterbury,

---

† David Mattingly: *An Imperial Possession*, p. 71
[6] Rosalind Niblett: *Verulamium*, p. 43.
[7] Francis Pryor: *Britain BC*, p. 415.

London and Wroxeter. This site was also at a crossing point of the River Ver, then a much bigger river than it is today.

The first site to be investigated in Verlamion, at Prae Wood, was excavated by Sir Mortimer Wheeler in the 1930s but since then it has become apparent that Prae Wood was just one of a number of sites making up the oppidum[8]. These were mostly situated on the edge of the higher ground above the river valley, convenient for grazing sheep and cattle on the plateau with arable farming on the upper valley slopes. Metal working, which required copious water supplies, would have been situated close to the river. Because the acidity of the soil on the plateau is not favourable to the preservation of pottery or other artefacts, and because all the buildings would have been constructed of timber, the layout and the appearance of Verlamion is largely conjectural. What remains are a number of enclosures – initially irregular in plan but later rectangular – formed by extensive ditch and embankment earthworks.

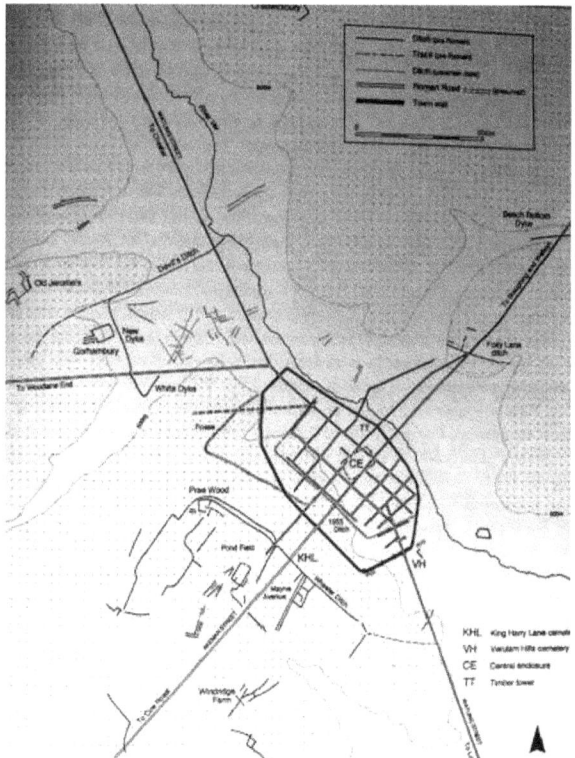

Plan of Verlamion. (After Niblett: Verulamium.)

---

[8] Rosalind Niblett: *Verulamium*, p. 37.

One enclosure, known as the Central Enclosure, was situated, atypically, in the Ver valley bottom and subsequently formed the site of the forum of the Roman city. From the finds of coin mould boards it seems likely that this enclosure was the site of Tasciovanus' mint, but it has also been suggested, in view of its size (2 hectares) that it could also have served as a pagan ritual centre.

Verulamium

The Claudian invasion[9]

Following Caesar's withdrawal from Britain there was a period of closer diplomatic contact between the southern British and Roman Gaul, which ushered in a sustained period of prosperity. As is noted previously, Tasciovanus, who became king of the Catuvellauni in succession to Casillvellaunus, presided over his kingdom from Verlamion as a client king, that is, always acknowledging his subservience to the Roman emperor. Tasciovanus was succeeded by Cunobelin (Shakespeare's Cymbeline), who ruled over an expanded Catuvellauni/Trinovantes kingdom from Camulodunum in relative peace from 10 to AD 40.

This politically calm period in late Iron Age Britain contrasted with the turbulence within the Roman Empire following the death of Augustus: the assassination of Julius Caesar in 44 BC precipitated civil war within the Republic and produced a succession of emperors: Augustus in BC 27, Tiberius in AD 14, Gaius in AD 39 and Claudius in AD 41. As relations with Britain became more tenuous, with the death of the treaty signatories on both sides of the Channel, all of these emperors toyed with the possibility of invasion to bring Britain firmly into the empire. It was only with the death of Cunobelin and the ensuing succession dispute between his sons that Claudius became convinced of the need for action.

And action there was, in the form of a 40,000-strong invasion force (four legions plus supports) sailing from Boulogne in AD 43 under the command of Aulus Plautius. The Roman army landed on the Kent and maybe the Sussex coasts virtually unopposed, their strategy being to cross the Thames west of London to take Colchester from the west, Colchester and the Trinovantes being perceived by Claudius and his generals as the enemy. By contrast Verulamium and the Catuvellauni, either because of genuinely good relations following Julius Caesar's settlement some ninety years earlier or more recent nimble diplomatic footwork on the

---

[9] David Mattingly: *An Imperial Possession*, Ch. 4.

part of Catuvellaunian chiefs, were seen as the good guys. The Roman army overcame resistance from the southern tribes. Safely over the Thames, they paused for a while to await the Emperor Claudius, who duly arrived complete with a detachment of elephants. Colchester succumbed within a few weeks, enabling Claudius to return to Rome victorious, leaving the consolidation phase to his generals. It is not known what became of the elephants.

The foundation of Verulamium[10]

Verlamion, together with Camulodunum (Colchester), would have been placed under martial law in the wake of the invasion, but as it had always been an administrative rather than a military centre, Verlamion was not heavily garrisoned by the Romans as was Camulodunum. The Romans therefore set about expanding, remodelling and adapting Verlamion rather than destroying it: their policy was to develop the right bank (south side) of the river floor. They chose to place their forum in Verlamion's central enclosure, which supports the hypothesis that the central enclosure had some religious importance in addition to being the site of the royal mint.[11]

Thus Verulamium was born. The contrast between the Roman treatment of Verulamium and Camulodunum was significant. Verulamium was initially designated a *civitate* – that is, it was recognised as the chief town of a distinct people, in Verulamium's case, the Catuvellauni. Camulodunum was given the status of a *colonia*, which was a chartered town of Roman citizens, founded on conquered territory for the settlement of discharged veterans. This involved the annexation of territory from the defeated population, who were not accorded citizenship and therefore had second-class status. This caused resentment and was a contributory factor in the Boudiccan revolt. It would also have meant that the town's economy was reliant on the Roman army, which therefore, with the steady decline of the strength of the army in the third century, was not so robust as that of Verulamium. It was possible for the more successful *civitates* to be promoted to the status of *municipium*, which is what happened to Verulamium, the only town in Britain to be so honoured. As with colonia, *municipia* also had chartered status in which ex-magistrates – in Verulamium's case mostly the Catuvellauni aristocracy – were granted Roman citizenship. The implication for Verulamium was more autonomy[12] and prosperity for local people.

---

[10] David Mattingly: *An Imperial Possession*, Ch. 9.
[11] Rosalind Niblett: *Verulamium*.
[12] David Mattingly: *An Imperial Possession*, P. 270.

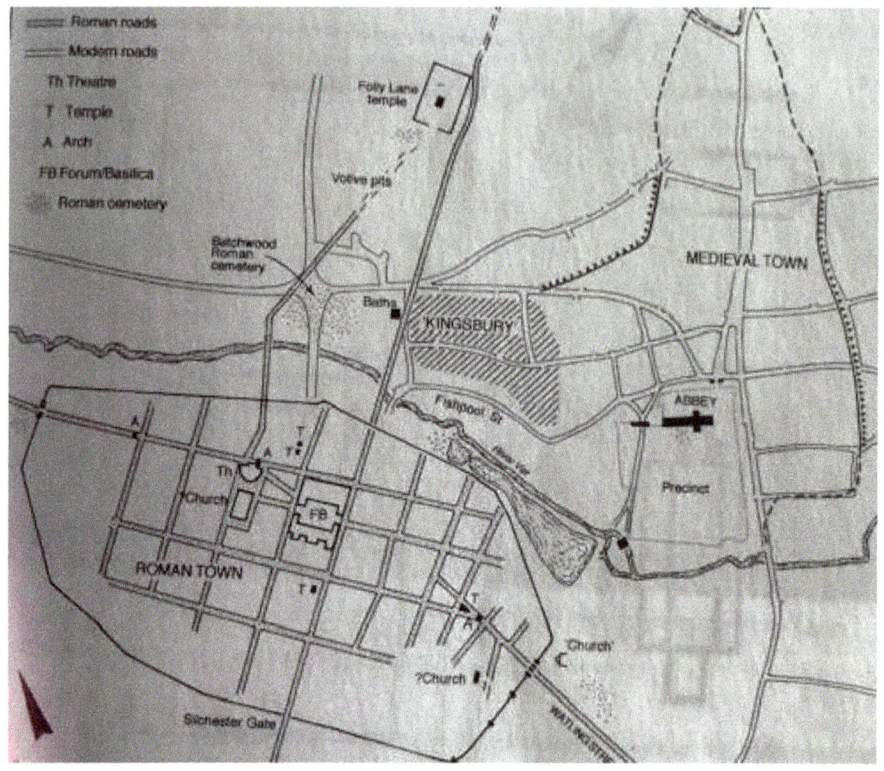

Verulamium and its surroundings. (After Niblett: Verulamium.)

Phases of development[13]

There were several phases of development at Verulamium:
- the first, in the period immediately following the conquest up to the Boudiccan revolt of AD 61, when Boudicca, queen of the Iceni tribe, mounted a spectacular but short-lived rebellion against Roman rule,
- the second following the Boudiccan revolt to a major fire in AD 155, known as the Antonine Fire,
- the third from AD 155 to the abandonment of Britain by the Romans in AD 409.

At the time of the Boudiccan revolt the town comprised little more than some timber workshops and possibly two masonry buildings, all situated near the common enclosure. At this time Verlamion had hardly changed and was largely unaffected by the attack. It took some time – at least a

---

[13] Rosalind Niblett: *Verulam*.

decade – for confidence in the future of the town to return, but when construction did resume it was focussed on public buildings and infrastructure, presumably under state initiative. The public buildings, including the magnificent forum-basilica complex, the commercial and administrative centre of the town that was built on the central enclosure of old Verlamion, and later the theatre; these buildings were built of masonry. The infrastructure included a rectilinear grid of metalled roads and a public water supply. The area of the town was 75 hectares and was protected on three sides by perimeter earthworks, the fourth being protected with the marshes associated with the River Ver. Once established, the commercial and residential buildings, still using traditional timber construction in all but the high status houses, developed rapidly to reach a peak in the first half of the second century.

In about AD 155 a major fire destroyed most of the lower side of Verulamium, including the forum and basilica, the public baths and many private houses. Reconstruction, which took up to fifty years to complete, testifies to the wealth and vitality of the city, as does the third-century flint and brick perimeter wall, which today is the most visible manifestation of Verulamium.

Verulamium in its prime viewed from the south east. (Courtesy of St Albans Museums.)

Verulamium after the Romans

Contrary to the earlier view that Roman civilisation rapidly deteriorated after the departure of the Romans in 410, more recent archaeological investigations have shown that the maintenance, repair and occupation of houses continued well into the fifth century indicate that the decline was gradual. Subsequently, into the sixth century, new buildings tended to be of timber construction as old masonry skills were lost, but Verulamium and its rural hinterland continued to be prosperous and quite possibly continued to function as a regional administrative centre.[14]

Religion

Religion is perhaps the area in which continuity between cultures, civilisations and ethnic origins is most evident. However, the religion of the pre-Roman British was very different to that of the Romans at the time of the invasion: this disparity was slowly eroded with the passage of time so that by the end of Roman rule the two religions were almost indistinguishable.

The religion of the pre-Roman British was Celtic in nature in that it was based on the natural world, and would have expressed a belief that the spirits of nature, which resided in water and the earth, deserved worship. In particular they venerated rivers and watery places – especially bogs and marshes, fertility and the seasons. Thus it is probable that the inhabitants worshipped the River Ver and its associated marshes – the name Ver, as with many rivers, is likely to be Celtic in origin[15]. The veneration of the earth was expressed by the construction of shafts suggesting a symbolic penetration to promote fertility. In common with most Celtic tribes the Catuvellauni would also have adhered to the tradition of a cult of severed heads, be they of local heroes or vanquished enemy.

By contrast the religion practiced by the Romans at the time of invasion was civic in nature, its main purpose being to uphold and support the empire with gods drawn from the classical Greek and Roman pantheon. Throughout the empire religion was more important to the army than any other group and its observance was led and more strictly enforced by the army. Religious observance in Verulamium, which was not an army base, might not have been so rigorously practiced as in the colonia but nevertheless there were seven temples in

---

[14] David Thorold: *Roman Verulamium*.
[15] K Rutherford Davis: *Britons and Saxons – The Chiltern Region 400–700*, p. 42.

Verulamium by the second century, but none so big or grand as those in Colchester.

The two approaches to religion co-existed in Britain without any serious disharmony. With the passage of time, through a process known as syncretisation, the Roman gods were merged with the Celtic deities so that a common religious practice emerged. A prime example of this merged religion is provided by the major temple in Verulamium, which incorporated both Iron Age and Roman elements[16]. The site was situated on the crest of a low hill known locally as Oysterfield, some 500 metres north east of Verulamium, from where it would have been quite conspicuous.

The Iron Age element comprised a mid-first century cremation burial of a high status – possibly royal – Catuvellauni chieftain. Archaeological excavations have revealed the construction of a single underground timber funerary chamber, set in a large earthworks enclosure where a feast was held, probably in the presence of the corpse, which was 'lying in state'. This feast would have been followed by the cremation of the corpse together with a large collection of expensive objects, including silver, a chain mail tunic, horse tackle and tableware. The ash and remains of the cremation were buried in an adjacent pit while the funerary chamber was destroyed and the excavation filled in. Subsequently access from the Verulamium forum/basilica was provided by a brushwood causeway over the river and its marshes. The western slopes of the hill either side of the access track were used for burials, with over forty shafts being dug. Nine of these have been excavated, providing evidence that these shafts may have had a ritual function: in one shaft the scalped and de-fleshed skull of a young man was found carefully placed on the shaft floor and buried, consistent with the skull cult mentioned previously.

The Roman component was the construction of a temple close to the burial site, which formed part of a more extensive complex which included baths at the bottom of the hill and, in Verulamium itself, temples associated with the theatre. This religious complex catered for large numbers of people, possibly 3–4,000, disproportionate to the town population, prosperous and well populated though Verulamium was. This suggests that Verulamium was a religious centre, attracting crowds for the surrounding countryside for major festivals.

---

[16] Rosalind Niblett: *Verulamium*, p. 111.

The decline of the Roman Empire in Britain

The decline of the Roman Empire, in which Britain and Verulamium were included, began in the third century (dubbed the 'third-century crisis') and was caused by both widespread and persistent incursions of Germanic tribes across the eastern border and by internal political turbulence in Rome, which, exacerbated by plague and hyperinflation, led to civil strife. In a fifty-year period the empire got through twenty emperors.

While Britain was spared the direct effect of both the incursions and civil strife, the army in Britain was severely depleted, losing some 40,000 soldiers – two-thirds of its strength – to provide reinforcements to the continental forces. Such a depletion must have had a considerable negative effect on the British economy, particularly on colonia and ports, as the army in Britain was clothed, shod, fed and equipped by British resources. At the same time the style of urban civilisation in Britain was evolving, exemplified by the widespread abandonment of prestige forum-basilica complexes in the main cities. These, inspired by Mediterranean models, were either eventually demolished or modified for alternative uses. It is not clear why this happened but it is possible the reason was that they were always 'vanity projects' and were never really either suitable for the British climate or necessary for public administration. If this were the case then their abandonment was not symptomatic of economic decline. In the fourth century this trend continued with the abandonment of temples, possibly as a result of the legalisation and the growth of Christianity. In part the gradual decline in the economy of the main cities was offset by the rise in small towns and the growth of the market economy.

Against this background of long-term decline, occasioned by empire-wide events, other more pressing local problems arose in the fourth century. One was a tendency of the British to instigate and support rival pretenders to the throne, to the extent that their reputation for this spread across the empire – St Jerome, a fourth-century priest and historian, described Britain as 'fertile in usurpers'. Another was the increase in frequency and severity of coastal raids from Picts and Scots (from Ireland and northern Britain respectively) and the lack of resources to repel them. Both of these problems hastened the final severance in 409.

Verulamium decline

It is likely that Verulamium, along with Silchester and other civitates not directly supplying the military, bucked the trend in decline to a certain extent. There is archaeological evidence in Verulamium that, late into the fourth century, a number of new and extravagant stone houses were built and refurbished and public infrastructure – water supply, drains and roads – were maintained. Because of this, and the deeper roots as a former Iron Age oppidum compared with the Roman colonia, Verulamium was in a better state to survive the withdrawal of the Roman Empire from Britain in 409. Nevertheless, the effects of this withdrawal were profound both economically and politically.

Rise of Roman Christianity

Christianity spread, as a minority religion, throughout the Roman Empire in the second and third centuries and there is no reason to suppose that Roman Britain was not included. Non-Roman religions were largely tolerated by the authorities provided they did not encourage sedition, weaken morality or otherwise threaten the dominance of the state religion. The Roman religion was centred on the worship of a range of gods, principally Jupiter but most importantly previous emperors, who had achieved the status of gods. Both Judaism and Christianity, being monotheistic, were treated with suspicion if not hostility, although Judaism was largely left alone because its antiquity commanded respect. This was not the case with Christianity, which was subject to three periods of persecution at the hand of the state: in the early third century under Emperor Severus, in the mid-third century, under Decius and Valerian and lastly in the early fourth century under Diocletian.

Once established in Jerusalem and Rome, Christianity spread fast in Asia Minor but rather less fast in the western empire. It began its western expansion with a foothold in the Rhone valley in the second century when the conversion of Gaul was boosted in 245 by Pope Fabian, who sent seven bishops to Gaul to found dioceses in Tours, Arles, Narbonne, Toulouse, Paris, Clermont and Limoges[17]. In the absence of any similar mission, the introduction of Christianity into Britain would have been more organic. It is not known when Christianity reached Britain but it is likely that the faith would have been transmitted to Britain fairly quickly, though informally, in the second century by maritime traders, both from North Africa and the Gallic channel coast. Both Tertullian and Origen, writing in the third century from Carthage and Alexandria respectively and doubtless informed by such traders, were aware of the existence of

---

[17] Henry Chadwick: *The Early Church*, p63.

the Roman province of Britain and equally positive that Christianity had reached it by 200[18].

At this time Christianity was an urban and mercantile religion. Because Britain was predominantly rustic and contained no big cities, compared with the heartland of the empire, its growth was slow, being further impeded by periodic episodes of persecution.

All the persecutions were triggered by the exclusivity of the Christians and their refusal to make even a token recognition to the pagan gods by not participating in the emperor cult or sacrifice.

Persecution of Christians

The Romans tended to be fairly relaxed about religion in general and tolerant of the observances of their conquered territories, provided that all their subjects made at least a token allegiance to the cult of the emperors. This token was normally in the form of participation of sacrifice. The only exception to this requirement was accorded to the Jews, in deference to the antiquity of their beliefs. Once the Christians emerged as a distinct group in Rome later in the first century, they could not claim antiquity (although they tried, invoking the Hebrew prophets) and so were required to toe the line. This they resolutely refused to do, although in all other respects they behaved like model citizens, supporting the empire, paying their taxes and obeying the civil law. Christianity was thus outlawed: worship had to be secret and its observance discreet. As time went on the regard in which Christians were held slowly changed. Initially they were suspected of incest and cannibalism, although their solidarity and charity towards widows, orphans, the sick and the imprisoned was admired. As their visibility and numbers grew the wild misunderstanding of their sacraments (the eucharist was perceived to be cannibalistic, for example) diminished while their success and self-confidence became apparent. But what persisted was their separateness, manifested by (amongst other things) their reluctance to participate in public life and their perceived pretensions to a superior level of morality, which successively bred suspicion, fear and ultimately persecution.

The first instance of persecution was confined to Rome itself and had nothing to do with dogma: it was brought about by the great fire of AD 64, rumoured to have been instigated by Nero, which destroyed much of Rome and for which Nero used the Christians as a scapegoat, setting an

---

[18] Charles Thomas: *Christianity in Roman Britain to AD 500*, p43.

unfortunate precedent: Christians were fair game. As Tertullian said of a later persecution, 'If the Tiber rises too high or the Nile too low, the cry is "The Christians to the lion!"'

Subsequently, until the middle of the third century, Christianity was regarded as a local problem and left to local Roman officials to deal with: persecution was sporadic in nature and erupted locally. Roman policy in dealing with the Christians was passive rather than proactive so that Christians were not to be sought out, but if brought to an official's attention as being a Christian they would be formally accused. If they confessed their faith they would be punished by death; if they recanted then they would be required to make the appropriate sacrifices to the gods and would be freed.

A prime example of this approach was the persecution in Lyon in 177. In this episode a mob attacked local Christians who were charged and imprisoned by the local magistrates, pending the arrival of the local Roman governor. The ensuing trial resulted in the conviction of some forty-eight Christians, the death sentences being carried out with the utmost ferocity in the arena. Only the bishop of Lyon, as a Roman citizen, was executed by beheading.

The first persecution that may have involved Britain was under the Emperor Septimus Severus in the early third century. Severus had become the emperor in 193 by means of a ruthless, bloodthirsty campaign against the previous emperor, senators and potential rivals. Severus was a violent man who considered that the Roman Christians had not welcomed his elevation with sufficient enthusiasm: he subsequently reacted by prohibiting any conversions[19]. Severus had two sons, Antoninus and Geta, by his second wife and following custom appointed the elder, Antoninus, as Imperator Designatus in 196 while Geta had to wait some ten years for the same honour. Having completed a series of campaigns strengthening and extending the empire's south-eastern and African limits, Severus turned his attention to Britain, determined to extend Roman rule to the entire island with a secondary objective of persecuting Christians.

Severus arrived in 208, accompanied by his wife, his two sons – both now deputy Augusti – and 40,000 troops. He took his army, together with Antoninus (nicknamed Caracalla on account of his habit of wearing a heavy hooded cloak), north to Scotland, leaving his younger son Geta as governor together with his mother. In the course of the three-year

---

[19] Diarmaid MacCulloch: *A History of Christianity*, p172.

Caledonian campaign, during which Severus died, it is possible that Geta, acting as governor, interpreted his father's passive persecution of Christians through the prohibition of conversions to an altogether more active level, that of the seeking out and the prosecution of Christians, of whom one could have been Alban. This scenario was first put forward by Dr John Morris[20] but was subsequently refuted – not wholly convincingly – by G R Stephens.[21]

The seizure of the Roman throne by Severus had ended a long and stable period in the second century during which there was an orderly transfer of power from one emperor to his successor. The Severan dynasty, and those that followed, relied on army support rather than on consensus, and army support was bought by increased pay, which resulted in inflation and debasement of the currency. The defence of the north-eastern and south-eastern borders became ever more demanding, as did the need to contain civil unrest within the empire, both leading to army expansion and further costs. By 250, the thousandth anniversary of the founding of Rome, the emperor of the time, Decius, construed this crisis as the gods' anger that due sacrifice had been neglected. His solution was simple: to require every person to respect traditional observance, with each person who complied being issued with a certificate. Those with no certificate were liable to punishment – either imprisonment or death. This persecution was implemented throughout the empire and it is quite possible that Alban was executed in this period. This persecution was abandoned with the death of Decius in 251 but re-introduced by the Emperor Valerian in 257, until his death at the hands of the Persians in 260[22].

The Emperor Diocletian (284–305) sought to end the third-century crisis and to restore the ancient splendour of Rome by root-and-branch reorganisation of the empire, which he divided into two parts, east and west. Each was ruled by an Augustus supported by an assistant Caesar: he ruled the eastern part with Caesar Galerius while the west, which comprised Italy, Spain, Gaul and Britain, was ruled by Maximian in Rome with Caesar Constantius as the assistant in Britain. Towards the end of the third century the religious conservatism of Diocletian turned into active persecution under the influence of the fiercely anti-Christian views of Caesar Galerius. This persecution, in 303, was far more aggressive than any previous episodes involving the destruction of churches, the banning of religious

---

[20] John Morris: *The Date of Saint Alban*.
[21] G R Stephens: *A Note on the Martyrdom of St Alban*.
[22] Diarmaid MacCulloch: *A History of Christianity*, pp. 173–4.

assembly and the requirement to sacrifice. Although this persecution was intended to be empire-wide, its implementation in the western part was perfunctory and all but ignored in Britain, as the governor of Britain, Caesar Constantius, was married to Helena, a committed Christian and the mother of Constantine, the future emperor, and could hardly have authorised any draconian persecution. This persecution, known as the Great Persecution, was the last. Diocletian abdicated in 305[23].

Christianity in the fourth century

After this episode the futility of persecution as a policy was recognised, resulting in the 313 Edict of Milan, which guaranteed religious freedom for all, Christians and pagans alike. By this time Christianity had grown to the point where formal ecclesiastical structure was in place with a metropolitan bishop presiding in each of the four provinces of Britain[24]. At the ensuing Council of Arles in 314 Britain was represented by three of the bishops – of London, York and Lincoln – while the fourth province of Wales and the south west was represented by a priest and deacon, the see being vacant at that time[25]. By the end of the fourth century, when Christianity became the formal religion of the empire, it has been suggested that all the twenty civitates listed by Bede, including Verulamium, would have had their own bishop. If this were the case, it is odd that Britain was only represented at the Council of Rimini in 359 by two bishops, both penniless, who had to be funded by their fellows.

Set against this impressive institutional growth there is a distinct lack of archaeological evidence of a thriving or prevalent church to back it up. Although Christianity was legalised in the Edict of Milan, church-building in a strongly pagan city like Verulamium may have been daunting. It was not until later in the century, as Christianity became more accepted and was made the empire religion in 380, would church-building have begun in earnest, but by then, or soon after, Roman Britain was in steep decline. Thus, not only have no remains of any building that could have been a cathedral been discovered, but even the remains of buildings that might have been churches are dubious.

At Verulamium there is evidence of three possible churches[26], two of which were within the city walls and one just outside. The archaeological

---

[23] Henry Chadwick: *The Early Church*, pp. 121–2.
[24] Charles Thomas: *Christianity in Britain to AD 500*.
[25] David Petts: *Christianity in Roman Britain*.
[26] Rosalind Niblett: *Verulamium*, pp. 136–7.

finds are meagre: there is evidence that late in the fourth-century alterations were made to the temple adjacent to the theatre that might indicate conversion to a church, although no supporting evidence has been found. The trace of another building, this one in the south-west corner of the city, is consistent with the floor plan of a simple church, but this plan, that of a basilica, was quite common in Roman architecture and could have been for other uses. The evidence of an extramural church, situated just outside (east) of the London Gate, comprises the footings of part of an apsidal building, which again could have been a church. In fact, no artefacts with any Christian symbols – memorials, art, baptismal fonts, jewellery – have been found in Verulamium. However, some seventy-five Christian graves, characterised by their east–west alignment and the absence of grave goods, have been found in three cemeteries immediately to the north of the River Ver.

That fourth-century churches were few in number and small in size is not necessarily in conflict with the health and vitality of Christianity at this time: congregations could assemble in the private houses of wealthy believers or in the open air as they did, in rural areas, for many centuries until the church-building boom in the twelfth and thirteenth centuries. Neither was the energy of the senior clergy in short supply. A British-born and educated priest, Pelagius, developed ideas that caught the imagination of many Christians in the empire and attracted a strong following in Britain. Pelagianism, as it became known, was deemed heretical and decisively rebutted by Origen but persisted in Britain to the extent that the British bishops appealed to Vitricius and then Germanus, bishops of Rouen and Auxerre respectively, to make extended visits to Britain to add weight to its rebuttal.

2

The Martyrdom of Alban

I am called Alban and I worship and adore the true and living God

Bede: *Ecclesiastical History of the English People*

Introduction

All the documentary evidence of the martyrdom of Alban dates from the very end of the Roman period in Britain and from the succeeding three centuries. There is no contemporaneous account and it is impossible, at this distance, to say with any confidence when and in what circumstances the martyrdom took place. Alban could only have been martyred in one of the episodes of persecution under the Emperors Severus, Decius/Valerian or Diocletian. As Charles Thomas points out[27], if Alban had been martyred in the Severan persecution it would have been an isolated event, which would have attracted widespread attention and is therefore considered most unlikely. The martyrdom would also have been most unlikely in the Great Persecution of Diocletian, as discussed previously. This leaves the mid-third century persecutions of Decius and Valerian as the most likely time of Alban's martyrdom, as suggested by Levison[28] and supported by Charles Thomas. Although it would be very interesting to know the date – or at least the period – of the martyrdom, it does not have a direct bearing on the story.

Mission of Vitricius

As recounted in Chapter 1, Christianity and its Church grew steadily throughout the fourth century, although it remained a minority religion in Britain and, as far as is known, was largely ignored by the parent Church in Rome: there are no records of any official mission or contact

---

[27] Charles Thomas: *Christianity in Roman Britain to AD500*, p. 44.
[28] Wilhelm Levison: *St Alban and St Albans*.

until that of Vitricius, the bishop of Rouen in 396. Vitricius (330–407), of Gallic birth, was a soldier in the Roman army, which he deserted when he converted to Christianity, whereupon he was tried and sentenced to severe flogging and allegedly death. He managed to escape this fate and in 393 was appointed Bishop of Rouen. In 396 he was invited to settle a dispute in Britain by unnamed British senior clergy assumed to have included the Metropolitan of the province of Maxima Caesariensis centred on London[29]. The nature of the dispute is not known but may have been related to Pelagianism or the heresy of Arianism, which denied the Trinity and held that God the Son was subordinate to God the Father. This had been refuted in the Council of Constantinople in 381. Vitricius was an enthusiastic proponent of the cult of saints as a means of promoting orthodoxy and had just received relics of Saints Vitalis and Agricola from Ambrose, Archbishop of Milan. In celebration of this gift he wrote a sermon, *De Laude Sanctorum* (In Praise of Saints), in which he states that he has just returned from a visit to Britain (described as a wild and hostile place), where he took the opportunity of introducing the notion of the cult of saints to his hosts, the better to support orthodoxy. Listing a number of well-known saints, such as John the Baptist, and not being aware of the name of any British saints, he was obliged to allude to several unnamed British saints, one of which 'in the hands of the executioners told the rivers to draw back, lest he should be delayed in his haste'. This has subsequently been taken, through its similarity with subsequent descriptions, to be a reference to St Alban.

There is no record of how long Vitricius' visit lasted or how much he achieved. It is odd that he wasn't able to obtain more information about British saints. That his hosts didn't reveal the identity of the saint who told the rivers to draw back could have been partly because the British bishops were disappointed that the visit hadn't been more successful – they may have felt disinclined to help him – and partly because they knew the name of the Verulamium saint but were unwilling to divulge it.

Would it be stretching conjecture too far to envisage a long standing envy between London and Verulamium? After all, Verulamium had its roots deep in the past and was possibly the base of the most powerful British aristocracy. London on the other hand was certainly more important as a commercial centre and the capital, but, lacking Iron Age roots, suffered a civic inferiority complex: a question of Rome to the empire's Athens or New York to America's Washington.

---

[29] Michael Garcia: *Saint Alban and the Cult of Saints in Late Antique Britain.*

Mission of Germanus

Germanus (378–442/8), was a Gallic aristocrat educated in rhetoric and law who initially practised as a senior government official. After having become a monk, promotion swiftly followed and he was appointed Bishop of Auxerre in 418, in which capacity he made two visits to Britain in order to suppress the widespread and popular Pelagian heresy. This heresy held that human nature was not tainted by original sin and that mortal will was capable of choosing good or evil without special divine aid or assistance. In the words of Charles Thomas[30], 'Pelagius, a late fourth-century Briton, preacher and philosopher, propounded views which elevated the role of Man as possessor of free will and considerable responsibility for his own destiny, against stronger views held by people like St Augustine (of Hippo) that stressed God's eternal, overwhelming, pre-determinism.' The cult of saints was potentially a key weapon in the armoury against this heresy: Alban was a heathen who was held not to confess his faith through an act of conscious free will but through the divine workings of ineffable grace.

Details of the two visits are recorded in the *Vita Germani* – Life of Germanus – written by Constantius of Lyon in about 480[31]. The first visit was made in 429 when Germanus was accompanied by Lupus, Bishop of Troyes, and was undertaken either on the order of Pope Celestine (according to the chronicle of Prosper) or at the invitation of orthodox British bishops (according to Constantius). In his Vita Germani he records an eventful visit, starting with the channel crossing:

> Thus they embarked upon the ocean under the leadership and inspiration of Christ, who, in the midst of danger, kept His servants safe and proved their worth. At first, when the ship put out to sea, she ran before light breezes blowing from the Bay of Gaul until she was in midchannel where, gaze as you might, you could see nothing but sky and water. Then it was not long before the ocean was assaulted by the violence of demons, haters of religion, who were livid with malice at the sight of such great men hastening to bring salvation to the nations. They heaped up dangers, roused the gales, hid the heavens and the day under a night of clouds, and filled the thick darkness with the terrors of the sea and air. The sails could not resist the fury of the winds and the

---

[30] Charles Thomas: *Christianity in Roman Britain before 500AD*.
[31] Nick Higham: *Constantius, St Germanus and 5th century Britain*.

fragile craft scarcely sustained the weight of the waters. The sailors were powerless and abandoned their efforts; the vessel was navigated by prayer and not by muscles. And at that point the leader himself, the bishop, his body worn out, in his weariness went to sleep.

Then indeed did the storm put forth its strength; it was as if a restraining hand had gone. Before long the vessel was actually being swamped by the waves that swept over it. At last the blessed Lupus and all the excited throng aroused their chief, to match him against the raging elements. He, all the more steadfast for the very immensity of the danger, in the name of Christ chided the ocean, pleading the cause of religion against the savagery of the gales. Then, taking some oil, he lightly sprinkled the waves in the name of the Trinity and this diminished their fury. Consulting his colleague, he now called upon everybody; and prayer was poured out by their united voice.

And there was God! The enemies of souls were put to flight, the air became clear and calm, the contrary winds were turned to aid the voyage, the currents flowed in the service of the ship. Thus the great distances were covered and soon all were enjoying repose on the desired shore.

Once recovered, Germanus and Lupus toured Britain, preaching and healing 'such were the crowds, not only in the churches, but at the crossroads, in the fields, and in the lanes.' Eventually the Pelagians agreed to a debate at which 'they came forth flaunting their wealth, in dazzling robes, surrounded by a crowd of flatterers.' Of course Germanus and Lupus won the day:

And indeed there was assembled at the meeting-place a crowd of vast proportions, wives and children among them, drawn by the occasion. The people were present both as spectators and as jurymen. The two parties faced each other, ill matched and on unequal terms. On the one side was divine authority, on the other human presumption; on this side, faith, on that side, bad faith; those owned allegiance to Pelagius, these to Christ.

The holy bishops gave the privilege of opening the debate to their opponents, who took up the time of their hearers with empty words drawn out to great length but to little purpose. Then the revered prelates themselves poured out the floods of their eloquence, mingling them with the thunders of the apostle and the Gospels, for their own words were interwoven with the inspired writings and their strongest assertions were supported by the testimony of Scripture. Empty arguments were refuted, the dishonest pleas were exposed, and their authors, as each point was made against them, confessed themselves in the wrong by their inability to reply. The jury of the people could hardly keep their hands off them and were not to be stopped from giving their verdict by their shouts.

Following this event, which presumably took place in London, 'the bishops visited the shrine of the blessed martyr Alban, to give thanks to God through him'. In a later episode Germanus took on the role as an army general against attack by the combined forces of Picts and Saxons. On his command, the British army, newly baptised, all shouted 'Alleluia' with such ferocity that the enemy threw down their arms and fled.

Thus, having defeated both the heretics and the heathen, Germanus and Lupus returned to Gaul, with a final reference to Alban: 'Their own merits and the intercession of Alban the Martyr secured them a calm voyage; and a good ship brought them back in peace to their expectant people.'

Germanus made a second visit, this time in the company of Bishop Severus of Trier in the mid-fifth century towards the end of Germanus' life, again to deal with another outbreak of Pelagianism. Constantius provides little detail of this visit, although it does confirm the ongoing contacts between the British and Continental churches long after the departure of the Roman administration.

Constantius' *Vita Germani* is widely regarded as a difficult text – historically acceptable but hagiographical in style so that Germanus is portrayed as superman. This tends to undermine our trust in Constantius as a reliable author: if we don't accept his story of miracle healing or miracle victories can we really believe the rest? From the point of view of his visits to Britain the *Vita* is unsatisfactorily vague: no names of people or places are given and the lack of any geographical description make it quite obvious that Constantius did not regard such details as important. The two references to Alban are cryptic in the extreme, but at least they were made. Constantius' aim was partly to present his subject as an almost Christlike figure quelling storms, performing miracles and vanquishing his enemies without the loss of any blood. It was also partly to provide a handbook for how bishops should ideally behave – ascetic, fearless, modest and resolutely orthodox and anti-Pelagian.

The lack of detail he provides on Alban may be explained by the fact that by the time he wrote the Vita his audience would already have been familiar with the Alban story. He doesn't mention that, according to the

Passio Albani, Alban revealed the story of his persecution and death – his Passion – to Germanus when he visited the tomb where he deposited the holy relics he had brought with him and, in return, took some earth, stained red supposedly with the blood of the martyr. In the revelation, which came to Germanus during the course of an all-night vigil, Alban instructed Germanus to publicise his story by means of writing an account on *tituli* (or placards). Such placards would normally be posted on the walls of the basilica housing a martyr's tomb but in this case Germanus prepared the placards on his return to Auxerre, it being too logistically difficult to do in Verulamium.

Many questions present themselves. Was the revelation genuine or did Germanus, acknowledged as a highly intelligent, highly educated and politically astute operator, invent it? After all a British martyr, touched by God's ineffable grace, suited his anti-Pelagian campaign perfectly. Was Germanus aware, from reading Vitricius' *De Laude Sanctorum* or from informal contacts with British bishops, of the existence of a unnamed British martyr before he set out for Britain? If not, did he normally take a collection of holy relics with him on his travels on the off-chance, as it were, of finding somewhere to deposit them? That he visited the tomb implies that the cult of the martyr already existed, but what about the name: was this the martyr's real name or was it given to him by Germanus, perhaps as a reference to Albion, the ancient name of Britain? If the British knew his name as Alban why had Vitricius not been told on his visit just 30 years earlier? Was that possibly due to the fact that the Pelagian camp wished to suppress his existence because they knew that the martyrdom didn't help their cause? Or did Vitricius either forget his name or simply ask the wrong people? It is easy to imagine a certain reluctance to divulge details to Vitricius, a 'local hire'. That certainly wouldn't have been the case with Germanus, a papal legate, a performer of miracles and a champion of orthodoxy. And did Alban really die on the 22 June, the summer solstice, or is this date freighted with allegorical meaning?

In the face of so many unanswerable questions, step forward archaeology: recent excavations have revealed the existence, just south of the present abbey, of a Romano-British cemetery that seems to have been taken out of use late in the fourth century and the area covered with a gravel surface on which large numbers of late Roman coins have been found[32]. This evidence is compatible with the manifestation of a

---

[32] Martin Biddle and Birthe Kjolbye Biddle: The Origins of St Albans Abbey: Romano-British Cemetery and Anglo-Saxon Monastery

pilgrimage site and supports the supposition that the cult of a Verulamium martyr existed before Germanus' visit.

The fugitive priest Amphibalus exchanging clothes with Alban. According to Eileen Roberts, in wall paintings of St Albans Abbey Amphibalus stands on the left and Alban on the right. If so, Amphibalus has already given the cross to Alban and has already received Alban's hat, so as to conceal his tonsure. There are , however, other interpretations.

From a thirteenth century wall painting in the nave of St Albans Abbey (author photo).

In conclusion we have to admit that none of the questions posed can be answered definitively and our response comes down to the bedrock of faith. Here I shall stick my authorial neck out: in my view the strong probability is that there *was* a tomb of a local Christian hero, as supported by Professor Biddle's archaeological work, probably constructed in the fourth century after the legalisation of Christianity, and that this tomb was, by the fifth century, a pilgrimage site. We know that the Iron Age religious background was that of hero-worship of decapitated skulls, which could have continued through to the late Roman period with the easy transfer of their hero veneration from pagan warlord to a Christian martyr. I also think that there was an unwritten folk memory of the story of the martyrdom that reached Vitricius as a faint rumour. All the evidence also points to the probability that Germanus was aware of the martyrdom – surely he had read *De Laude Sanctorum* before he left Gaul – and brought with him holy relics with the intention of visiting the tomb. He may not have known the name of the martyr, or his background, or the date of the execution, or the story of the martyrdom and these details he may have invented or embellished.

A later source from Auxerre tells us that Germanus founded a basilica of St Alban within the walls of Auxerre, dedicated in honour of the martyr, where he deposited the blood-stained soil he brought from Britain. This would have been where the story of Alban, either on placards or by text painted directly on the walls, would have been displayed.

The Passio Albani

A Passio is a written account of a saint's martyrdom. Two German scholars, Wilhelm Levison and Wilhelm Meyer, independently came across two versions of the Passio Albani in 1903: one in Turin (the so-called T version) dated from the late eighth century and the other in Paris (the P version) dated from the ninth/tenth century[33]. Shortly after this the evidence of a shorter version was found in four manuscripts, two in London and two in France. This was thought to have been an extract from the T and P versions and was called the E version. This view went unchallenged until it was recently shown by Richard Sharpe that the E version was in fact the original text and was likely to have been based on the placards that Germanus wrote on his return to Auxerre[34]. Subsequently Michael Winterbottom has reconstructed and translated the earliest Passio from the London and French manuscripts[35]:

> **1.** In the time of the persecution, the holy Alban, who had not yet been baptised, and was (according to the report of olden days) still a pagan, gave shelter to a cleric who was fleeing from his persecutors, put on his clothing – the hooded tunic he was wearing – and offered himself up instead of him. He was at once handed over to the judge.

---

[33] Wilhelm Levison: *St Alban and St Albans*.
[34] Richard Sharpe: *The Late Antique Passion of St Alban*.
[35] Michael Winterbottom: *The earliest Passion of St Alban*.

The Martyrdom of Alban

2. Since he declared under torture that he was a Christian (Christianity not yet having been recognised), he was sentenced to execution by the sword.

3. And when he was being led away to be sacrificed, he came to the river that separated with its swift course the walls and the arena where he was to be struck down. And he saw there that a great crowd of people, of both sexes and every age and status, who without doubt were being summoned by God to attend on the martyr, had so thronged the river bridge that he could hardly have passed over before evening.

4. In fact, the judge had been left in the city with no one to attend on him. The holy Alban made his way to the river across which he had to pass (?) to reach his martyrdom. As he looked up at heaven, the river bed at once became dry, and the water yielded to – or rather went ahead of – his footsteps.

5. And when he had come to the place assigned for his death, the executioner, who was going to execute the martyr, met him with drawn sword. But praying to be punished in the martyr's place and throwing away his impious blade, he grovelled at the feet of the holy Alban: he had suddenly become his companion instead of his persecutor.

6. But while the sword lay on the ground and the executioners hesitated, not without reason, the holy martyr climbed the hill with the crowds of people. The hill rises conveniently about fifty paces from the arena. It is unspeakably beautiful, painted – or rather clothed – with diverse flowers. There is nothing steep, precipitous or sheer about it; nature brings it down with long wide slopes to look like a flat plain.

7. The hill had undoubtedly been made ready for the martyr even before it was consecrated by his holy blood, for its beauty had made it like his merits. At the top the holy Alban asked to be given water, and at once, incredibly enough, there came forth before the martyr's feet an unfailing spring, so that all might realise that the river too had paid homage to the martyr.

8. For it could not have come about that the martyr should ask for water on the high hill top, when he had left none at all behind in the river, if he had not seen the river. For, its service quite finished, its holy work complete, it returned to its natural course, leaving behind evidence of the duty it had done. And I did not think I should pass over the fact that the eyes of the executioner, who brought impious hands to bear on that pious neck, fell to the ground roots and all, along with the martyr's head.

9. And there the executioner who had previously refused to strike down the holy one of God was also put to the sword. Then the terrified judge, stunned by such an extraordinary turn of events, even without instructions from the principes ordered an end to the persecution, pronouncing that religion is rather strengthened by the slaughter of holy men, the very thing which they thought led to the name of Christianity being blotted out.

10. When the holy bishop Germanus came to the basilica with relics of all the apostles and diverse martyrs, meaning to house the precious gifts there, he ordered the grave to be opened up, so that the bodies of holy men who had been received by heaven as equal in merit, though brought together from different regions, should be taken in by a single place of burial.

11. When the relics had been honourably laid to rest next to each other, he took a clod of earth from the very place where the martyr's blood had flowed forth. This devout act was violent indeed, but its temerity was occasioned by a believer's piety. The piece of earth retained traces of blood, making it clear that the ground had grown red with the martyr's blood even as his persecutor grew pale. After these things had been manifested and revealed, a great crowd of men turned to God on that day, thanks to our Lord Jesus Christ, to whom is honour and glory for ever and ever. Amen.

It should be noted:
- no mention is made of Verulamium as being the location of the martyrdom or the tomb;
- no name is given to the cleric in paragraph 1;
- execution by sword described in paragraph 2 implies that Alban was a Roman citizen;
- the similarity between 'the river bed at once became dry' in paragraph 4 and 'told the river to draw back' in Vitricius' *De Laude Sanctorum*;
- the distance of the hill is given as 50 paces, which is at odds with the 500 paces of later versions;
- paragraphs 10 and 11 were probably added to the Passio after Germanus' death as Germanus would never have described himself as 'the holy bishop';

The Turin version, until recently considered as the earliest and therefore definitive text apart from incorporating a long introduction, departs from the earliest version in two main respects: it specifically states that the martyrdom took place in the Severan persecution, with Caesar acting as the judge and that the date of the execution was 22 June. The P version does not mention Severus but does retain the date.

The account of Gildas

Gildas (500–570), also known as Gildas the Wise, was a churchman who wrote a scathing polemic entitled *De Excidio Britanniae* (DEB), or *On the Ruin of Britain*, in which he recounts the history of Britain at the end of the Roman period and the coming of the Anglo-Saxons. Effectively this is a hell-fire sermon not intended to be an objective chronicle – his overall stance is that the departure of the Romans and the takeover of the eastern half of Britain by the heathen Anglo-Saxons was an unmitigated disaster and castigates both the British kings and churchmen for allowing it to happen.

The account, loosely based on one of the versions of the *Passio* and probably written early in the early/mid-sixth century comprises three parts: the first being a setting out of the historical context and the second and third being devoted to the shortcomings of Gildas' contemporaries.

In the first part, before the first reference to Alban in his paragraph 10, he describes the persecution of Christians, which he 'conjectures' to have taken place in the reign of Diocletian:

> God, therefore, who wishes all men to be saved, and who calls sinners his own free gift, kindled up among us bright luminaries of holy martyrs, whose places of burial and of martyrdom, had they not for our manifold no less than those who think themselves righteous, magnified his mercy towards us, and, as we know, during the previously-named persecution, that Britain might not totally be enveloped in the dark shades of night, he, of crimes been interfered with and destroyed by the barbarians, would have still kindled in the minds of the beholders no small fire of divine charity. Such were St Alban of Verulam, Aaron and Julius, citizens of Carlisle, and the rest, of both sexes, who in different places stood their ground in the Christian contest.

He continues with an account of the martyrdom of Alban, which appears to be loosely based on the earliest version of the *Passio Albani*, which was as we have seen probably written less than 100 years before.

> The first of these martyrs, St Alban, for charity's sake saved another confessor who was pursued by his persecutors, and was on the point of being seized, by hiding him in his house, and then by changing clothes with him, imitating in this example of Christ, who laid down his life for his sheep, and exposing himself in the other's clothes to be pursued in his stead. So pleasing to God was this conduct, that between his confession and martyrdom, he was honoured with the performance of wonderful miracles in presence of the impious blasphemers who were carrying the Roman standards, and like the Israelites of old, who trod dry-foot an unfrequented path whilst the ark of the covenant stood some time on the sands in the midst of Jordan; so also the martyr, with a thousand others, opened a path across the noble river Thames, whose waters stood abrupt like precipices on either side; and seeing this, the first of his executors was stricken with awe, and from a wolf became a lamb; so that he thirsted for martyrdom, and boldly underwent that for which he thirsted.

As has been mentioned, Gildas was not a historian and would have had to rely on scarce and probably fragmentary evidence, both oral and written. Thus, never having visited either Verulamium or London, he confuses the

The martyrdom of Alban as depicted in the fourteenth century shrine in St Albans Abbey.

River Thames with the River Ver. (A London/Thames location for the martyrdom does not fit with the topography described in the *Passio*.) In the main, however, this account follows the earliest version of the *Passio Albani* reasonably closely. The DEB provides the first reference we have of Verulamium, but falls short of stating that it was the scene of the martyrdom.

The account of the Venerable Bede

Bede's (672–735) most famous work, *The Ecclesiastical History of the English People*, completed in 731, contains the longest and most detailed account of St Alban, based on the Passio Albani and Gildas' De Excidio Britanniae, and has become the standard account[36].

> ### Conversion and arrest of Alban
> This Alban, being yet a pagan, at the time when at the bidding of unbelieving rulers all manner of cruelty was practised against the Christians, gave entertainment in his house to a certain clerk flying from his persecutors. This man he observed to be engaged in continual prayer and watching day and night; when on a sudden the Divine grace shining on him, he began to imitate the example of faith and piety which was set before him, and being gradually instructed by his wholesome admonitions, he cast off the darkness of idolatry, and became a Christian in all sincerity of heart. The aforesaid clerk having been some days entertained by him, it came to the ears of the impious prince, that a confessor of Christ, to whom a martyr's place had not yet been assigned, was concealed at Alban's house. Whereupon he sent some soldiers to make a strict search after him. When they came to the martyr's hut, St. Alban presently came forth to the soldiers, instead of his guest and master, in the habit or long coat which he wore, and was bound and led before the judge.
>
> ### The Trial
> It happened that the judge, at the time when Alban was carried before him, was standing at the altar, and offering sacrifice to devils. When he saw Alban, being much enraged that he should thus, of his own accord, dare to put himself into the hands of the soldiers, and incur such danger on behalf of the guest whom he had harboured, he commanded him to be dragged to the images of the devils, before which he stood,

---
[36] Bede: *The Ecclesiastical History of the English Nation*, Book 1 Chapter 7.

saying, 'Because you have chosen to conceal a rebellious and sacrilegious man, rather than to deliver him up to the soldiers, that his contempt of the gods might meet with the penalty due to such blasphemy, you shall undergo all the punishment that was due to him, if you seek to abandon the worship of our religion.' But St. Alban, who had voluntarily declared himself a Christian to the persecutors of the faith, was not at all daunted by the prince's threats, but putting on the armour of spiritual warfare, publicly declared that he would not obey his command. Then said the judge, 'Of what family or race are you?'—'What does it concern you,' answered Alban, 'of what stock I am? If you desire to hear the truth of my religion, be it known to you, that I am now a Christian, and free to fulfil Christian duties.'—'I ask your name,' said the judge; 'tell me it immediately.'—'I am called Alban by my parents,' replied he; 'and I worship ever and adore the true and living God, Who created all things.' Then the judge, filled with anger, said, 'If you would enjoy the happiness of eternal life, do not delay to offer sacrifice to the great gods.' Alban rejoined, 'These sacrifices, which by you are offered to devils, neither can avail the worshippers, nor fulfil the desires and petitions of the suppliants. Rather, whosoever shall offer sacrifice to these images, shall receive the everlasting pains of hell for his reward.'

The judge, hearing these words, and being much incensed, ordered this holy confessor of God to be scourged by the executioners, believing that he might by stripes shake that constancy of heart, on which he could not prevail by words. He, being most cruelly tortured, bore the same patiently, or rather joyfully, for our Lord's sake. When the judge perceived that he was not to be overcome by tortures, or withdrawn from the exercise of the Christian religion, he ordered him to be put to death.

The Martyrdom
Being led to execution, he came to a river, which, with a most rapid course, ran between the wall of the town and the arena where he was to be executed. He there saw a great multitude of persons of both sexes, and of divers ages and conditions, who were doubtless assembled by Divine inspiration, to attend the blessed confessor and martyr, and had so filled the bridge over the river, that he could scarce pass over that evening. In truth, almost all had gone out, so that the judge remained in the city without attendance. St. Alban, therefore, urged by an ardent and devout wish to attain the sooner to martyrdom, drew near to the stream, and lifted up his eyes to heaven, whereupon the channel was immediately dried up, and he perceived that the water had given place

and made way for him to pass. Among the rest, the executioner, who should have put him to death, observed this, and moved doubtless by Divine inspiration hastened to meet him at the appointed place of execution, and casting away the sword which he had carried ready drawn, fell at his feet, praying earnestly that he might rather be accounted worthy to suffer with the martyr, whom he was ordered to execute, or, if possible, instead of him.

Whilst he was thus changed from a persecutor into a companion in the faith and truth, and the other executioners rightly hesitated to take up the sword which was lying on the ground, the holy confessor, accompanied by the multitude, ascended a hill, about half a mile from the arena, beautiful, as was fitting, and of most pleasing appearance, adorned, or rather clothed, everywhere with flowers of many colours, nowhere steep or precipitous or of sheer descent, but with a long, smooth natural slope, like a plain, on its sides, a place altogether worthy from of old, by reason of its native beauty, to be consecrated by the blood of a blessed martyr. On the top of this hill, St. Alban prayed that God would give him water, and immediately a living spring, confined in its channel, sprang up at his feet, so that all men acknowledged that even the stream had yielded its service to the martyr. For it was impossible that the martyr, who had left no water remaining in the river, should desire it on the top of the hill, unless he thought it fitting. The river then having done service and fulfilled the pious duty, returned to its natural course, leaving a testimony of its obedience. Here, therefore, the head of the undaunted martyr was struck off, and here he received the crown of life, which God has promised to them that love him. But he who laid impious hands on the holy man's neck was not permitted to rejoice over his dead body; for his eyes dropped upon the ground at the same moment as the blessed martyr's head fell.

At the same time was also beheaded the soldier, who before, through the Divine admonition, refused to strike the holy confessor. Of whom it is apparent, that though he was not purified by the waters of baptism, yet he was cleansed by the washing of his own blood, and rendered worthy to enter the kingdom of heaven. Then the judge, astonished at the unwonted sight of so many heavenly miracles, ordered the persecution to cease immediately, and began to honour the death of the saints, by which he once thought that they might have been turned from their zeal for the Christian faith. The blessed Alban suffered death on the twenty-second day of June, near the city of Verulam, which is now by the English nation called Verlamacaestir, or Vaeclingacaestir, where afterwards, when peaceable Christian times were restored, a church of wonderful workmanship, and altogether worthy to commemorate his martyrdom, was erected in which place the cure of sick persons and the frequent working of wonders cease not to this day.

The Venerable Bede: eighth century copy of a page of the Ecclesiastical History. (By courtesy of the British Library, Cotton MS C11.)

It should be noted that while Gildas was unsure of the period in which Alban was martyred ('it is conjectured that the martyrdom took place in the reign of Diocletian'), Bede ignores the conjecture and asserts it as a fact. Furthermore:
- Both the judge's question about Alban's background and his response was a standard part of many martyrdom accounts.
- The portrayal of the hillside as paradise was also a common feature of such accounts, done to emphasise the contrast of the spiritual state of the martyr with the horrors about to come[37].

Myth or reality?

Was the story as related by Gildas and Bede a myth or was it real? There are three possibilities to consider:

---

[37] Robin Lane Fox: Pagans and Christians.

- The martyrdom was true in all but the more obviously legendary details.
- The entire story is mythological. In this scenario the church leaders and/or civic authorities, or Germanus invented the story of a Verulamium martyr for their various purposes in the late fourth or early fifth centuries.
- The martyrdom was actual but the details, including the name Alban, were invented. In this scenario there was a genuine Verulamium martyrdom in an episode of Roman persecution which led to the veneration of the saint as a local hero/martyr. The visit by Germanus was genuine, but as the promotion of a local martyr suited Germanus' anti-Pelagian campaign very well, the revelation by Alban at the tomb vigil was possibly an invention.

The first possibility is a matter of faith, but there are some considerations to give one pause:
- While Gildas implies a considerable number of holy martyrs, ('such were St Alban of Verulam, Aaron and Julius of Carlisle, and the rest'). Is it just coincidence that Verulamium, the only *municipium* in Britain, is home to the only named martyr from lowland Britain?
- Why is the martyrdom given such an auspicious date, the summer solstice?
- Why is there such a paucity of supporting archaeological evidence of Christianity in fourth-century Verulamium if the martyrdom were real? On the other hand, a lack of archaeological evidence of fourth-century Christianity is not just limited to Verulamium – there is none in London either, for example.

For the second possibility, that the entire story was invented, it is necessary to examine the motives. For the Verulamians the prime motive may have been to enhance the prestige of Verulamium at the end of Roman rule. This would have been in the context in which Verulamium was attempting to wrest the leadership of Britain from London as the latter city went into deep decline with the fall-off in trade and the economy at the end of the fourth century. To be credible as a capital, any city had to have a patronal saint, and if needs must it would have to invent one. Having done this, then the endorsement of the 'martyr' by a senior churchman (i.e., Germanus) leading to the initiation of a cult would be necessary. In this fraud the Verulamians would also have had the opportunity to promote the cult of their invented martyr by grafting it onto the rootstock of the ancient Celtic cult of skull veneration at Verulamium, in decline in the fourth century, thereby achieving a near-seamless transfer of allegiance.

Alternatively Germanus could have been the author of the martyrdom story for the purpose of combating Pelagianism, although this motive is not strong. However, it is difficult to follow the account of Germanus' life without being convinced of his integrity and complete lifelong devotion after his first visit to St Alban – a devotion which surely was not and could not have been fabricated.

If the story was a complete fabrication then it was an extraordinarily successful one: it fooled everybody until modern times. Were our forebears so gullible? Do not most – possibly all – myths have a kernel of truth somewhere in their foundation? Perhaps the third possibility is, after all, the most probable.

Who was Alban?

It is probable that Alban was a Roman citizen, otherwise he would have been killed in the gladiatorial arena and not beheaded. He was, probably, British or Romano-British, although this, then as now, does not tell us much about his ancestry. In Bede's account Alban replies to the judge's question about his ancestry with, 'What does it concern you of what stock I am?' He was evidently well-off with a house in or near Verulamium – he might have been a *municipium* official, a trader or even the owner of a villa. There is no evidence that he was a soldier, and this would have been unlikely as Verulamium was not any army base: it seems that this portrayal as a centurion was a fabrication of medieval chroniclers. Surely the fugitive priest would not have risked trusting his luck to a government official. Because there is no mention in any of the accounts of a wife or family it has always been assumed that Alban was unmarried.

In summary my mental picture of Alban, based on Bede, is that he was young and probably single, well educated, as is shown in the nature of his replies to the judge's inquisition, and quite possibly an owner of a villa big and secluded enough for Amphibalus to feel safe for the several days of his stay, during which time he converted Alban. This would not have been practical in a smaller, city centre house.

There is no certainty that his name was really Alban[38]. It might be – as has been suggested – that he came from Balkan stock, possibly even from Albania. More probable is that he was known, pre-Germanus, as simply 'the Albion martyr', Albion being an ancient alternative name for Britain.

---

[38] Philip Thornhill: St Alban and the end of Roman Britain.

After all, at that time he might have been the only Briton that anybody in the wider Roman Empire had ever heard of, the two other saints named by Gildas, Julius and Aaron, lacking sufficient profile.

Where did the martyrdom take place?
The only account of the martyrdom that specifically identifies the place of martyrdom as Verulamium is that of Bede: Gildas refers to St Alban of Verulam, but does not say that Alban was martyred there. Although an alternative location of Caerleon in Wales (the place of martyrdom of Julius and Aaron) has been suggested, the similarity between the description of the hill where Alban was executed and the site of the abbey is compelling.

Given this, then the trial, or rather the encounter with the judge, must have taken place in the temple situated in the forum. From here Alban's route would have been north-east along Akeman Street to the Ver river crossing and then up Fishpool Street to the cemetery on the south-facing side of the hill, which is now known as the Abbey Orchard – a distance of about half a mile.

What was the name of the priest that Alban sheltered?
We do not know anything about the priest whom Alban sheltered other than that he was on the run. When the soldiers came to arrest the priest Alban swapped clothes with the priest, putting on his tunic and *caracalla*, a sort of hooded greatcoat. That the priest would have worn a *caracalla* in midsummer is unlikely and the use of the word may be due to a confusion in the Turin version of the Passio Albani with the nickname of Severus' elder son. Because the word *caracalla* passed out of common use in Latin, later copyists substituted the word amphibalon, an overcoat. Subsequent confusion resulted in the priest being named Amphibalus.

When did the martyrdom take place?
The Turin version of the Passio Albani and both Gildas and Bede say quite specifically that the martyrdom took place on 22 June, the summer solstice. Summer is also implied in all versions, where the hill of martyrdom was described as: 'It is unspeakably beautiful, painted – or rather clothed – with diverse flowers', although it should be noted that such a description was perhaps a standard device in hagiography[39]. Midsummer would also explain the presence of large crowds blocking the

---
[39] Robin Lane Fox: Pagans and Christians.

bridge over the River Ver: they would have come to Verulamium for the pagan midsummer festival. But the midsummer of which year? As mentioned previously, the martyrdom could have taken place in either of the two third-century episodes of persecution. After much debate the consensus seems to agree the mid-third century as being the most likely. But whichever date is supposed, the event took place nearly 200 years before Germanus' visit and his rejuvenation – or initiation – of the cult of St Alban.

Continuity of veneration

By the time of Germanus' visit there was a tradition, at least 400 years old, of ritual activity at Verulamium in the centuries before the martyrdom[40]. The object of veneration was the extraordinary burial site at Oysterfield described previously, around which a large Romano-Celtic temple was built, surrounded by pits used for ritual deposits including a scalped, defleshed head. The grave was occupied by a body lying on an ivory couch surrounded by Roman grave goods. This grave, and the complex in which it was located, was the object of mass veneration at festivals including that at midsummer. Such veneration died out in the early fourth century when its place seems to have been taken over by the veneration of the Verulamium Christian martyr Alban, which continued through to the arrival of Germanus. Here then we have a long tradition of the veneration of a local hero/saint, which is very old indeed – sufficiently firmly established to survive the turbulent times in the near future.

Early in this period the observance of Christianity was prohibited and in this time the story of the martyr would have been sustained orally by the Verulamium faithful. There may have been a simple tomb – or just a stone or a post – marking the grave on the edge of the pre-existing cemetery. After the Edict of Milan in 313, when Christianity was legalised, 100 years would have elapsed, during which time there would have been a growth in Christianity, its institutional development and church-building. It is probable that, at this time, a basilica was built around the tomb, the basilica that Germanus visited. Was this, then, the building which Bede described as 'a church of wonderful workmanship, and altogether worthy to commemorate his martyrdom', was erected? Or was this church built after Germanus' visit and the major boost to St Alban's status resulting from the visit and the establishment of the cult?

---

[40] Robin Fleming: *Britain After Rome*, p. 122.

3

The Anglo-Saxon Transition

The masonry is wondrous; fate broke it.

Courtyard pavements were smashed; the work of giants is decaying

> *The Ruin*, an anonymous Old English elegy of the eighth century.

The mole shouldered the clogged wheel, his gold solidus; where dry-dust badgers thronged the Roman flues, the long-unlooked-for mansions of our tribe

> Geoffrey Hill: from *Mercian Hymns IV*.

Overview

The 150-year period following the breakdown of Roman administration in the mid-fifth century falls within the 'Dark Ages', a designation now discredited, but in terms of contemporary documentary evidence dark it certainly was. It's an important period in the Alban story because what happened in Britain, now recognised as a relatively peaceful and gradual takeover by the Saxons rather than conquest, enables us to take a view on the possible continuity of the cult of St Alban.

Britain's secession from Rome – or the Roman abandonment of Britain – was a long time a-coming, but when it came was sudden, unplanned and dramatic[41]. The build-up was a toxic combination of coastal attacks requiring a big capital investment in defences, funded by a ruinous level of taxation and internal political instability. It became inevitable when, in the early 400s, the army went unpaid due to a lack of money. Their response was to back a series of usurpers to the emperor culminating in Constantine III, who left Britain in 408, taking the army with him to defend Gaul against Germanic invaders. In this he was

---
[41] David Mattingly: An Imperial Possession, ch 17

successful and was recognised briefly and reluctantly, although he was killed in 411 on Emperor Honorius' orders. Meanwhile Britain was attacked by the Picts (from Scotland) and the Scots (from Ireland). In the absence of any support from Rome and in the light of deep disaffection on the part of the British due to ruinous taxation, Britain organised her own defence and simultaneously seceded from the empire in 409: in the words of the Greek historian Zosimus, the Britons 'were obliged to throw off Roman rule and live independently, no longer subject to Roman law'.

On secession there was a trend to revert to the former tribal divisions, complete with the re-fortification of the Iron Age hillforts, mostly based in the west of Britain and led by a chieftain known as Vortigern, referred to by Gildas as 'the proud tyrant'. In inland areas of southern Britain there was more of a continuation of Roman-style administration and orthodox Romano-British Christianity. In the mid-fifth century, this faction was led by Ambrosius Aurelianus, whose parents, according to Gildas, 'had worn the purple' that is his father had been governor of Britain in the post-Roman period. He was also perhaps related to Ambrose, the great Archbishop of Milan whose father was also named Aurelius Ambrosius.

This fissiparous situation precluded a coordinated defence of the Island against coastal raiders with the result that Germanic federated troops, known as *foederati*, were employed as mercenaries. This arrangement was initially successful but inevitably, as time passed, it broke down. Because either the British failed to honour their obligations to pay and supply the *foederati* or the *foederati* made increasingly excessive demands – or a combination of the two – the *foederati* expanded out of their allotted enclaves to terrorize the interior. Such incursions, resisted by sporadic battles, culminated at the end of the fifth century, with the battle of Badon Hill, thought to be near Bath, in which the British forces, possibly under the command of Ambrosius and possibly with the support of King Arthur, comprehensively defeated the raiders. The breathing space that this victory provided was, however, wasted in internecine conflict between the faction previously led by Vortigern and that led by Ambrosius, their mutual animosity perhaps fuelled by Vortigern's support of Pelagianism[42]. This political vacuum provided the opportunity for a resumption of Anglo-Saxon immigration – and on a much larger scale.

---

[42] Michael Wood: *Domesday A Search for the Roots of England*.

The Saxon *Adventus*: continuity or conquest?

Gildas, writing in the early sixth century[43]:

> Then all the councillors, together with that proud tyrant Gurthrigern [Vortigern], the British king, were so blinded, that, as a protection to their country, they sealed its doom by inviting in among them like wolves into the sheep-fold, the fierce and impious Saxons, a race hateful both to God and men, to repel the invasions of the northern nations. Nothing was ever so pernicious to our country, nothing was ever so unlucky. What palpable darkness must have enveloped their minds – darkness desperate and cruel! Those very people whom, when absent, they dreaded more than death itself, were invited to reside, as one may say, under the selfsame roof.
>
> From that time the germ of iniquity and the root of contention planted their poison amongst us, as we deserved, and shot forth into leaves and branches. The barbarians being thus introduced as soldiers into the island, to encounter, as they falsely said, any dangers in defence of their hospitable entertainers, obtain an allowance of provisions, which, for some time being plentifully bestowed, stopped their doggish mouths. Yet they complain that their monthly supplies are not furnished in sufficient abundance, and they industriously aggravate each occasion of quarrel, saying that unless more liberality is shown them, they will break the treaty and plunder the whole island. In a short time, they follow up their threats with deeds.
>
> For the fire of vengeance, justly kindled by former crimes, spread from sea to sea, fed by the hands of our foes in the east, and did not cease, until, destroying the neighbouring towns and lands, it reached the other side of the island, and dipped its red and savage tongue in the western ocean. In these assaults, therefore, not unlike that of the Assyrian upon Judea, was fulfilled in our case what the prophet describes in words of lamentation; 'They have burned with fire the sanctuary; they have polluted on earth the tabernacle of thy name.' And again, 'O God, the gentiles have come into thine inheritance; thy holy temple have they defiled,' So that all the columns were levelled with the ground by the frequent strokes of the battering-ram, all the husbandmen routed, together with their bishops, priests, and people, whilst the sword gleamed, and the flames crackled around them on every side.

---

[43] Gildas DEB paragraph 23 & 24.

> Lamentable to behold, in the midst of the streets lay the tops of lofty towers, tumbled to the ground, stones of high walls, holy altars, fragments of human bodies, covered with livid clots of coagulated blood, looking as if they had been squeezed together in a press; and with no chance of being buried, save in the ruins of the houses, or in the ravening bellies of wild beasts and birds; with reverence be it spoken for their blessed souls, if, indeed, there were many found who were carried, at that time, into the high heaven by the holy angels. So entirely had the vintage, once so fine, degenerated and become bitter, that, in the words of the prophet, there was hardly a grape or ear of corn to be seen where the husbandman had turned his back.

Well, he certainly doesn't mince his words! Gildas was of course exaggerating in order to make a point: that the calamity that befell Britain was all down to the sloth of the British leaders, both temporal and spiritual. Something of this view persisted amongst historians until quite recently. Certainly Edward Gibbon, in his *History of the Decline and Fall of the Roman Empire*, had no doubts that fierce British resistance, after initial success of containment of invading forces, eventually gave way to the Saxons, who extended their control over southern, central and eastern Britain. This resulted in the vanquished peasantry being reduced to servitude so that 'the arts and religion, the laws and language which the Romans had so carefully planted in Britain, were extirpated by their barbarous successors.'

This approach was accepted as the authorised version of events and maintained through to the mid-twentieth century by established historians. Susan Oosthuizen[44] provides numerous examples of nineteenth and twentieth-century historians using phrases such as 'overwhelming Anglo-Saxon superiority', 'scenes of desolation' and 'hopeless servitude' in their description of the supposed Anglo-Saxon invasion.

This view began to change in the mid-twentieth century when a more critical approach took hold, based on a review of documentary, archaeological and genetic evidence.

First, documentary evidence. There are three contemporary documentary sources that offer relevant evidence of the situation in fifth- and sixth-century Britain: Constantius' *Life of Germanus*, *The Gallic Chronicle* and Gildas' *De Excidio Britanniae*.

---

[44] Susan Oosthuizen: The Emergence of the English.

It is possible to discern, from Constantius' work, elements of continuity in Britain at the time of Germanus' two visits: meeting a man of tribunian authority (whose daughter he cures of blindness) in his first visit and a prominent citizen Elaphius in the second. Both indicate some continuity of civil administration, although Germanus' key role in the successful Alleluia battle (if Constantius is to be believed) seems to imply the absence of a regular army.

In the Gallic Chronicle of 452, it is noted that 'Britain was lost to the empire, having come under the authority of the Saxons'. This was written from hearsay evidence by a writer based in Provence, and it is hard not to detect a whiff of schadenfreude.

Gildas, as we have seen previously, is less concerned with objective factual historical record than with a polemic description of the deteriorating relationship between the Britons and the Anglo-Saxons during the Saxon incursions of the fifth century. The larger scale, more extensive wave of immigration took place after Gildas had completed *De Excidio Britanniae*.

Two hundred years later Bede drew heavily on Gildas' work to present his account of the Saxon transition but doesn't add any new insight.

Thus it seems there is no contemporary or near-contemporary documentary evidence to support the conquest hypothesis. Nor does archaeology provide any support, because no mass graves of Britons have been found and relatively few obviously Anglo-Saxon funerary remains. A recent study found that the cause of death of only 2 per cent of all skeletons dating from this period was found to be violent. Very few fifth century coins have been discovered because the main supply of coinage was that with which the Roman garrison was paid. In the absence of a supply of coinage the urban economy would have suffered a steep decline, but this decline predated the transition period by at least a century. The rural economy, by far the biggest economic sector, was never highly monetized and so continued unaffected by the transition. It was affected by the climatic repercussions of a major volcanic eruption suffered in the 530s which may have been responsible for a shift of emphasis from arable to pastoral[45].

Lastly, genetic evidence indicates the contribution of Saxon genes to the English population is low, ranging from 15 per cent in East Anglia to 5 per cent in the bulk of England and less than 5 per cent in Wales and the west of England[46]. The numbers of Anglo-Saxon immigrants must have

---

[45] Nicholas Crane: *The Making of the British Landscape*.
[46] Stephen Oppenheimer: *The Origins of the British*.

been relatively small, far too small to support the conquest hypothesis, but there is no denying their enormous cultural impact, especially in language. The impact of the introduction of a new language would have been somewhat ameliorated, in lowland Britain at least, by the fact that even in Iron Age times Britons were exposed to a Germanic language spoken by the Belgic tribes with whom they traded. This familiarity probably continued throughout the Roman period, helped no doubt by the large numbers of soldiers recruited for the Roman garrison from the Germanic tribes. The overall period of exposure to Germanic languages was thus some five centuries – evolution rather than revolution.

The fifth- and sixth-century immigrants were heathen, with a polytheistic belief system. Their principal gods were Woden, Tuw and Thor but there were many others, with a supporting cast of elves, goblins, dragons etc. Nothing is known about their interaction with either the remains of Roman paganism or the remnants of Roman Christianity. Because there is no indication that the Anglo-Saxons insisted, as had the Romans, on a token acknowledgement of their religion, it is assumed that friction between the various believers was minimal[47]. There would have been little contact between the paganism of the rural dwelling Anglo-Saxons and Christianity, which was essentially an urban religion. Certainly nothing is known of any attempt by the British Christians to convert the Anglo-Saxons, which drew the contempt of the later Augustine mission.

Patterns of immigration

On its secession from the Roman Empire Britain soon fragmented into its constituent parts, loosely based on Iron Age polities. In the north and west of Britain, areas which were only lightly Romanised, the fragmentation resulted in rule by local or regional strong men or *tyranni*, one of whom may have been King Arthur. In the Romano-British heartlands a semblance of civil administration from the *civitates* continued, although the money economy and countrywide tax system collapsed. However, enough inter-regional cooperation was available to mount some measure of coastal defence in the decades immediately following secession.

Immigration to Britain from the near continent had been going on for many centuries before secession, but naturally increased in volume in the

---

[47] Barbara Yorke: *The Conversion of Britain*.

fifth century. The principal sources of immigrants were Angles, confusingly from Jutland, Saxons from the base of the Danish peninsula, and Jutes from the Rhine delta, and probably not from Jutland[48]. As noted previously, immigration was boosted in the mid-fifth century when contingents of Germanic soldier/settlers were invited by Vortigern to help defend the south and east coast from attacks by the Picts and Scots as *foederati*, that is, their military service was provided in return of grants of land and provisions. Within six years of their arrival the Kentish contingent, led by Hengist, rebelled against these terms and defeated the British forces in Kent, Hengist's son taking the Kentish throne. Similarly the Angles and the Saxons were invited to defend the East Anglian and Sussex coast. These forces grew in number and migrated ever westwards until in the late fifth century they were confronted by a combined British army. In the ensuing battle, at Badon Hill, supposedly near Bath, the British forces won a convincing victory that caused the Anglo-Saxons to withdraw eastwards and paused any further settlement for a generation. Indeed it was probably responsible for a significant emigration, noted by Procopius, of Saxons back to the Continent, implying that some, at least, abandoned their effort to build a new life in Britain.

When migration resumed in a second wave, early in the sixth century, Anglo-Saxon penetration of lowland Britain advanced rapidly, with the south/west Saxons pushing up from Sussex, settling in the upper Thames Valley and the East Saxons and Angles pushing westwards via the Rivers Ouse, Nene, Welland and Cam. The Chilterns, including Hertfordshire and Bedfordshire, remained largely Saxon-free until, in 571, the two waves of migration – east and west – met the Britons in battle at a place called Bedcanford (Bedford), as a result of which they took four settlements: Luton, Aylesbury, Benson and Eynsham.

By the end of the sixth century much of lowland Britain would have been under Anglo-Saxon control, organised into a large number of small kingdoms that would eventually coalesce to form the principal seventh-century English groupings: Northumbria, Mercia, East Anglia, Essex, Kent, Sussex and Wessex – known as the Heptarchy.

Verulamium in the fifth and sixth centuries

Verulamium, as with other British Roman cities, underwent a long slow period of decline from the mid-fourth century, by which time

---

[48] Frank Stenton: *Anglo Saxon England*, p. 10.

Christianity had been adopted as the official empire religion. This period of decline intensified after the early fifth century when the Roman army left Britain, although it is likely that the main structures of Roman civilisation, including Christianity, survived. Even on a material level there is evidence of some continuity of occupation of Verulamium in the early fifth century with the maintenance of the water supply and the adaptation of buildings to a more rustic use: Roman city life it wasn't, but it was continuity nonetheless[49]. Then there is the evidence of Germanus: in the account of both his visits the background is one of a functioning civic administration and functioning ecclesiastical hierarchy, albeit riven with heresy. This situation could have continued for some considerable time with the heresy resolved by Germanus and civil governance being provided by the elite, deeply rooted in their Catuvellauni ancestry.

Archaeological and place-name evidence indicates that there was no Saxon incursion into Verulamium and its hinterland in the second half of the fifth century. Higham[50] acknowledges that the commonly held view of a divided Britain – a Celtic west and an Anglo-Saxon dominated east – is open to challenge; there is a strongly held counter-argument that pockets of sub-Roman culture and autonomy survived. It is probable that Verulamium was one of these pockets – if so it would only have been through good organisation of its defences, which would have played an important role in rallying the pan-British forces prior to the battle of Badon Hill. Certainly, Verulamium would have played a pivotal role in the absence of Colchester and London, both having succumbed to mid-fifth century raids. It can be argued that Verulamium aspired to the leadership of fifth century Britain[51]. It had good reason to be proud:

- It was based on Verlamion, the capital of the largest and most resourceful of the Iron Age tribes, the Catuvellauni.
- It had secured excellent terms with the Roman invaders, becoming a *municipium* – the only one in Britain – with virtually self-governing power.
- It was home to Alban, the proto-martyr of Britain, recognised as such by Germanus, a representative of the pope. It successfully transformed itself from a centre of Romano-Celtic paganism to a centre of Romano-British Christianity.

---

[49] Rosalind Nebitt: *Verulamium*, p. 131.
[50] Nick Higham: *From Sub-Roman Britain to Anglo Saxon England – Debating the Insular Dark Ages*.
[51] Philip Thornhill: *St Alban and the end of Roman Britain*.

– Its main rivals, London and Colchester, had been overrun by pagan immigrants. Other comparable *civitates* in the region, notably Silchester and Winchester, had not achieved the same status as Verulamium and were far more vulnerable to powerful attack from the south and west Saxons: neither had a patronal saint at this time.

In the power vacuum that existed after the secession from the Roman Empire, the promotion of the cult of St Alban would have been in perfect harmony with the aspirations of the Verulamium elite. What Verulamium lacked, however, was the manpower for a large standing army, situated as it was in a region of relatively low population density. It could not prevent, despite the generational Anglo-Saxon set-back following their defeat at the battle of Badon Hill, a second wave of Saxon infiltration in the mid-sixth century. The spread of immigration was very uneven, however, and there is plenty of evidence – archaeological and place-name studies – to suggest that the Verulamium cantonal area was relatively unaffected by immigration until the end of the sixth century.

First, archaeology. By the early fifth century the prevailing custom was, for pagan and Christian British alike, to be buried in an approximately east–west orientation. The Saxon immigrants followed their tradition of cremation followed by burial of their remains, together with grave goods, dateable by archaeologists. There are no known Anglo-Saxon cemeteries or even graves in the area[52]. Second, place names, which would have either Celtic, Roman or Anglo-Saxon provenance. For instance the name Ver, as in the river, is a Celtic name of great antiquity, while Alban is a Latin name first used in this context by Germanus in 429. Early Saxon place names typically end in ~*ingas* meaning a folk group, or ~*ham*, meaning a village, quite possibly incorporating both, as in Birmingham. There are no Saxon place names with an *inga* or *ham* ending in the vicinity of Verulamium that can be dated to the fifth or sixth centuries. The closest places with names ending in ~*ham* are Aldenham and Borehamwood to the south east and Studham to the north west. For names ending in ~*ingas* the closest is Hertingfordbury to the east. All of these names originate after the sixth century[53].

Following the battle of Bedcanford a Saxon tribe, the Waeclingas, settled in Verulamium, which became known as Waeclingacaester from which the name Watling Street was derived. By the end of the sixth

---

[52] Tom Williamson: *The Origins of Hertfordshire*.
[53] K Rutherford Davis: *Britons and Saxons – The Chiltern Region 400–700*.

century Waeclingas was surrounded by embryonic kingdoms: Essex to the east, London and Middlesex to the south (although these were in reality part of Essex), Wessex to the west and Mercia/Middle Anglia to the north.

There can be no doubt that the profile and prestige of Christianity in general and of Christianity in Verulamium was immeasurably boosted by Germanus' visits and the publication of his biography and the early versions of the *Passio Albani*. It is impossible to know, but not an unreasonable conjecture, that the basilica in which Alban's tomb was housed was a modest building. In view of Bede's description of the church as being of 'wonderful workmanship' the probability of an extension or reconstruction of the basilica in the fifth century is not unlikely. After all, in the absence of Roman taxes the local economy probably had the resources and retained the masonry skills. Could it have resembled St Martins Church, Canterbury, dating from the immediate post-Roman period, a conjectural model of which is shown:

A model of the post-Roman St Martins Church, Canterbury.

London was probably thoroughly paganised from the late fifth century and consequently organised diocesan Christianity in the south east ended. The Verulamium Christians, together with their cult of St Alban, would have found themselves alone and isolated until the widespread Christianisation of England took place in the middle of the seventh century. From the time when Verulamium came under Saxon control, in the mid-sixth century, it is probable that a satisfactory accommodation would have been reached with the Waeclingas, who may have regarded the city with a sense of some awe. It is likely that aspects of the Alban story would have resonated with the pagan Waeclingas: Alban was portrayed in Gildas as 'the highest spirit in the battle line of Christ, a hero who willingly left his home to engage in a struggle for his belief, a victor rather than a victim'. Here there are parallels to Beowulf's struggle with Grendel[54]. Furthermore, the references to water miracles in the story – the river drying up in Alban's path to martyrdom and the spring of water to quench his thirst – would have resonated with the pagan water cult. Maybe the Waeclingas grew to venerate their adopted saint, a Saxon hero of their very own. Thus, it is entirely possible there was continuity of the cult of St Alban through the relatively short period of Waeclingas dominance between the end of the sixth century and the nominally Christian Mercian hegemony of the mid-seventh century.

---

[54] Kyle Potter: *A Cult Between Cultures: Reading St Alban as an Anglo-Saxon Hero*

4

Political Consolidation, Religious Conversion

First the rough seed, sown in rougher soil.

                               Horatius Bonar (nineteenth-century hymnodist).

Fruitful Britain holy Alban yields.

                               Venantius Fortunatus (sixth-century Roman poet).

Introduction

If, as I firmly believe and hope I have shown, the memory and cult of St Alban survived the existential threat of the 'Dark Ages' it might seem that we enter the seventh and eighth century as if we are emerging from the dark valley of despair. These two centuries saw the beginnings of the rule of law and the conversion of the the constituent kingdoms of Britian to Christianity, notional and superficial though that might have been. Plain sailing for St Alban then? Maybe, but somehow he seems to have been forgotten – the harvest of the Augustine's Oak synod? (See Chapter 5.)

Political consolidation

The various kingdoms and other territories that made up lowland Britain went through a process of consolidation that took several centuries to complete but which affected the speed and the character of the process of religious conversion. Both these processes affect the Alban story.

    The territories that had the greatest effect on Verulamium – or Waeclingascaester as it was known in the seventh century – were Essex, Middle Anglia and Mercia, which amalgamated over the course of the seventh century. Of these the kingdom of Essex was the oldest and weakest of the kingdoms, having been formed in the first wave of immigration in the mid-sixth century. By the early seventh century it was subservient to Kent. It was more extensive than the modern county – it incorporated London and its western boundary took in the eastern part of modern day Hertfordshire.

The kingdom of Mercia emerged from a group of Angle immigrants who settled in the Trent valley in the late sixth century under a dynasty believed to have descended from Woden, which gave Mercian kings greater than usual authority. Their history begins with King Penda in the early seventh century, a fierce pagan who expanded the Mercian territory in all directions, assimilating both the satellite territories of Magonsaete and Hwicce in the west and Middle Anglia in the east. The Middle Angles inhabited what is now the east Midlands, stretching from the foot of the Chilterns in the south to the Wash in the north and bounded by East Anglia and Essex in the east. Thus by the mid-seventh century Waeclingas became contiguous with, and subservient to, Mercia.

In the south Waeclingas bordered on Middlesex, which, together with London, was nominally controlled by, or was part of, Essex, but by the second half of the seventh century had been absorbed into Mercia.

Conversion – the Gregorian mission

Christianity may have survived, in places, the waves of Anglo-Saxon immigration and cultural takeover in the fifth and sixth centuries but the numbers of Christians would have been small, and only in the west and in a few former *civitates*, notably at Verulamium, would any vestiges of the Romano-British church structure have survived. Both Gildas and Bede were highly critical of the British bishops, all with dioceses in the west of Britain, for not attempting to evangelise the pagan Anglo-Saxons – but it was just too difficult. Nor was there any external help from Rome or the former empire until the end of the sixth century, some 150 years after the last visit by a senior churchman, Germanus.

Towards the end of the sixth century informal contacts between the peoples of Kent and the south Saxons with the Franks of north-east Gaul had been growing primarily through trade, which may have familiarised the British population with Frankish Christianity. In 580 King Aethelberht of Kent married Bertha, a Christian Merovingian princess who brought Bishop Luidhard with her as chaplain. Thus King Aethelberht would have had seventeen years exposure to Christianity before the arrival of the Augustinian mission, during which time the bishop restored the Roman stone-built chapel dedicated to St Martin at Canterbury.

The idea of a mission was perhaps sown in the mind of Gregory by a chance incident in Rome. The story is well known but bears repetition[55]:

> There is a story told by the faithful that, before he became pope, there came to Rome certain people of our nation, fair skinned and light-haired. When he heard of their arrival he was eager to see them: being prompted by a fortunate intuition, being puzzled by their new and unusual appearance, and above all, being inspired by God, he received them and asked what race they belonged to. They answered, 'the people we belong to are called Angles.' 'Angels of God,' he replied. Then he asked further, 'what is the name of the king of that people?' They said, 'Aelli,' whereupon he said, 'Alleluia, God's praise must be heard there.' Then he asked the name of their own tribe, to which they answered, 'Deire*,' and he replied, 'They shall flee from the wrath of God (*de ira dei*) to the faith.'

When Gregory became pope in 590 he was determined to mount a mission to Britain. His motives, prompted by the memory of his meeting with the Angle boys, were primarily pastoral, heeding the need to spread the word to the 'ends of the world' which Britain certainly was. There also may have been a secondary political motive. Perhaps Gregory was aware of the missionary activities of Ninian and Columba in northern Britain: he may also have been aware of Columbanus' work revitalising religious zeal in Francia. He had to act to ensure that the future Christianity of the Anglo-Saxons was inspired and controlled by Rome rather than by the Celts.

Gregory chose Augustine, a monk from his own former monastery, to lead the mission. As prefect of Gregory's monastery, he had been responsible for enforcing monastic discipline and the supervision of its estates. Gregory could not have been fully aware of the state of the Church in Britain as it seems he thought all that Augustine had to do was to re-invigorate an existing, but moribund organisation. He (and Augustine) was unaware of the traditions of the British Church and of their pride in maintaining the faith for nearly two centuries since secession from the Roman Empire without any further contact or support from Rome.

On arrival in Kent in 595 Augustine made short work of converting Aethelberht, whose wife was already Christian. He established a base at

---

[55] Henry Mayr Harting: The Coming of Christianity to Anglo-Saxon England.
* Deire: Northumberland.

Canterbury and then proceeded to found a new see at Rochester. In 601 he convened a synod with bishops representing the British Church at a site that became known as Augustine's Oak, in the Severn Valley. The British were from the outset suspicious of Augustine, who came under the protection of the enemy, the Anglo-Saxons. There were two sessions of meeting: in the first Augustine told the British that they should:
- help preach the gospel to the heathen;
- adhere to the Roman method of estimating the date of Easter;
- correct other matters that did not conform to the unity of the Roman Church.

After much wrangling Augustine requested that an infirm person should be brought in so the two sides could indulge in what was effectively a miracle-healing competition. The British were not happy with this proposal but nevertheless produced a blind man whom Augustine healed. The British replied they would need the consent of their people before they could abandon their ancient traditions and that a second session would be required, at which more of their number would be present. In this interval, the bishops consulted with a holy man, a hermit, asking him whether they ought, at the request of Augustine, to forsake their traditions. In the words of Bede[56], the following dialogue ensued:

> 'If he is a man of God, follow him.' 'How shall we know that?' said they. He replied, 'Our Lord saith, 'Take my yoke upon you and learn of me, for I am meek and lowly in heart: if, therefore Augustine is meek and lowly of heart it is to believed that he has taken upon him the yoke of Christ and offers the same to take upon you. But if he is stern and haughty it appears that he is not of God nor are you to regard his word.' They insisted again, 'And how shall we discern even this?' 'Do you contrive,' said the anchorite, 'that he may first arrive with his company at the place where the synod is to be held, and if at your approach he shall arise to you, hear him submissively, being assured that he is the servant of Christ: but if he shall despise you and not rise up to you whereas you are more in number, let him also be despised by you.'

Needless to say Augustine did not rise to greet the British and the synod ended badly with no agreement and with Augustine cursing the British with 'the vengeance of death'. It is thought that Bede included this

---
[56] Bede: *The Ecclesiastical History of the English Nation*, Book 2, Chapter 2.

detailed account of the synod in his Ecclesiastical History to demonstrate the insularity and stubbornness of the British Church. In this he succeeded but in so doing he showed up Augustine's arrogance and inflexibility – he was just too prefectorial. Neither side had a good meeting with the result that relations were soured between the two churches for a century or more. Perhaps the gulf between the two sides reflects a more fundamental difference than that of the alternative methods of calculating the date of Easter, or between stubbornness on one side and arrogance on the other. Is there not an echo here of the changes in teaching and practice that evolved in Rome in the 250 or so years that elapsed between the time when the British Church was formed and the time of this encounter?

This attitude on the part of the Roman Church was to have a considerable negative effect on the acceptability to the English Church of the Romano-British St Alban.

Perhaps Pope Gregory sensed Augustine's inflexibility, because in 601, the same year as the synod, he sent a second mission led by Mellitus bearing letters for Augustine instructing that the Anglo-Saxon pagan temples should be adapted for Christian use and not destroyed (as previously stipulated) and that a more softly-softly approach should be followed in the process of conversion.

Meanwhile, Augustine's mission continued. King Aethelberht was exhorted by Gregory in a letter brought by Mellitus[57]: 'Let your glory hasten to infuse, into the kings and people that are subject to you, the knowledge of one God, Father, Son and Holy Ghost.' Accordingly, as the overlord and uncle of King Salbert of Essex, he prevailed on him to accept the faith with Mellitus appointed as Bishop of London in 604 just before Augustine's death in 605. Unfortunately neither King Aethelberht or King Salbert had succeeded in converting their sons, so on their deaths, in 616/617, Christianity was extinguished in Essex and very nearly so in Kent. There was one last chance: a marriage was arranged in 616 between Aethelberht's daughter Ethelburga and King Edwin of Northumberland on condition Edwin was baptised. She travelled north with Paulinus, one of the monks from Gregory's mission, and eventually in 625 Edwin was baptised and Paulinus was consecrated Bishop of York. However, in 632 Edwin was killed in the battle of Hatfield Chase by an alliance of Cadwallon, King of Gwynned, and Penda, the pagan King of Mercia. Ethelburg and Paulinus fled south.

---

[57] DW Barrett: *Sketches of Church Life – Diocese of St Albans*.

Conversion of Northumberland and Mercia

Edwin had come from the Deira component of the united Northumbrian kingdom and on his death Oswald, a prince on the Bernician side, avenged Edwin's defeat by attacking and defeating Cadwallon near Hexham. Oswald, a Christian who had been baptised at Iona, was thus accepted as the new king of the united Northumbria and immediately requested the abbot of Iona to send a suitable monk to act as Bishop of Northumbria. Iona sent Aidan, who established a monastery on Lindisfarne as his base, and within thirty years Aidan thoroughly Christianised Northumbria. Meanwhile Oswald, who had married the daughter of King Cynegils of Wessex, stood godfather to his father-in-law at his baptism conducted by Birinus in Dorchester-on-Thames.

Subsequently Oswald was killed in a battle near Oswestry by Penda and the Northumbrian throne passed to Oswius, Oswald's brother. A marriage was then proposed between Oswius' daughter and Peada, the son of King Penda, the pagan King of Mercia. But a condition was made, and accepted, that Peada be baptised first, and so the cause for which Oswald died was vindicated. Once this was settled Peada asked Finian, Aidan's successor at Lindisfarne to send missionaries to evangelise the Middle Angles. One of these, Diuma, became the first Bishop of Mercia with his see at Lichfield: another, Cedd was consecrated Bishop of Essex and converted the East Saxons, for a second time. In the midst of this evangelical activity the main source of friction between the Roman and the Celtic Church, the method of calculating the date of Easter, was resolved in Rome's favour at the Synod of Whitby. With Wessex, Middle Anglia and Essex all firmly Christian by 660, it didn't take long for London and Middlesex to fall into line, so that the 'island' of the Waeclingas, although not receiving any direct mission, could not fail but to be assimilated into the Anglo-Saxon Christian world.

Church organisation

In the Roman Empire church organisation mirrored the civil organisation in that that each *civitate* would have its own bishop, and each province, of which there were four in Britain, its own metropolitan bishop[58]. We see this in the British representation at the 314 Council of Arles. Thus in the fourth century there would have been fifteen bishops: Verulamium, being

---

[58] Barbara Yorke: The Conversion of Britain 600–800.

not just a *civitas* but a *municipium* no less, would certainly have had its own bishop. The bishoprics of western Britain would have survived after the secession of the Roman Empire – these were the men who attended Augustine's synod in 601. However, the metropolitan of the British province in which Verulamium was situated, Maxima Caesariensis, based in London, did not survive the *adventus saxones* and the position of bishop of Verulamium must have been a lonely one: not only the London but other neighbouring dioceses – Winchester, Colchester and Silchester – would have been overwhelmed in the first wave of Saxon incursions. So Verulamium was isolated with Cirencester likely to have been its closest neighbour. Ultimately all or most lowland British bishoprics would have been abandoned by the time Augustine landed in Kent in 597.

Pope Gregory's intention was that Augustine would restore the organisation of the British Church with two provinces based on London and York. Each province would be administered by a metropolitan (archbishop) and twelve bishops and these would broadly reflect tribal regions and kingdoms. This proved to be impractical and in the event Augustine set up his base at Canterbury with subsidiary dioceses at Rochester and London, under Bishop Mellitus, and York, under Bishop Paulinus. However, neither the bishoprics of London nor York survived the death of the supporting kings, Aethelberht and Edwin respectively. As the conversion of Anglo-Saxon Britain proceeded new dioceses were established, but these were instigated by the various kings and their missionaries, not by central control from the Archbishop of Canterbury. Such central control did not emerge until the appointment of Theodore as archbishop in 669.

At the time of its foundation in 656, the Mercian diocese of Lichfield covered a vast area which would have extended as far as Waeclingascaester. Soon after its foundation the diocese was split up with the creation of the Leicester diocese in 680. Even so, the distances of these bishoprics from Waeclingasceaster were so great that diocesan control would have been minimal.

Conclusion

The conversion of Anglo-Saxon Britain was achieved by largely peaceful, unplanned and uncoordinated missionary efforts lasting about sixty years from 597 to 660. In this the role of kings was decisive and the influence of women possibly even more so. Queen Bertha of Kent was instrumental in the conversion of her husband King Aethelberht. Her daughter

Ethelberga was responsible for the conversion of her husband King Edwin of Northumberland, while Oswiu's daughter caused the conversion of Peada of Mercia. There were other factors at work as well, one of which was that pagan kings began to notice that Christian countries at the time were wealthier than pagan ones and won more battles as a result.

Once Christianised it was the kings who had the biggest voice on where to found bishoprics, because this was a matter of kingly prestige: in Mercia, Lichfield was the obvious first choice while Leicester, the centre of the Middle Angles, the next. It is doubtful whether the Mercian king in question, Wulfhere, had ever even heard of Verulamium and St Alban, but even if he had Verulamium wouldn't have made the cut; Waeclingas was just too peripheral, too small and too unimportant – and maybe too British.

5

The Saxon Monastery of St Alban

A prophet is not without honour except in his own country.

St Mark's Gospel 6/4.

Rood was I reared. I lifted a mighty king, Lord of the heavens, dared not to break.

From *The Holy Rood*, an anonymous Old English poem.

Introduction

After an inexplicably long delay, a monastery was founded at the site of Alban's execution just outside Verulamium. Tradition has it that Offa, effectively the King of England, founded the monastery as a Benedictine community in 793, but this 'foundation' is not supported by available evidence. Irrespective of Offa's precise role, the monastery got off to a very shaky start and required a refoundation at the end of the tenth century before it could flourish.

The cult of St Alban

Saints are holy men or women who act as mediators between heaven and earth and provided an inspiration for ordinary people. The cult of saints was a concept developed by the Church in the fourth century as an aid to the conversion of western Europe and to the sustaining of that conversion. Essential elements of the development of a cult were both a *Passio*, or life of the saint, and relics of the saint. After the visit of Germanus in 429 Alban had both and so his cult was born.

As we have seen, most of the Anglo-Saxon conversions took place in the first half of the seventh century when Waeclingasceaster and Alban were obscure. Despite the resonances the Alban story may have had with the Anglo-Saxons, described in Chapter 4, and despite the subtle downplaying of Alban's Britishness in Bede's account (where Alban avoids a direct response to the judge's question concerning his origins), the Romano-British cult of St Alban evidently failed to make the transition to Anglo-Saxon acceptance outside the immediate vicinity of Verulamium – the Anglo-Saxon calendar does not mention St Alban's feast day, although it mentions those of several Irish saints[59]. Only in Worcester was there a British seventh-century dedication to St Alban, although other dedications followed in the late Saxon and Norman periods.

At this early stage there was no claim made, by his cult followers, that St Alban was Britain's proto-martyr: this status was achieved gradually over several centuries.

By contrast in France and Merovingia the cult initiated by Germanus was very vigorous, with a total of over a hundred dedications to St Alban by the end of the millennium. Of these about forty were made before 750. These are mostly concentrated in Burgundy and Provence but extend as far west as Brittany and east to Switzerland, as shown in the next figure. The identification and authentication of these are the result of painstaking research. The subject is confused by name changes – Albanus to Albinus and Auban for example, and by the appropriation of Alban of Verulamium to Alban of Mainz. These two cults are now thought to be identical and the result of anti-British bias on the part of Boniface, the Anglo-Saxon missionary who introduced the cult to Mainz.

The early dedications in France are concentrated in north-east France and above all in Provence and Burgundy. There is a body of opinion that the Germanus mission to Britain of 429 was ordered by the metropolitan Hilary of Arles and that this explains the concentration of dedications in Provence. The dedications in Riez, Vienne and Lyons all date from the fifth century and seem to follow personal visits of Germanus to these cities, while Bishop Lupus of Troyes, who accompanied Germanus to Britain, was undoubtedly responsible for the dedication in that city. The cult spread, helped by lines the poet (later Bishop of Poitiers) Venantius Fortunatus wrote in the late sixth century:

'Fruitful Britain holy Alban yields'.

The quotation from Mark's gospel that heads this chapter can equally be applied to saints as to prophets.

---

[59] Mark Laynesmith: Translating St Alban: Romano-Brirish, Merovingian and Anglo-Saxon Cults.

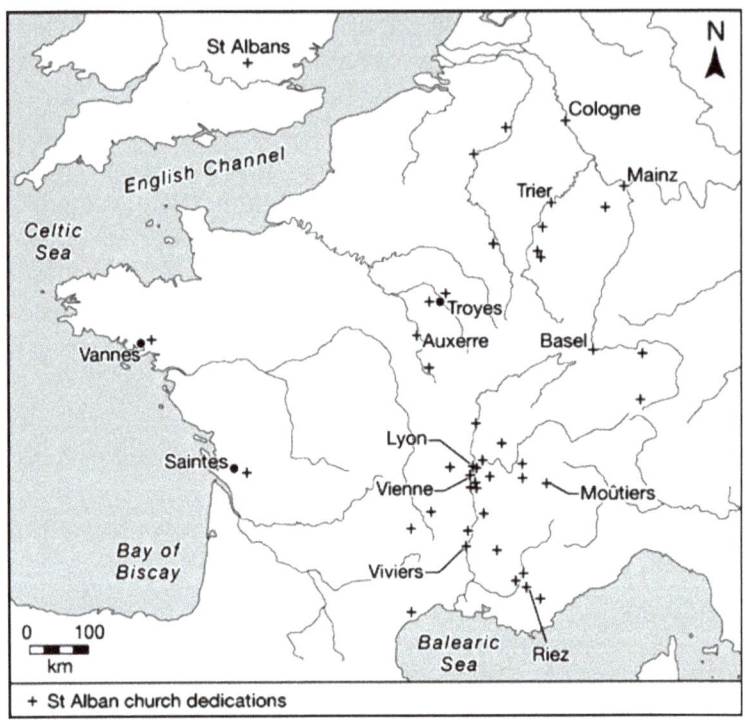

Churches dedicated to St Alban in France, Germany and Switzerland before 750 (after Laynesmith).

Monasticism

Monasticism first appeared in the fourth-century Roman Empire when hermits, reacting against the perhaps too cosy alignment between civil and ecclesiastical administrations, sought isolation for spiritual peace, abstinence and prayer in the Egyptian and Syrian deserts. These hermits attracted ever more followers, which led to the formation of religious communities, each under the rule of an abbot. This became very popular and spread rapidly throughout Gaul to Britain in the sixth century, although it is thought that Tintagel may have been the first monastic site in Britain dated to the end of the fifth century[60]. It became well established in England following the first wave of conversions, before the establishment of defined dioceses. Although an important part of a bishop's responsibilities was the conversion of pagans in his diocese, this was difficult to achieve before the creation of the parish system.

---

[60] Charles Thomas: Christianity in Roman Britain to AD 500, p348.

The Saxon Monastery of St Alban

Monasteries, however, were more community-based and became sufficiently numerous to play an effective part in the conversion process.

English religious communities founded in southern England (author sketch).
O founded in 7th century
+ founded in 8th century but before 793

Religious communities were normally founded by individuals other than the bishop and supported by the appropriate king or aristocrat. In England south of the Humber about thirty religious houses were set up by the end of the seventh century, with a further forty in the eighth, as shown. Those founded in the seventh century were mostly concentrated in the ancient kingdoms – Essex, Wessex, Hwicce (Severn valley) and above all Kent. The houses founded subsequently evened out the spatial distribution to a certain extent but there were still areas with a significantly low density of religious houses: Sussex, which was long a bastion of paganism and the area covered by modern Hertfordshire, Buckinghamshire, Bedfordshire and Essex (outside London).

The foundation of the monastery of St Alban

Up to the time of the foundation of its monastery at the end of the eighth century, it has to be assumed that the martyrial church, as described by Bede as being of 'wonderful workmanship', must have continued to exist and to be in use. By this time the church would have been some 300 years old and may have undergone various modifications and restorations, the extent and nature of which cannot even be guessed. But with the cult of St Alban having such a high profile in Europe and with relatively good communication between the religious communities of the countries of western Christendom it is unimaginable that the fabric of the mother church would not have received some maintenance and care.

It is likely that there would have been a resident priest or even a small community to watch over the tomb and its priceless relics and, if nothing else, to collect the alms of pilgrims. Nevertheless, it is odd, to say the least, that there are no records of the foundation of a religious community before the end of the eighth century, by which time some seventy communities had been founded south of the Humber. Perhaps it had been politically impossible to found a religious house dedicated to a British saint before the Council of Whitby in 664, which effected a reconciliation of the British and Roman churches. But was the further delay, after 664, because the martyrial church was already acting as a quasi-monastery? Or was it because Waeclingasceaster had become such a backwater there was no king, warlord or aristocrat associated with the area sufficiently interested or motivated to found a new monastery?

King Offa and the Church

Offa, a descendant of the pagan King Penda, became King of Mercia in 757, but it wasn't until he had been on the Mercian throne for twenty-eight years that he could proclaim himself as the 'King of Mercia and all the nations around' – he was overlord to the Kings of East Anglia, Essex, Wessex, Sussex and Kent. He was the most powerful king ever to have ruled in Britain, controlling all the territory south of the Humber, and was treated with respect by both Pope Hadrian and Charlemagne, king of the Franks and later to be Holy Roman Emperor. He had achieved this status, however, only after putting down a long rebellion by the Kentish King Egbert, which left a legacy of suspicion and distrust of both him and the Archbishop of Canterbury, at that time Jaenberht, a distant kinsman of the king. This distrust was exacerbated by the creation, in 735, of the ecclesiastical province of York, which lay within the Kingdom of Northumbria. Thus, Mercia and its dependent nations lay entirely within the province of Canterbury. Offa's plan to resolve this issue was the creation of a third province, based on an archbishopric in Lichfield: he felt the pride of Mercia required no less.

By chance, possibly, Pope Hadrian (who entertained doubts about Offa's good faith) sent a mission to Britain in 786 – the first since Augustine's mission nearly 200 years earlier – in order to reinforce papal authority. The mission comprised two Italian bishops, George of Todi and Theophylact of Ostia, accompanied by an unnamed Frankish abbot, surely Charlemagne's man. (Charlemagne, even before his election as Holy Roman Emperor in 800 had assumed Europe-wide responsibility for the Church.) The mission received a warm welcome from Offa. Bishop George visited Northumbria, where he agreed various Church reforms, while Bishop Theophylact toured Mercia: George filed a report to Pope Hadrian while Theophylact unfortunately neglected to do so – his impressions of the Mercian Church would have been of interest. At their final council, Offa agreed to all the Church reforms already agreed by the Northumbrians and also agreed an annual payment to Rome (which became known as Peter's Pence) of 365 mancuses per year (1 mancuse = £200 in today's money). No mention was made of Offa's Lichfield project.

Offa did not give up on Lichfield, however: he pursued it in a letter to Pope Hadrian who reluctantly agreed on the understanding it was the unanimous wish of the twelve suffragan bishops of the Canterbury province. Offa called a council at Chelsea where, after a stormy meeting, he obtained majority, but certainly not unanimous, support, which was not accurately conveyed to the Vatican. Hadrian's successor Pope Leo III accordingly sent a pallium (an ecclesiastical vestment conferred by the pope to symbolise episcopal authority) to Hygeberht, who was installed as Archbishop of Lichfield in 788.

The foundation of St Albans Abbey – the legend

There is a strong but unsubstantiated tradition that King Offa founded St Albans Abbey in 793, a few years before his death. Like all good legends, this one starts, as recounted by Peter Newcombe, an eighteenth-century intellectual,[61] with a dream: King Offa, while visiting Bath, dreamed that an angel instructed him to go to Verulamium to raise the body of the first British martyr, Alban, and place his remains in a shrine, suitably ornamented. Accordingly, Offa arranges to meet his senior clergy at Verulamium: Hygeberht, recently consecrated as Archbishop of Lichfield with his two suffragans, Unwona, Bishop of Leicester, and Ceolwulf, Bishop of Lindsey. While they were searching for Alban's burial place, a 'light of heaven was vouchsafed to assist the discovery: a ray of fire stood over the place of burial'. The ground was opened and the remains placed

---

[61] Peter Newcombe: The History of the Ancient and Royal Foundation Called Abbey of St Alban.

in a small chapel until a more noble edifice could be constructed. After further consultation with his nobles and prelates Offa journeys to the pope in Rome to procure his approval and the desired privileges of the new monastic foundation, which of course were granted. On his return Offa founds the new monastery under Benedictine Rule and appoints a kinsman as the first abbot. This legend was invented, or at least first written down, by Matthew Paris, a thirteenth century monk and chronicler, some 500 years after the event. It supposes that the original Church had been destroyed by the Saxons and St Alban's tomb lost, directly contrary to Bede's account.

King Offa directs the discovery of the grave of St Alban. (Matthew Paris, courtesy of St Albans Cathedral archives.)

Documentary and archaeological evidence

So, did Offa found a monastery at St Albans? It was certainly believed so in the later Middle Ages on the evidence of Matthew Paris' account based on various charters granting land and privileges to the new monastery. These charters are now known to be forgeries, possibly in existence by 1122, well before Paris' time, and there is no firm evidence either that the monastery was founded in 793, the traditional date of foundation, or that Offa was the founder[62]. There is no evidence that Offa ever visited Rome or that any specific privileges were granted by the pope: indeed there is no mention of St Albans Abbey in any Vatican records for several hundred years.

---

[62] Julia Crick: Offa, Aelfric and the Refoundation of St Albans.

There is, however, pre-conquest evidence that associates Offa with St Albans: the substantially authentic diplomas of King Aethelred (of Unready fame) refer to the restoration by Aethelred of estates formerly granted by Offa. The endowments for which authentic charters exist would not have been sufficient to sustain the monastery in the pre-conquest period. The 'authenticated' endowments are not sufficiently extensive to account for the sum of the assets recorded in the Domesday Book. The monastery must have been in possession of one or more substantial assets for which no records exist, which may have been endowed by Offa.

It is also relevant that the other twelfth-century historians, Henry of Huntingdon and William of Malmesbury, neither of whom had any motives for exaggerating the antiquity of the foundation of a religious community at St Albans, took the view that Offa was connected with the early formation of a religious community. They both agree that Offa caused the translation of St Alban's relics to a new and more splendid shrine and assembled a group of monks under an abbot bound by the Rule of Benedict.

There is, as yet, no direct archaeological evidence supporting the foundation of a new monastery at St Albans. Such evidence that exists is presented under 'The development of St Albans Abbey' later.

Circumstantial evidence

There is strong circumstantial evidence to support Offa's involvement in the foundation of St Albans Abbey:
- Offa was a powerful king and an astute politician who, while probably not particularly pious, took a close interest and was heavily involved in Church affairs.
- Although he was 'King of Mercia and surrounding nations' he was a Mercian and operated a Mercia-first policy. His project to establish an archdiocese at Lichfield was in pursuit of strategic aims, but also to boost Mercian pride. His gratitude for the pope's acquiescence needed a grander gesture of thanks than the Peter's Pence grant (see King Offa and the Church previously).
- He was in awe of Charlemagne, who considered himself as the defender of the faith and consequently interested himself in British Church affairs. Offa perhaps regarded him as a mentor. Charlemagne's wife Fastrada died in 794 and was buried in St Albans Abbey, Mainz, which at that time was under reconstruction, funded by Charlemagne. It may be that Offa was encouraged to found a

monastery at St Albans by Charlemagne, as suggested by GG Scott[63].
- Alcuin, a confidant of Charlemagne, wrote to Offa exhorting him to read, in Bede's *Ecclesiastical History* (Book 1, Ch 32) Pope Gregory's letter to King Æthelberht of Kent on the duties of a Christian king, which included the promotion of the Christian faith through the example of good works.
- Offa was full of remorse at the murder, at his instigation, of King Aethelberht of East Anglia, and full of terror of the prospect of eternal hell and damnation as a consequence: the foundation of St Albans Abbey may have been in propitiation of this.
- St Albans shares the same flag (a golden saltire on a blue field) with Offa's Mercian capital Tamworth: coincidence or a vestige of an ancient link?

The foundation of St Albans Abbey would have satisfied all these motives and would have added to the lustre of Mercia – an act of gratitude to the pope, an emulation of his mentor Charlemagne, a response to Alcuin's exhortation and a penance for the execution of Aethelberht.

The establishment of St Albans Abbey would have required the endowment of land, for which there is no record, but the absence of an authentic record doesn't mean that it didn't happen. If the abbey was not founded, and the land not endowed, by Offa, then by whom? Certainly not Offa's predecessor Aethelbald, who was accused by Alcuin of promiscuity and thieving from monasteries, and almost certainly not any of Offa's Mercian or Saxon successors. As FM Stenton says, referring to Offa: 'He is the obscurest leading figure in Anglo-Saxon history and it is easy to under-estimate his achievement.'[64] Offa should be given the benefit of doubt – he was at least associated with the foundation.

St Albans monastery in the eighth and ninth centuries

The establishment of a new religious community at St Albans would have entailed, if not the construction of a new abbey church, at least the extension of the pre-existing martyrial church, to house a new shrine, and also the construction of conventual buildings to house the monks. No

---

[63] Sir GG Scott: *Report on the Restoration of St Albans Abbey*.
[64] F M Stenton Anglo-Saxon England, p 224.

information is available about any such building work.

The *Gesta Abbatum Monasterii Sancti Albani* – Deeds of the Abbots of St Albans Monastery – compiled in St Albans Abbey in the thirteenth century by Matthew Paris from twelfth-century texts written by Adam the Cellarer, gives the supposed names and dates of all the abbots, although even this basic information is full of errors and inconsistencies. The account, as presented by Rushbrook Williams,[65] of the first nine abbots from 793 to 960 is open to doubt, not being corroborated by any independent source. It makes dismal reading, the first five abbots being mostly incompetent, corrupt and most certainly in breach of the Benedictine Rule.

The new community got off to difficult start with both the king and his chosen abbot, his friend or kinsman Wilegod, dying just three years after its foundation: Wilegod perhaps was not the dynamic resolute leader of men required to launch a new venture of this sort, even if he was a kinsman of the king. It is quite possible the *Gesta Abbatum* is guilty of exaggeration or even of inventing fake news, the better to illustrate the glory of the post-conquest monastery, but it is easy to imagine, after an uncertain start, difficulties continuing under a new abbot and under a possibly indifferent king. By 880 the monastery seems to have reached a nadir with Abbot Wulsig who 'prayed little and hunted much', who discarded the monastic habit and who established an adjacent nunnery to ensure a ready supply of young virgins. Tradition has it that Wulsig was eventually poisoned by his monks, the monastery barely functioning as a religious community.

Wulsig's successor, Wulnorth, began his abbacy with some attempt of reform, perhaps inspired by King Alfred, who was attempting the same objective on a countrywide scale. This attempt was not sustained and the monastery slipped back to its bad old ways. By the time of the first Viking raids in about 860 the monastery may not have comprised much more than the church and a collection of typically wooden conventual buildings and as such it might not have offered a particularly tempting prize for the heathen Vikings. St Albans is likely to have avoided the earliest raids but tradition has it, as recounted in *Gesta Abbatum*, that in a later raid a band of Norsemen broke into the shrine and took the saint's relics to Odense in Denmark. This story is not credible as Denmark was still firmly pagan territory at that time and as such the relics would have been valueless. Such an event may well have taken place in the eleventh century and the

---

[65] Rushbrook Williams: The History of St Albans Abbey.

question of the ownership, theft, recovery and whereabouts of the holy relics is a recurring theme and seems to have been a major preoccupation of the early history of the abbey.

The Viking raid seemed to have a positive effect on Wulsig, who mended his ways towards the end of his abbacy, but too late, alas. His successor, Eadfrith was hopeless: 'guilty of sloth, weakness and incompetence'. At this point the monks found it difficult to agree on a successor and an appeal was made to the bishop in whose diocese the monastery was situated, Dorchester-on-Thames. The result was the appointment of Wulsin, which marked the beginning of a period of genuine reform and recovery. As the abbey became more prosperous it found the presence of a royal burgh – Kingsbury – just half a mile distance, increasingly irksome. The village that had sprung up immediately to the north of the abbey, the embryonic St Albans, suffered from bullying by Kingsbury and it was Wulsin's strategy to boost the economy of St Albans to the detriment of Kingsbury. He did this by diverting Watling Street through St Albans and by establishing a weekly market. He is said also to have founded three churches to the west, north and south east of the abbey, marking the main approaches to the monastery and the founding of a grammar school. All these actions certainly happened but it is by no means clear that they happened in the ninth century – mid-tenth century is rather more likely.

The two successive abbots, 'Alfric I' and Ealdred, pursued Wulsin's policy of degrading Kingsbury by purchasing the fish pools on which the Kingsbury economy partly depended with the result that more of the Kingsbury population moved to St Albans. Indeed it was so successful that many – the rougher element – moved to squat in the ruined city of Verulamium. The challenge to law and order that this represented led Abbot Ealdred to demolish many of the buildings of Verulamium and to stockpile the re-usable materials – brick and stone – for future monastery use.

Refoundation

The most determined movement to reform monastic life in England was instigated in the mid-tenth century by Dunstan, Archbishop of Canterbury from 958, with the help of, amongst others, Aethelwold, Abbot of Abingdon. Dunstan had been a monk at Glastonbury where, as abbot, he was responsible for its refoundation, the introduction of Benedictine Rule and the reconstruction of the ruined buildings. After a brief spell of exile in Flanders, where he experienced first-hand the rigours of life in a Benedictine monastery, he returned to England at the call of King Edgar eventually to become Archbishop of Canterbury. His reforms were in due course codified in the *Regularis Concordia*, prepared by Aethelwold while Bishop of Winchester. In 975 Aelfric, a distinguished monk-scholar from Abingdon Abbey, who may have been a novice in Aethelwold's time as abbot, was appointed Abbot of St Albans and with this appointment St Albans at last began to emerge from the shadows. Aelfric naturally, with Dunstan's support, led a programme of monastic reform at St Albans where he remained abbot until 990 when he was made Bishop of Ramsey and subsequently Archbishop of Canterbury, just six years after the resignation of Dunstan. He was succeeded as abbot by his brother Leofric, who remained in post until 1030. Aelfric maintained a close interest in St Albans throughout his tenure at Canterbury and the two brothers worked well together in transforming the fortunes of St Albans Abbey, in which they were strongly supported by King Aethelred (978–1016): this period has been called the refoundation of the abbey, in which Aelfric would have been strongly influenced in his formative years by the refoundation of Abingdon Abbey by Aethelwold. If it was not a refoundation it was certainly a significant rejuvenation. Both Aelfric and Aethelstan encouraged reference to the abbey's early history and the role of Offa as benefactor, based either on lost documentary evidence or that of a strong tradition within the monastery[66]. King Aethelred issued four charters in favour of St Albans, which restored estates thought to have formerly been granted by Offa. However, the bulk of the endowments made in this period came from Aelfric and Leofric rather than Aethelred[67].

Because the status of a monastery depended largely on that of its patron saint, Aelfric and Leofric realised the long-term strategic benefits to the abbey in promoting Alban as England's protomartyr, as well as establishing its royal foundation. St Alban had not been defined as the British protomartyr in the early texts: for Constantius of Lyon he was simply 'the blessed martyr'; for Venantius Fortunatus he was 'the egregious Alban'. It is in the third of King Aethelred's four charters that St Alban is first described as *'Anglorum protomartyr'*[68]. This marked the beginning of a campaign for the recognition of St Alban as the English

---

[66] Pamela Taylor: *The Early St Albans Endowment and Its Chroniclers.*
[67] Julia Crick: Offa, *Aelfric and the Refoundation of St Albans.*
[68] Paul Hayward: *The Cult of St Alban, Anglorum Protomartyr, in Anglo-Saxon and Anglo-Norman England.*

protomartyr, which was not fully accepted until after the Norman Conquest.

Leofric, whose abbacy lasted some fifty years, is said to have governed the monastery with 'rare prudence and skill' so that the abbey's endowments, influence and reputation continued to flourish after Alfric's and then Aethelred's death. Leofric managed to purchase – and subsequently demolish – the pesky Kingsbury and assert increased independence from episcopal control. He also acquitted himself well on the perennial subject of St Alban's relics: the *Gesta Abbatum*[69] credits him with sending the relics to Ely for safe keeping in the face of a threatened Danish invasion. Except he didn't; the relics he sent were fakes and when, after the Danish threat had passed, he requested the return of the relics the abbot of Ely sent back yet another set of fakes. Whereupon Leofric produced the originals and a century-long dispute as to who possessed the true set ensued. The matter was not resolved until Pope Adrian IV (Nicholas Brakspear, the only English pope and formerly associated with St Albans Abbey) intervened in the twelfth century, although the affair enhanced Leofric's prestige, at least locally.

The development of St Albans monastery

There is no reference in *Gesta Abbatum* of any development of the monastery in the centuries following 'foundation' before the Norman conquest, although there are plenty of references and other evidence of the increasing wealth, influence and reputation of the monastery, especially after the 'refoundation'. Within the murky context of the Alban story it is known that the martyrial basilica existed in the fifth century when it was visited by Germanus and it is likely that the same church, possibly rebuilt or renovated, existed in 730 as reported by Bede. It is likely that this church, possibly further extended, served as the original abbey church. The site of the original basilica/martyrial church/abbey church is not known with any certainty but could be either at or a short distance to the south of the present cathedral, in the Abbey Orchard.

---

[69] Rushbrook Williams: *The History of St Albans Abbey*.

THE SAXON MONASTERY OF ST ALBAN

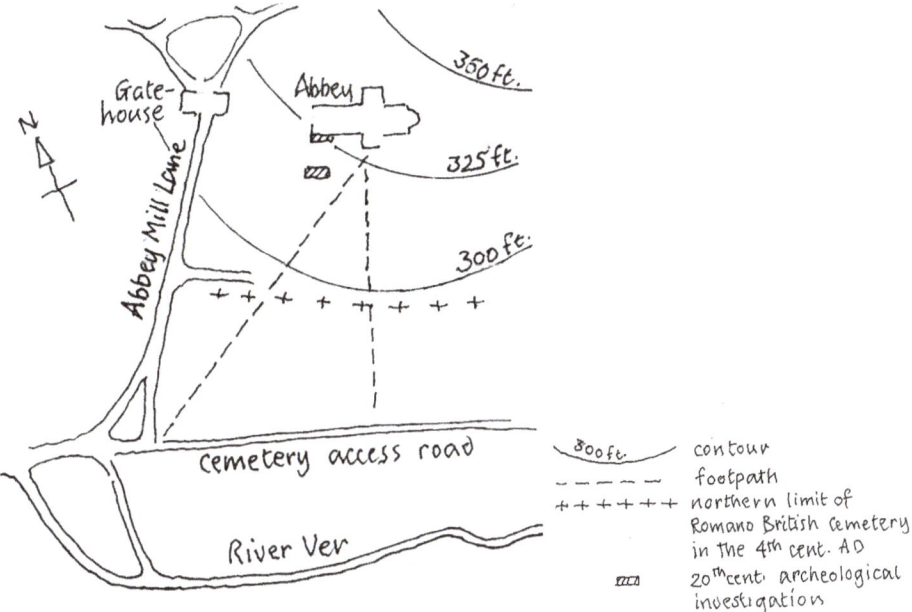

The site of the Romano British cemetery south of St Albans Abbey

Archaeological evidence

Three archaeological investigations, led by Professor Biddle, were carried out between 1978 and 1995 to throw more light on Anglo-Saxon development in the area immediately south of the present abbey.[70] The purpose of these investigations was to test the theory proposed by the historian Wilhelm Levison in his seminal paper[71] that the origins of the abbey lie in a martyrial basilica erected over the grave of Alban outside Roman Verulamium, and that therefore it was quite possible that the veneration of St Alban had survived unbroken from the Roman period.

The conclusions of the three archaeological campaigns, 1978, 1982–4, 1994–5 are summarised as follows:

1. A large Roman cemetery developed northwards from an east–west Roman access road running along the bottom of the Abbey Orchard, as shown in the layout sketch. By the time of Alban's martyrdom the cemetery extended halfway up the hill, and this is where he is likely to

---

[70] M and BK Biddle: 'The Origins of St Albans Abbey: Romano-British Cemetery and Anglo Saxon Monastery' – included in *Alban and St Albans: Roman and Medieval Architecture, Art and Archaeology*.
[71] Wilhelm Levison: *St Alban and St Albans*.

have been buried. The cemetery continued its northern expansion up to and possibly beyond the location of the nave until the early fifth century.

2. An area of the Romano-British cemetery was sealed by a gravel surface, laid towards the end of the fourth century. The finds on this surface were remarkable: 108 coins, 70 fragments of glass and 718 sherds of pottery, which are consistent with what would be expected from pilgrims visiting a martyr's shrine on feast days and is similar to other Romano-British sanctuaries elsewhere.

3. Evidence of an Anglo-Saxon monastic buildings in the Abbey Orchard south of the present abbey, constructed in several stages, the earliest of which may have incorporated the martyrial church. The evidence includes the footprint of the west limb of a 12m diameter apse orientated north–south, which bears some resemblance to the north apse footprint at Winchester Saxon Abbey that once formed part of the double-apsed martyrium constructed around St Swithin's grave in Winchester Old Minster[72].

4. Evidence of a late tenth century Anglo-Saxon church situated under the nave of the present abbey. The finds show that this church had plastered and painted walls, glazed windows and a floor paved with glazed and decorative tiles – a level of embellishment associated only with the most important churches such as those at Canterbury, Winchester and Bury St Edmunds.

5. A 38m long, 6m wide stone corridor possibly linking the older monastic buildings, south of the present abbey, with the later church described previously.

6. Two Anglo-Saxon cemeteries, one immediately to the south of the present south transept with eleven graves and the other below the north-west corner of the cloister garth, containing eighteen graves. All these graves contained only the bodies of adult men – presumably monks.

7. The discovery of a number of sixth- to eighth-century pieces – ornamented pins and a disc – point to a continuity of activity in this area.

---

[72] M and BK Biddle: *The Origins of St Albans Abbey: Excavations in the Cloister 1982–1983*.

THE SAXON MONASTERY OF ST ALBAN

The outline of the foundations of the Saxon Winchester Old Minister showing the shape of the north–south apses. Was the floor plan of the Saxon abbey church at St Albans similar?

In summarising the implication of the archaeological finds, Professor Biddle states: 'It is hard to avoid the conclusion that the St Albans complex is part of a major Anglo-Saxon church of several structural periods lying east and west below the south part of the (Norman) cloister...' The earliest of these periods may have included the church described by Bede as being of 'wonderful workmanship', any subsequent modifications or extensions to this church effected at the time of the foundation and a possible rebuild after the Viking raids. The case for continuity of veneration through the sixth to eighth centuries, implied by Bede, is supported by the archaeological evidence. Certainly, it is likely that by the time of the 'refoundation' the original church would have been too small and looking its age. Nevertheless, a church originating from the Roman period housing the original shrine of St Alban would have commanded huge respect and there could be no question of its demolition. In the last of the structural periods Aelfric and or Leofric felt the need to bring the monastery up to a similar level to that of other first-ranking monasteries and had the energy, the will and the resources to do so: they decided on a new church linked to the old by a grand corridor.

On the other hand, Levison[73] points out the parallels between the development of St Albans and that of Bonn and Xanten in Germany. In both these locations a martyrial church was built where the patronal saint had been executed, at a cemetery outside the Roman city. In both cases a medieval city grew up around the martyrial church, which became the foundation of a cathedral. In both cities archaeological investigations has

---

[73] Wilhelm Levison: *St Alban and St Albans*.

revealed the ancient tomb of the saint directly beneath their respective chancels. So the possibility that the shrine in the present cathedral marks the place of the original martyrium cannot be ruled out.

The appearance of the Saxon Abbey

Although the account of Offa's foundation of the St Albans monastery is quite clear that Offa built a new church to house the new shrine, this seems unlikely in light of the less than smooth inauguration process, especially following the death of both Offa and his abbot. It would seem much more likely that the abbey church of the Offa 'foundation' was an adaptation of the ancient martyrial church, with the addition of transepts and a tower, the ancient church perhaps forming the chancel. Perhaps the first abbey church of St Alban resembled St Mary's Church Breamore in Hampshire. The tower of this Saxon church is typical of the Carolingian tradition, built like a pagoda in receding stages.

St Mary's Church, Breamore, Hampshire.

Another Minster church, All Saints at Wing in Buckinghamshire, is the most local of all Saxon churches to St Albans, although externally only the polygonal chancel is Saxon.

The Saxon Monastery of St Alban

The Saxon chancel of All Saints Church in Wing, Buckinghamshire.

As for the new 'refoundation' abbey church, there is very little information on which to speculate its appearance: as we have seen it was richly ornamented and the builders had at their disposal large quantities of Roman brick and stone recovered by Abbot Ealdred earlier in the tenth century. Professor Biddle makes the point that the linking of buildings by covered walks is a particular medieval trait in both secular and ecclesiastical contexts[74] and cites, as does Eileen Roberts[75], the example of the abbey church of Saint Riquier in northern

The abbey church of St Riquier, Picardy.

---

[74] M and BK Biddle: *The Origins of St Albans Abbey*.
[75] Eileen Roberts: *The Hill of the Martyr – An Architectural History of St Albans Abbey*, p. 18.

France where a processional way linked the main and two lesser churches. This abbey church, built between 790 and 799 by the son-in-law of Charlemagne, became highly influential on northern French church architecture.

An artist's view of how the new Saxon abbey church of St Alban may have looked is shown below.

The Saxon Abbey of St Alban? Watercolour by Caddy Attewill.

6

The Norman Abbey

He destroys well, who builds something better.

Goscelin, an eleventh century monk and biographer.

Locus iste a Deo factus est,   This place was made by God,
inaestimabile sacramentum   a priceless sacrament;,
irreprehensibilis est.   it is without reproach.

An antiphon from the Catholic liturgy.

Background

William (the Conqueror), Duke of Normandy, decided as a young man in his twenties that he should marry, and selected Matilda of Flanders, daughter of the Duke of Flanders and niece and granddaughter of kings of France, as the object of his affections. He sent an emissary to arrange the marriage and was somewhat put out when she turned him down on the grounds of his illegitimacy. Being a man of action, William rode the 300 miles to Bruges where he accosted her riding to church. To the horror of her attendants he pulled her from her horse 'by her long braids' and held her until she agreed to marry him. Well, it's one way of doing it! The marriage was forbidden by the pope on consanguinity grounds but they married anyway, in 1050. However, retrospective papal approval was vital and so William sent Lanfranc, Italian by birth and education and at that time the Prior of Bec in Normandy, to Rome to secure a dispensation from the pope. In this he succeeded, winning him the lifelong gratitude of both William and Matilda. The penance was heavy, however: both William and Matilda were required to build a monastery each, in Caen. The result was the Abbaye aux Hommes and the Abbaye aux Dames, both supreme examples of Romanesque architecture. No token compliance, then. Duke William appointed Lanfranc as the first abbot of the Abbaye aux Hommes in 1059.

Following his Westminster coronation in December 1066, William, as part of the consolidation phase following his conquest, removed nearly all the Saxon bishops of England and replaced them with Normans, all except for the Archbishop of Canterbury, Stigand, whom he found useful in this initial phase. Although William had undertaken the conquest with the broad support of Pope Alexander II, an approval secured by Lanfranc, he needed more – the pope's explicit endorsement that he was God's chosen leader of the English. Thus in 1070 he welcomed the arrival of three papal legates who came to participate in a second coronation, this time in Winchester. The legates also participated in discussions concerning major reforms that William intended to make to the English church. William wanted to reaffirm the Rule of Benedict, but more broadly he wanted to transform the Church from a loose association run by semi-autonomous bishops into a more strictly controlled and coherent unit under the king, working through his Archbishop of Canterbury.

While William was prepared to pay an annual tax to the Catholic Church in Rome (the Peter's Pence) he refused to swear fealty to the pope, ostensibly on the grounds that neither Charlemagne nor Alfred, amongst others, had set this precedent. As soon as Stigand, the incumbent Saxon Archbishop of Canterbury, was deposed William appointed Lanfranc archbishop in his place and required Thomas, the Archbishop of York, to swear allegiance to Lanfranc. William was a devout man and genuinely believed that he was responsible for his own soul as well as those of his subjects and that a lifetime of warfare had put him and his subjects in jeopardy. Penances were therefore required – from himself, the foundation of Battle Abbey, and from his knights, the construction of parish churches. As William of Malmesbury later wrote: 'everywhere you could see churches rising up in the villages and minsters in the towns and cities, built in a style of a new kind'.

William, Lanfranc and St Albans

Although William made an almost clean sweep of the Saxon bishops, his policy was to allow Saxon abbots to remain in post, provided they did not become involved in rebellion. His attitude to Frederic, Abbot of St Albans, appointed in 1064, is unclear. The *Gesta Abbatum*, seemingly intent on presenting King William in the worst possible light – and conversely Archbishop Lanfranc in the best – reports that Abbot Frederic stood up to William, as a result of which the abbey's assets, the manors, farms, houses and woodland, were devastated and Frederic went into hiding at Ely, leaving the abbacy vacant for several years. There is no evidence that any of these things happened: indeed, careful research by Mark Haggar[76] has shown there was no significant loss of the income of St Albans Abbey in the years following the conquest. However, the *Gesta Abbatum* may be partially correct: before the conquest, Abbot Frederic was a prominent figure at the court of Edward the Confessor and a close friend of both Stigand, Archbishop of Canterbury up to 1070, and Harold Godwinson, Edward's successor. Moreover, Stigand had a financial interest in St Albans in that he held the manor of Redbourn from St Albans. But the fact that Frederic remained as abbot until 1075 must mean that he was not implicated in any subversive activity, at least until that time. There is therefore no evidence that William was hostile to St Albans, as shown in a writ: 'by the prayers of Archbishop Lanfranc, my sworn man, I have granted to the church of St Alban soke and sake*, toll and team and all customs in all places as well as honestly as Stigand had on that day when King Edward died'.

The newly appointed archbishop wasted no time in implementing William's root-and-branch reforms of the English Church, which included the reconstruction of St Albans Abbey. Lanfranc nurtured the campaign, initiated by Aelfric and Leofric earlier in the eleventh century to establish St Alban as protomartyr with a special claim on the devotion of the English people. St Alban was chosen in preference to rival saints of Saxon origin partly because of his British ethnicity – the Normans were guilty of racial prejudice – but mainly because of his undoubted and well-attested antiquity and the widespread observance of his cult throughout continental Europe. This confirmation of St Albans pre-eminence inspired Lanfranc to replicate, in his reconstruction of St Albans Abbey, what he had achieved in his Caen Abbey, which he had also dedicated to a protomartyr, St Stephen. Such a parallel required St Albans Abbey to be built on a similarly grand scale.[77]

Although it is quite possible that William was not familiar with the cult of St Alban, the project to reconstruct the abbey dedicated to Britain's protomartyr on such a scale presented an unrivalled opportunity to promote himself as a caring Christian monarch, especially since he may have been seen in Rome as a rough diamond, on account of his illegitimacy, his illiteracy and his unlawful marriage.

---

[76] Mark Haggar: *Gesta Abbatum Monasterii Sancti Albani: Litigation and History of St Albans*.

* Subject to monastic as opposed to national jurisdiction.

[77] Paul Hayward: *The Cult of St Alban, Anglorum Protomartyr, in Anglo-Saxon and Anglo-Norman England*.

The Norman abbey

Paul of Caen

Work on St Albans Abbey could not begin until the reconstruction of Canterbury Cathedral was complete, in 1077. Lanfranc used the abbey of St Etienne in Caen as a model, the architecture of which hints at the influence of his humanist education and his sense of Lombardian space, as the model for both Canterbury and St Albans. For the reconstruction of St Alban Lanfranc summoned his kinsman Paul, his nephew most probably, to oversee the work as abbot. Abbot Paul without doubt also came from the Lombardian city of Pavia, the name Paul being uncommon in Normandy at the time.[78] He was probably born about 1030 and as a young man he would have witnessed the reconstruction of the great church San Michele in Pavia. Like his uncle before him he crossed the Alps to complete his education and to seek his fortune in France. He joined Lanfranc at the school in Bec and subsequently became a monk in Caen when the Abbaye aux Hommes was consecrated in the 1060s. There he stayed until 1077. So he knew Lanfranc very well and together they made a formidable team.

Abbot Paul was horrified by the state of St Albans monastery when he arrived, above all by the disparity between its substantial revenues and the meanness and dilapidation of the conventual buildings. He despised his predecessors, the Saxon abbots, whom he described as *'rudes et idiotas'* and is thought to have made a clean sweep of all the buildings. As well as rebuilding the monastery, he implemented Lanfranc's reforms with the strict observance of the Rule of St Benedict, the creation of a scriptorium which would in due course became world-renowned, the founding of outlying cells and daughter houses at Tynemouth, Binham, Wallingford and Hatfield, and the restitution of abbey property illegally seized by Norman nobility immediately after the conquest.

The abbey church: a rebuild or a modification of the Saxon abbey church?

As we have seen, there is archaeological evidence that a new church was built in the late tenth century to the north of the older, possibly original, Saxon abbey church, with a covered walkway linking the old and the new churches. Remains of the new Saxon church are likely to extend under

---

[78] Christopher Brooke (ed. Robert Runcie): *St Albans the Great Abbey in Cathedral and City*.

the nave of the present abbey, but we have no knowledge of its extent or design.

Until recently it has long been assumed[79] – based on Matthew Paris' account – that the Saxon church was demolished to provide a clear site, partly greenfield, on which to build the Norman abbey church.

In a recent paper, however, Jill Franklin[80] has suggested that the Norman builders adapted the late tenth century church rather than demolishing it and then reused the materials. This supposes the Saxon church comprised an aisleless building, cruciform in plan, built on a very grand scale, which the Norman masons modified by the addition of nave and presbytery aisles. Her hypothesis is based on the evidence that the windows in the west-facing walls of the north and south transepts adjacent to the corners where the transept walls meet the nave walls were blocked up when the Norman builders constructed the nave aisles. Dr Franklin shows that such remodelling of unaisled churches in this period was not uncommon, as at York Minster and Worksop Priory, for instance. But if this were indeed the case it would follow that the great arches supporting the tower, and maybe even the tower itself, or at least it's first stage, were the work of Saxon masons

On balance, I think the rebuild option is the more likely, for a variety of reasons:
- If the Norman masons had modified a Saxon church they surely would not have achieved the coherence of design possessed by the present abbey.
- Could the Saxon masons – *rudes et idiotas* as they were described by Abbot Paul – really have constructed a church on such a a large scale, complete with the great arches that support the central tower, and indeed the tower itself?
- The evidence provided by the blocked-up apertures is not entirely convincing: they were surely too small and too close to the transept/nave corner to be windows. They may have been built for temporary access or ventilation or even by mistake on the part of the part of the builders of the transepts – or a lack of communication with the master mason.

---

[79] Eileen Roberts: *The Hill of the Martyr – An Architectural History of St Albans Abbey*.
Martin Biddle & Birthe Kjolbye Biddle: *The Origins of St Albans Abbey from Alban and St Albans*.
John McNeill: *The Monastery Church, from St Albans: Cathedral and Abbey*.
[80] Jill A Franklin: *The Anglo-Norman Abbey Church of St Alban and the Aisleless Nave of its Cruciform Predecessor – The Material Evidence*.

The abbey church of the reconstructed monastery was planned on a truly vast scale: it was to be the largest church in England at the time, to be surpassed only by Durham Cathedral in the twelfth century and considerably bigger than Lanfranc's own new cathedral at Canterbury. Why so large? Certainly not for strategic reasons – political or military – as at Durham: it could only be because it was intended to be a statement of intent to the wider Church community that the Norman dynasty was going to be one that took its Christian duties with the utmost seriousness. Although the new Abbot Paul would have a great deal of autonomy in all other aspects, the question of scale was one likely to have been agreed at the outset between William and Lanfranc.

Although Abbot Paul despised his Saxon predecessors, he would have held St Alban, and his shrine, in the greatest veneration. For this reason it is likely that he chose to build the new church on an adjacent (almost) greenfield site so that the old church could be kept in use until the new church was complete, minimising disruption to worship. Naturally an uphill site, to the north, was attractive as it offered a more commanding position. There would have been no question that the church plan would be anything other than cruciform with a central tower at the crossing. Despite the convention of an east–west orientation Paul had to work within topographical constraints and orientate the church to be parallel to the contours that run west–south–west to east–north–east. An east–west alignment would have resulted in a 6m difference in floor level between the ends of the church that would be impractical. The other imperative constraint was foundation conditions – the stability of the tower required the most favourable geology and this governed the siting of the crossing.

In the absence of any local stone there was no choice but to reuse materials – Roman bricks, flints and some limestone from the adjacent ruined city of Verulamium, much of which had already been collected and stockpiled by the Saxon abbots. Some of this material had already been used in the construction of the tenth century Aelfric/Leofric church, which had to be demolished to make way for the Norman nave, so it would have been doubly recycled.

Abbot Paul appointed a gifted Norman mason/architect, known simply as Robert the Mason, to take charge of the construction. John Harvey in his biographical dictionary of medieval architects writes that Robert 'reused Roman materials with beauty and ingenuity.'[81] The design

---

[81] Eileen Roberts: The Hill of the Martyr – an Architectural History of St Alba.

The Norman Abbey

of the abbey church would have been based on the Abbaye aux Hommes in Caen where Paul had spent fifteen years as a monk. It is also just possible that the image of San Michele in Pavia lingered in his mind. The interior of these two churches are shown:

Interior views, looking east, of San Michele, Pavia (left) and S. Etienne, Caen (right).

The similarities of the corresponding view, looking east, of the interior of St Albans Abbey are striking.

The church was very long – fifteen bays from end to end – giving a total length of about 110m. Although there was an internal division separating the secular area (the nave) from the monastic area there were no high screens so the church was very much open plan. The shrine, the focus of the whole edifice, was situated at the centre of the chord of the main, central apse and, raised on a dais, would have been visible even from the west end of the nave. There were seven apses altogether, each with its own altar, and to accommodate these, the transepts had to be more pronounced than was normal. The high altar was situated immediately to the west of the shrine. The apses, presbytery and its aisles were vaulted to accentuate the sepulchral air of the east end of the church. The internal brick surfaces were plastered and painted to simulate masonry joints and decorated with lozenge and chevron patterns. In the transepts Saxon baluster shafts, crudely turned from limestone, were reused at triforium level.

(Courtesy of St Albans Cathedral)

Externally the Roman brick walls of the tower, and maybe the brick and flint walls of the nave, transepts and presbytery would have been plastered in lime, which would have given it a creamy colour. The roofs would have been pitched (but at a slightly flatter pitch than now). A pyramidal roof would have completed the tower, which was not embellished with battlements at that time. The west front of the nave would have been, in the absence of the customary twin towers, quite plain and perhaps rather underwhelming. Maybe at even that early date they had plans to extend the nave so there was no point in constructing towers that would soon become redundant.

The abbey was consecrated on 28 December 1115 in the presence of King Henry II and Queen Matilda in a very splendid ceremony. A watercolour painting of what the Norman abbey would have looked like – so familiar to us yet subtly quite different – is reproduced as the end piece of Part One of this book.

Let these stones speak: Eileen Roberts opens her architectural history with these words, and so I will end this account: what they say, at St

THE NORMAN ABBEY

Albans, more eloquently through the austere design and the intractable materials than would be possible with more sophisticated architecture, is *'Credo in unum Deum'*.

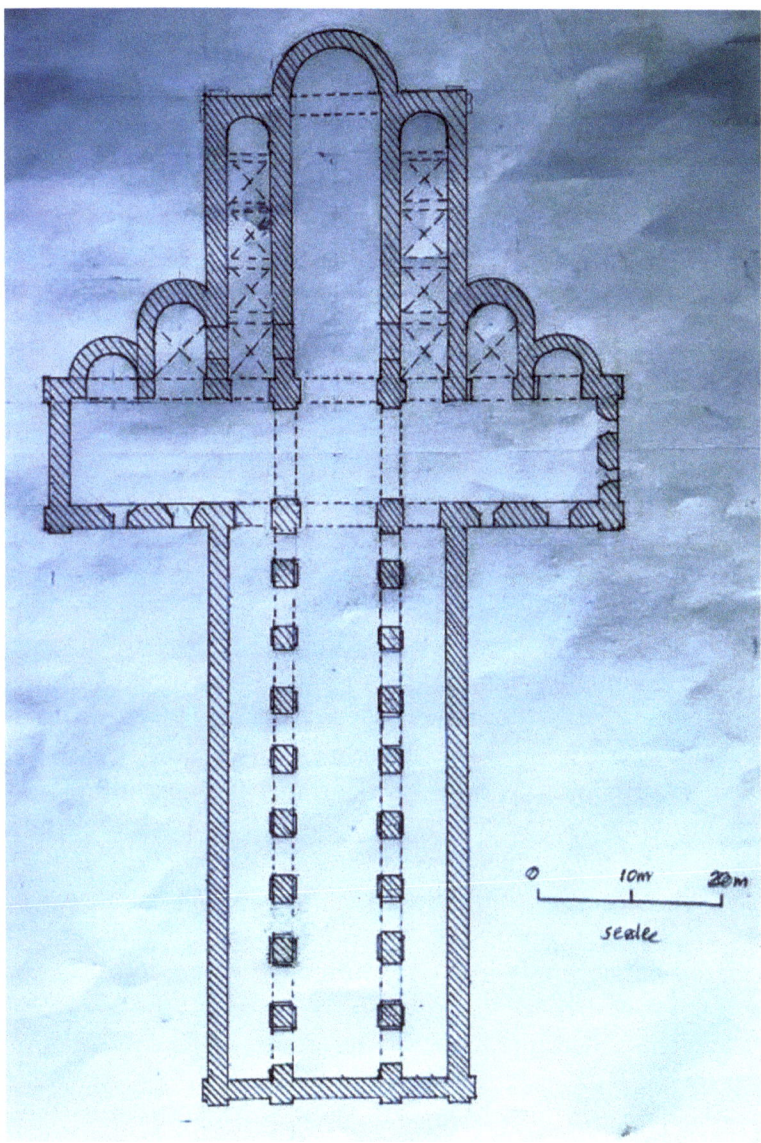

Plan of the Norman abbey.

7

Conclusion to Part One

The Alban story in the first millennium is one of continuity and chance. To unpick the succession of seemingly specific and unexpected historical events – the Roman conquest of the Iron Age British, the Anglo-Saxon takeover of the Romano-British and the Norman conquest of the Anglo-Saxons – it is possible to discern the thread of continuity. Indeed what may have seemed at the time as an abrupt event appears much less abrupt in hindsight, with each such event being followed by a period of assimilation in which the new arrivals were gradually absorbed by the host population.

The oppidum of Verlamion was founded by an Iron Age tribe on a not particularly obvious site where two tracks crossed – one leading eastwards to the main port at Colchester and the other leading northwest to Anglesey: a good location but nothing special. With luck and hard work the founding tribe, the Catuvellauni, became one of the most powerful in Britain and Verlamion became their capital. After their conquest of Britain the Romans founded a town at Verlamion but because it was not a particularly good site from a military point of view it was not used as a military base but was left to flourish in its own way. The Romans did not make changes for change's sake and didn't even feel it necessary to change the name – Verlamion became Verulamium. The agriculture and field patterns also continued with little change – a British peasant would hardly have been aware that he had been conquered. Over the next 360 years the Romans were assimilated by the British and in time adopted an island outlook in place of a continental one. Similarly with religion – the British concept of religion was quite different to that of Rome – the one naturalistic, the other state orientated. By the end of the colonial period the two religions had fused together, spectacularly so in Verulamium. A further fusion took place when the object of people's veneration, the severed head of a British hero, was replaced by the severed head of a Romano-British saint/hero. For the small number of Christians the martyrdom of Alban was a paradigm shift but Christians at the time were a small minority. For the vast majority the conversion to Christianity would perhaps been a more gradual process.

Conclusion to Part One

After the Romans withdrew, civic life and administration continued in Verulamium for over a century. By chance, the effects of the secession at Verulamium were ameliorated by the visits of Germanus, which had two profound consequences:
- It established Alban as the protomartyr of the British whose cult became important to both ecclesiastical and civic leaders in Verulamium;
- It established the cult of St Alban on the Continent, which secured the recognition, support and authority of the Roman Church.

The eventual occupation of Verulamium by the Saxons was, as elsewhere, an evolutionary rather than a revolutionary event in which the consequences of Germanus' visits and the ongoing Augustinian mission would have eased the acceptance of Alban by the Waeclingas – who settled in the Verulamium region – as a Saxon hero: continuity assured.

King Offa for all his faults should be credited with the foundation of the first St Albans monastery, even if he did so in emulation of his mentor Emperor Charlemagne and for the prestige of Mercia rather than an act of piety. This foundation, if such it was, led to what was perhaps the greatest existential threat to the survival of the cult of St Alban in Britain at the hands of the incompetence (at best) of the ninth century abbots. The monastery, however, survived and was rescued in the refoundation of the end of the tenth century

Finally, the Normans. William the Conqueror appointed his closest adviser Lanfranc, Archbishop of Canterbury, who had helped him at every turn. Lanfranc was highly educated, unafraid of the fearsome William, and widely respected. For different reasons this rather disparate couple agreed on the rebuilding of St Albans Abbey: William impelled by conscience, perhaps piety, and prestige, certainly; Lanfranc driven by the desire to do the right thing for Britain's protomartyr, historically under-valued by the Saxons.

Thus the cult of St Alban survived three major existential threats in its first millennium:
- When Christianity was outlawed in the third-century Roman Empire;
- During the *adventus Saxones* in the sixth century;
- A period of neglect in the ninth century.

But it *did* survive, and survived gloriously. With such an abbey as the Normans built, the real work of ministry could begin.

How the Norman abbey church may have appeared from the south, before the construction of the cloisters and other conventual buildings. Watercolour by Caddy Attewill.

Conclusion to Part One

Timeline of relevant events: part one

Century	Year	Event	Period
First BC	Early 100s	Formation of British tribes	Iron Age
	55, 54	Julius Caesar's expeditions to Britain	
AD First	43	Conquest of Britain: foundation of Verulamium	Roman Empire
	61	Boudiccan revolt: destruction of Verulamium	
	64	Fire in Rome: Christians blamed and persecuted by Nero	
Second	155	Antonine Fire at Verulamium: reconstruction of the municipium	
	177	Persecution of Christians at Lyon	
Third	208	Severus persecution: earliest year of Alban martyrdom	
	250	Decian persecution: probable year of Alban martyrdom	
	257	Valerian persecution: alternative year of Alban martyrdom	
Fourth	303	Diocletian persecution: Britain largely unaffected	
	313	Edict of Milan legitimises Christianity	
	380	Christianity adopted as official religion of the empire: construction of the martyrial church (basilica)?	
	396	Visit by Vitricius	
Fifth	409	Britain secedes from Roman Empire	Anglo-Saxon
	429, 445	Visits by Germanus	
Sixth	Late 400s	Battle of Badon Hill: Saxon advance temporarily halted by British	
	Early 500s	Gildas writes De Excidio Britanniae	
	563	Foundation of Iona monastery by Columba	
	571	Battle of Bedcanford allowing the Saxon takeover of Verulamium	
	597	Augustine mission to Britain: foundation of Canterbury diocese	
Seventh	600	Conversion of Kent and Essex – Rochester and London dioceses	
	601	Synod of Augustine's Oak – Augustine and British bishops	
	605	Augustine's death	
	625	Conversion of Northumberland: foundation of York diocese	
	635	Aidan founds Lindisfarne monastery	
	633	Arrival of Birinus – subsequent creation of See of Dorchester	
	642	Conversion of Wessex	
	Mid-600s	Cedd reconverts Essex	
	656	Foundation of Lichfield diocese by Cedd	
	664	Synod of Whitby	
	731	Bede completes Ecclesiastical History of the English People	
	757	Offa crowned King of Mercia	
	793	Offa 'foundation' of St Albans monastery – rebuilding the shrine?	
Ninth	800s	Mismanagement at St Albans – Viking raids	
Tenth	Late 900s	Refoundation of St Albans monastery by Aelfric & Leofric	
	1066	Norman Conquest	Norman
Eleventh	1077	Paul de Caen appointed Abbot of St Albans Abbey: reconstruction starts	
	1097	Death of Paul de Caen – Richard d'Albini appointed second abbot	
Twelfth	1115	Consecration of the new St Albans Abbey	

PART TWO

The Medieval Monastery

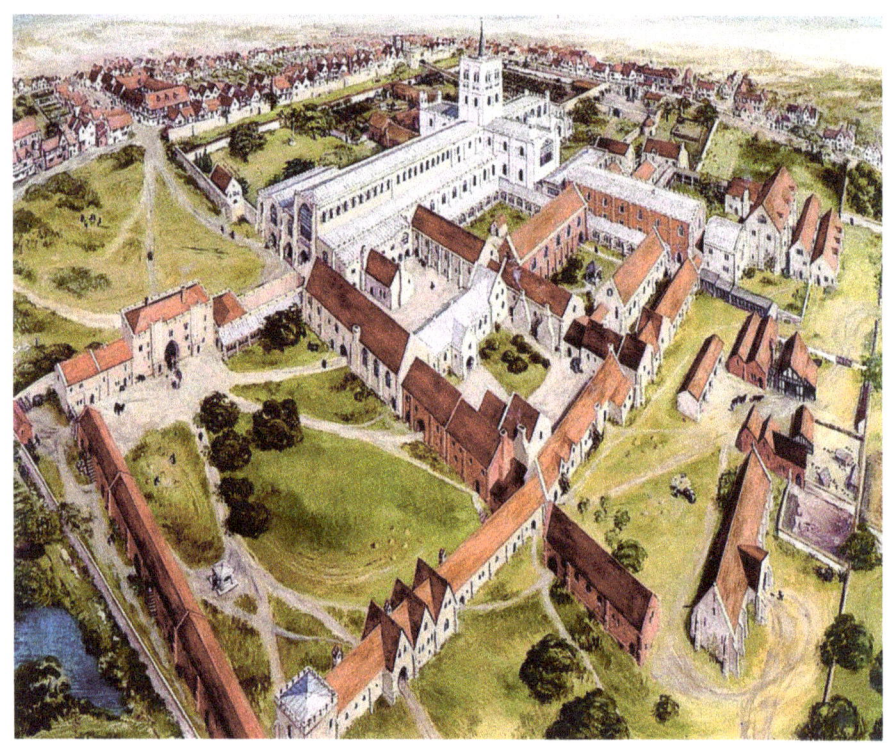

The layout of St Albans monastery, showing the extent of the conventual buildings to the south of the abbey church.
(Courtesy of St Albans Cathedral.)

8

Historical Setting

Introduction

Part One of this account of the story of St Alban ended with the consecration of the new Norman abbey in 1115. Part Two continues the story up to 1539, when the monastery was dissolved by King Henry VIII. This period of 424 years saw the revolutionary changes brought about by the Norman conquest take root, and the monastery flourish under, for the most part, the primacy of some outstanding abbots together with the participation of some gifted monks and lay people. That is not to say that its voyage, which ultimately ended in shipwreck on the rocks of the Reformation, was easy: it was beset by the storms of a particularly turbulent period of history, with endemic warfare, a continuous tussle for ascendancy between the monarchy and the papacy and profound social changes that saw the demise of feudalism and the rise of the individual.

The main strands of the historical context affecting St Albans monastery can be broadly divided into three groups. First was the appetite of English kings for waging war against the Welsh, the Scots and the French and the expense of these wars requiring funding from monasteries. Second was the growth in power of the papacy, which enhanced the importance of the Church and the senior churchmen but led to an ongoing struggle for supremacy with the monarchy. Finally was the inevitable decline of the feudal system on which monastic houses were founded, a decline accelerated by the Black Death and the corresponding emergence of Parliament, the market economy, literacy and the universities.

In the medieval life of the St Albans monastery, England was ruled by a succession of twenty-two monarchs drawn from three dynasties: the Normans until 1154, when the Plantagenets took over until the advent of the Tudors in 1485. Although these monarchs were born of only three extended families in a limited gene pool of French and English aristocrats, they differed widely from each other in many ways – in terms of character, ability and motive. From the point of view of ferocity and military prowess, a key attribute of a successful medieval monarch, the spectrum ranged from King Henry III, who despised and avoided warfare, to King Richard I, for whom warfare was his life-blood. A similar range is to be seen in their competence as rulers where King John's incompetence, which led to the brink of total breakdown, is in sharp contrast to the ability of his father Henry II, an educated and diligent monarch who left England in a more stable and prosperous condition than that which he inherited.

Warfare

Warfare was endemic in England in the Middle Ages with uprisings and rebellions at home, battles with our island neighbours Wales and Scotland and wars with our continental neighbours, particularly with France. Internal conflicts also occurred: in the twelfth century, occasioned by the Stephen/Matilda dispute, known as 'the Anarchy'; in the thirteenth century following King John's disastrous reign and the consequent rebellion, and most notably in the Wars of the Roses of the fifteenth century. Benedictine monasteries were originally founded partly to provide a haven of peace and stability in a turbulent world where monks could worship God and pray for the salvation of the world. Therefore civil strife was the normal background for monasteries, but carried with it the very real risk that the combatants might not respect monastic sanctity. St Albans was at the front line in all three of these episodes of civil conflict. In the first, the abbey was inclined to support the Empress Matilda in her conflict with her nephew King Stephen and sumptuously entertained her after Stephen's defeat and imprisonment at Lincoln in 1141: the abbey was subsequently punished by Stephen's military commander William of Ypres by the extortion of a great deal of money.

The next episode of unrest, the Barons' Revolt of 1215, followed the sealing of the Magna Carta, which was originally conceived in St Albans at a council summoned by King John. In this revolt the barons' dissatisfaction with King John's reluctance to follow the provisions of the charter was such that they deposed King John and invited Louis, the eldest son of the King of France, who had a tenuous claim to the English crown. In the campaigns that followed, Louis occupied St Albans and was bought off from burning the monastery by the payment of a ransom of 80 marks. After the withdrawal of Louis in 1217, King John's and Henry III's strongman, Falkes de Bréauté, attacked St Albans and its abbey as punishment for coming to terms with Louis and blackmailed Abbot

William de Trumpington for a further 200 marks. The total loss to the abbey, including the theft of some 100 horses and other livestock, was severe.

This conflict was followed by the uprising, in St Albans as well as in other monastic towns, in 1327 and the Peasants' Revolt of 1381. The last brush with civil strife was during the fifteenth-century Wars of the Roses, when again the abbey had to steer a delicate path between the warring factions in order to avoid attack. There were two battles of St Albans: the first, in 1455, was won by the Yorkists, with King Henry VI being injured, but at least the victors respected the sanctity of the abbey. In the second battle, six years later, Lancastrian forces defeated the incumbent Yorkists and went on the rampage, looting the abbey and devastating its estates.

The battles with Wales, Scotland and France had a smaller direct effect on St Albans but the indirect effect, particularly economic and financial, was considerable. Wars were expensive and as time went on, with increasing dependency on professional as opposed to feudal armies, became more so. Brimming with optimism, kings convinced themselves that wars would pay for themselves or even make a profit, but this was rarely the case, especially in the ultimately unsuccessful Hundred Years' War. In addition to the direct cost of the army, England spent a great deal in subsidising France's enemies in the Low Countries, to little effect. Monasteries, especially big rich ones like St Albans, were regarded by kings as milk-cows, an easy source of funds, to the extent that St Albans was brought to the brink of bankruptcy at the end of the thirteenth century.

Foreign wars, especially against France, nurtured the spirit of nationalism and xenophobia, which resulted in increasing disenchantment with the papacy and provided fertile ground for resentment against ecclesiastical wealth and power.

The Papal Revolution

Wars with their neighbours were not the only fights that the English kings had to wage: there was a lower level but equally important struggle with the Roman Church for ascendancy.

The fall of the Western Roman Empire on the sixth century left the church, led by the papacy, as the dominant institution in western Christendom, secular authority being fragmented into a number of embryonic states. Hitherto the church had distinguished sacred and secular matters following Christ's injunction 'to render unto Caesar those things which are Caesar's and to God those things which are God's.' After the fall, however, the Church became increasingly involved in secular affairs to the extent that, especially in continental Europe, bishops came to dominate municipal governments. This trend was boosted by a document known as the *Donation of Constantine* – an eighth-century forgery – purporting to be a letter from Emperor Constantine to Pope Sylvester I granting the pope and all his successors not just the primacy of the Universal Church but temporal power over all the territories of the western empire.[82] Despite attempts to assert papal sovereignty, which in any case was totally unrealistic, the power exerted by papacy, drawn as it was from a limited pool of Roman aristocrats, remained passive rather than active. In due course there was a movement towards reform, driven by both the German emperors, who introduced reform-minded clerics into the papal court[83] and by Benedictine monasticism, led by the abbey of Cluny, to restore stricter adherence to the Benedictine Rule: in particular, the right of monks to elect their own abbot.[84] This movement, which became known as the Papal Revolution, led to the election of a series of energetic and reformist popes who put an end to the cosy entente that existed previously. The first of such popes was Leo IX (1048–54), who was committed to asserting the Church's right to elect its own senior clergy and its independence of secular powers. To this end he created, or nurtured, a clerical elite – later known as cardinals – intent on systematic reform.

One of Leo's successors, Gregory VII (1073–85) – he who humiliated the excommunicated Emperor Henry IV at Canossa in 1076 – had an even more ambitious agenda: he regarded the pope's primacy not as a gift of an emperor as implied in the *Donation*, but of Christ himself. This resulted in popes of that period styling themselves as 'Vicars of Christ' instead of 'Vicars of St Peter' to underline their universality. Gregory VII set out a new order in his *Dictatus Papae* which, in the words of Siedentop[85], 'takes us into a new world, a world in which papal sovereignty is asserted to be the fulcrum of Christian civilisation'. This document reverses the hierarchy implicit in the *Donation* that the papacy is subservient to the secular power and included key claims:[86]

- The pope can be judged by no one.
- The Roman Church has never erred and never will err till the end of time.

---

[82] Diarmaid MacCulloch: *A History of Christianity*, p 351.
[83] Larry Siedentop: *Inventing the Individual – The Origins of Western Liberalism*, p. 185.
[84] Ibid p. 186.
[85] Ibid p. 203.
[86] RW Southern: *Western Society and the Church in the Middle Ages*.

- That the Roman pontiff alone is by right called 'universal'.
- That all princes kiss the feet of the pope alone.
- That he is permitted to depose emperors.

These claims were unprecedented and, if implemented, would have transformed Europe into a theocracy. Since the time of Offa successive English kings had thought it expedient to maintain the approval of, and good relations with, Rome, had paid taxes demanded by popes but, despite their faith in the papacy, had consistently refused to concede sovereignty: this situation had been tacitly accepted by all popes prior to the Papal Revolution. It was not, however, tacitly accepted by Gregory and the legally-trained reformist popes that succeeded him, and this unresolved claim of supremacy was a running sore between monarchs and Rome for centuries to come. It was, however, a claim bound to fail. The papacy had only 'soft' power at its disposal – that of interdict and excommunication – and these powers were deployed sparingly as they could result in extensive collateral damage, both political and economic. They also had a relatively short shelf-life as long familiarity taught monarchs to look on their terrors with equanimity. Even so, the extent of papal power was extensive, with papal approval required for the appointment of all senior ecclesiastical posts – bishops and abbots – in all western countries. Further, all clerics – numbering some 50,000 in England alone – were to be exempt from the reach of secular justice for all crimes, civil and criminal.

The attempt by the reformist popes to wrest temporal supremacy reached its peak when Pope Innocent III, in 1208, placed England under an interdict and King John under an excommunication, over a dispute concerning the appointment of the Archbishop of Canterbury. John, fearing that Pope Innocent III might organise and authorise a crusade against him, pledged fealty, with the result that the popes did in fact for a short period exert considerable direct power in England.

The early fourteenth century saw a marked change in papal outlook[87]. During the 200 years of expansion of papal power from Gregory VII to Boniface VIII, secular society also expanded and developed. The increase in trade and urban population, together with the intellectual freedom enjoyed in the universities, resulted in new ideas, some of which aroused papal hostility, manifested in the condemnation of the spiritual wing of the Franciscan Order (the so-called Fraticelli) and of the teaching of

---

[87] RW Southern: *Western Society and the Church in the Middle Ages.*

William of Ockham. Previously, the self-confident lawyer-popes of the twelfth and thirteenth centuries had embraced independent thought: the reversal in their attitude in the fourteenth century belied a deeper malaise. The attention of the papacy was increasingly absorbed by internal divisions and rivalries and the inherent impossibility of Gregory's temporal ambition became more and more apparent, to the extent that it was eventually abandoned in the fifteenth century. The papacy was further weakened by the Great, or Western Schism, when for thirty-nine years there were two rival popes, one in Rome and one in Avignon (and for a brief period a third in Pisa) and then by the succession of the 'renaissance popes', some of whom (especially Alexander VII) were manifestly corrupt. It took the Protestant Reformation and the consequent Counter-Reformation for the papacy to recover.

Social and economic evolution

The Papal Revolution was a manifestation of a more profound societal change, that of the rise of the individual. Larry Siedentop's insight[88] was that Christianity's insistence that each person has a personal relationship with God led to the primacy of the individual and conscience in western thought. This fundamental moral equality of individuals formed the basis of the emerging legal system – pioneered by canon law of the Papal Revolution and subsequently adopted by secular law. This freedom and sense of justice took no account of the feudal stratification of society, which was founded on radical social inequality with the ownership of land carrying with it the right to govern the serfs who were tied to the land; the new sense of justice spelled the end of the assumption of inequality.

While this almost tectonic change was taking place other events were re-shaping society. The social environment and economic conditions prevailing in the early medieval period, up to the mid-twelfth century, when many monasteries were founded – and in the case of St Albans, re-founded – were very different to those that pertained at the end of the fifteenth century, the eve of the Dissolution.

First of all, population. While the economy throughout the entire medieval period remained overwhelmingly agrarian, the population rose from about 2 million in the early twelfth century to over 6 million at the start of the fourteenth, with the bulk of the growth concentrated into the period of 1180 to 1220. This increase, due primarily to a sustained period

---

[88] Larry Siedentop: *Inventing the Individual*.

of good harvests caused by a prolonged solar maximum[89], also required an increase in the area under cultivation. However, this increase was insufficient to match that of the population and this, together with declining yields due to a reduction in soil fertility[90], caused levels of nutrition to decline in the late thirteenth century. The economic repercussions were an increase in the price of grain and of land, and a decrease in the rates of pay of labour and inflation. Landowners (including the Church, the biggest landowner of all) were enriched at the expense of the peasantry, whose land holdings and income declined as the labour supply increased. To make matters worse – much worse – a period of famine from 1315 to 1320, probably caused by a gigantic volcanic eruption, resulted in a five year long 'nuclear winter' which killed about 10 – 15 per cent of the English population – between about 600,000 to 900,000 people – with the survivors suffering malnutrition[91]. Within a generation this disaster was followed by the Black Death, which together with subsequent waves of plague killed some 40 per cent of the remaining population so that by the end of the fourteenth century the population was little more than it had been 300 years earlier. This depopulation had serious long-term impacts on the availability and price of labour. The population only slowly recovered in the fifteenth century and although both the famine and the plague affected other European countries, England remained underpopulated and poorer relative to her neighbours.

The social repercussions of the Great Famine and the Black Death, which between them killed half the population, or 3 million people, over just two generations, must have been profound. In all God-fearing societies natural disasters were ascribed to God's punishment for the sins committed by society: more specifically, in a still predominantly feudal society, they were seen as the sins of the ruling elite: the monarchy, nobility and the Church. Against a background of increasing nationalism, the Church, perceived to be controlled by foreign interests, could have taken much of the blame and this, in part, may have been the origin of the anti-clericalism that was an ever-present feature in subsequent centuries.

At the same time another remarkable transition was taking place: an increase in the proportion of the population living in towns, both new and ancient, that were engaged in trade and manufacture, particularly that associated with the export of wool and the building boom. Associated

---

[89] Nicholas Crane: *The Making of the British Landscape*.
[90] J L Bolton: *The Medieval English Economy*.
[91] Miri Rubin: *The Hollow Crown*.

with this was a measure of de-population of the rural poor resulting from the replacement of arable farming by sheep rearing. It is estimated that the urban population increased, as a percentage of the total, from 6–7.5 per cent in the early twelfth century to between 10–15 per cent in the fourteenth, a fivefold increase in numbers. This gave rise to the granting of charters for some 170 new towns, while existing towns and cities also underwent considerable expansion. Medieval towns came to be seen as non-feudal islands in a feudal sea which, by promoting trade and the money economy, helped in the decline of feudalism, which tended to inhibit trade by restricting personal liberty and freedom of contract.

Legal reforms

Other societal changes were taking place, critically driven by far-reaching law reforms and the establishment of universities at which law, both canon and civil, was taught. Law reform emanated from the canon, or ecclesiastical law developed by the reforming popes, was gradually adopted by secular rulers – in England as well as in Europe – and slowly replaced the primitive law heavily based on custom and superstition[92]. It was King Henry II's foundation of the common law, described by David Carpenter[93] as a watershed in English history, who responded to the challenge. His wholesale law reforms included:
- The appointment of professional judges, mostly French and from a clerical background and handpicked by Henry, to make regular visitations that covered the entire country every two years.
- The abandonment of trial by ordeal – fire or water – initially for civil cases and later criminal cases as well. Following the banning of this barbaric practice, usually administered by clergy, by the fourth Lateran Council in 1215, all trials thereafter, both civil and criminal, were tried by jury.

These reforms had the effect of reducing the number of cases heard in baronial courts, thus reducing their power and influence.

Growth of Parliament
Kings of England had long used a council, composed of the great barons and senior churchmen, to advise on law making and, later, to approve

---
[92] Larry Siderup: *Inventing the Individual*.
[93] David Carpenter: *The Struggle for Mastery*.

emergency taxation. Membership of the council, which became known as Parliament, was extended by Edward I to include two knights and two burgesses to represent each shire and borough respectively. Thus the two Houses of Parliament became established: the Lords, comprising the barons, bishops and abbots; and the Commons, comprising the knights and the burgesses. Both houses had to approve any tax raising and other financial legislation.

Decline in feudalism

Naturally both the fluctuations in the population and the rise in the urban population resulted in major social repercussions, the biggest of which was the decline of the feudal system, in which the nobility, both lay and ecclesiastical, held lands from the king in exchange for an oath of allegiance which obliged them to provide military service to the king whenever required. In turn these land-holders required the peasantry, who were tied to the land, to provide labour to work the land. Feudalism was widespread throughout Europe and had existed in Anglo-Saxon England, but in a rather looser form: it was the Normans who implemented it in a typically thorough-going way.

The decline in feudalism, which had a profound impact on the development of society, was due to a multiplicity of causes, including:
- The change from feudal dues being paid by the provision of labour to payments by cash, a trend initiated by the landlords themselves.
- The rise of the market economy, with the growth of towns, markets and fairs, in response to the population growth.
- The chronic need of successive kings for money to pay for foreign wars from taxation that had to be approved by the fledgling Parliament.
- Legal reforms leading to the centralisation of justice by strengthening royal courts at the expense of manorial courts.
- Crusades and the emancipation of villeins.

This decline, gradual and spread over several centuries, received an enormous boost from the strengthened bargaining power of the peasantry in the late fourteenth century with the shortage of labour caused by famine and plague.

Rise of the universities

At the turn of the millennium a young mathematically minded monk of humble birth, Gerbert of Aurillac, was befriended by the Count of

Barcelona, who took him to Vic in Catalonia to study the liberal arts, including mathematics and music. This gave him the opportunity of studying Greek texts together with their Arabic and Hebrew commentaries then being collected in the Emirate of Cordoba[94]. This material slowly found its way to the Spanish marches and in particular to the Benedictine monastery of Santa Maria di Ripoll, close to Vic. Gerbert was the first scholar of note to bring this revelatory new learning to mainstream Christian Europe and his subsequent election as pope – Sylvester II – ensured the support of the papacy and a wide and rapid dissemination.

It was the eleventh century that saw the emergence of universities. This was in response to a number of disparate factors – the growth of urban communities, the awakening of the realisation that the bible alone could not provide the answer to questions about the natural world, the increasing need for literate clerks to provide the administration that was required by the ecclesiastical and secular governments and the limited capacity of cathedral and monastic schools to provide them. Bologna was the first, in 1088, specialising in law, followed by Paris, theology, and then in the twelfth century by Oxford and Cambridge in the thirteenth. Although closely associated with the Church, especially in their teaching of canon law and theology, these universities were essentially secular in their foundation and were relatively independent of papal or episcopal control. This was especially the case in England where the territorial extent of dioceses was larger than in continental Europe; this applied particularly at Oxford because of its distance from Lincoln, its diocesan capital. This led to a tradition of free-thinking that found expression in the radical, possibly heretical views propounded by Ockham and Wyclif.

Naturally these nascent universities embraced the flood of material from the east with great enthusiasm: this material provided a boost to the study of the humanities including natural sciences and a broadening of the study of theology, in which much attention was given over to the study of Aristotle.

Benedictine monasteries

Foundation and purpose

As was said in Part One, St Albans Abbey was originally founded on the Rule of St Benedict, which was written in the mid-sixth century and

---

[94] James Hannam: *God's Philosophers – How the Medieval World Laid the Foundation of Modern Science*.

which enjoyed a near-monopoly of monastic foundations until the arrival of the new orders, notably the Augustinians and the Cistercians, in the late eleventh century. Benedict's rule had the advantage of simplicity and flexibility: it was predicated on celibacy and total obedience to the abbot, who was to act as a benevolent father figure, a representative of Christ on earth 'whose commands and teaching should be a leaven of divine justice, kneaded into the minds of his disciples'[95]. The regime was to be austere, with equal time devoted to prayer, study and manual labour. The rule stipulated that worship was to be systemised into daily divine services or offices: at midnight and seven daytime offices of Matins, Prime, Terce, Sext, Nones, Vespers and Compline, with every monk expected to attend every office. There were to be three classes of recruits (in order of priority): laymen of mature years, clergy and the sons of nobility, with laymen providing the bulk of the novitiates. In the course of time most of the recruits were the children of noblemen, which ultimately had dire consequences.[96]

Their original purpose was to recreate the potentialities of a self-governing society run on Christian principles under a rule that recognised the moral equality of all brothers, in which the abbot governed by consent of the governed with minimal use of compulsion. It was not intended to provide means of personal salvation to the monks, although it did this by providing a refuge in which salvation could more easily be achieved. The main purpose of monasteries was to achieve salvation for society in general. They were the spiritual equivalent of secular armies: monks were the soldiers, the enemies supernatural. They also battled for the safety of the souls of their benefactors and it was this double purpose which induced great men to lavishly endow the monasteries. Thus the Benedictine Order established itself, by the end of the eleventh century, as the seemingly unshakeable institution on which Christianity was based.

The growth and decline of Benedictine monasticism

The Benedictine Order grew vigorously throughout the early medieval period and reached its peak in terms of numbers and reach in the eleventh century. In England, which lagged a little behind the continent, it grew steadily until the late twelfth century. This growth, however, proved to be unsustainable when, in the thirteenth century, the net income of monasteries came under increasing pressure. As time wore on monastic

---

[95] The Rule of St Benedict. Chapter 2.
[96] RW Southern: *Western Society and the Church in the Middle Ages*.

priorities and characteristics changed. Benefactors tended to prefer their monasteries to exemplify the dignity and solidity of the Christian faith: show and elaborate ceremony mattered. The proportion of the intake from noble families increased and the ritual consequently became more elaborate. The manual labour element of a monk's day dwindled, that function being taken over by lay brothers and servants. In order to keep the larger number of monks busy they were engaged in administrative instead of manual work. An administrative system in which the more senior monks managed the smooth operation of the monastery had existed for many centuries but in the twelfth century there was a proliferation in the numbers of posts and in the number of monks – known as obedientiaries – engaged in administrative duties – and this trend continued throughout the medieval period.

Abbots, as well as acting as a benevolent father figure to the monks, as required by the Rule, also had to fulfil the role of a feudal lord with many tenants and bonded villeins under their control – not at all what St Benedict had in mind. This combination of conflicting demands – temporal vs spiritual – was almost impossible for abbots to reconcile. As feudalism declined in secular society Benedictine monasteries, for financial reasons, resisted change and thus appeared increasingly anachronistic. At the end of the twelfth century the Cistercians, in direct competition to the Benedictines, claimed to be the true adherents to the Benedictine Rule and in the thirteenth century the number of Cistercian foundations grew to some 740 monasteries in one century: it seems that austerity was popular, highlighting the complacency in the Benedictine Order. This was indeed recognised by Pope Innocent III, whose fourth Lateran Council (1215) advocated reform requiring Benedictine monasteries to adopt a federal structure, country by country, and to hold triennial parliaments or chapters. This was widely ignored except in England, where it was very successful: in 1277 the English chapter drew up revised statutes, intended of attracting 'men of outstanding dignity, education and religion' to the Benedictines by shortening and simplifying the divine office and by sending monks to university. These reforms were neither widely popular nor accepted; indeed, Archbishop Peckham, being a Franciscan with no interest in reinvigorating the rival order of the Benedictines, forbade their adoption [97].

However, despite the reforms, Benedictine decline was inevitable: the intellectual hegemony once enjoyed by the monasteries passed to, or had

---

[97] RW Southern: *Western Society and the Church in the Middle Ages*.

to be shared with, the embryonic universities while the spiritual leadership was assumed by the new orders – Franciscan, Dominican, Cistercian. The pastoral role of the Benedictines was increasingly taken over by university-educated secular clergy – the parish priests.[98]

Above all society was changing. The legal reforms initiated by the Papal Revolution, taken up by secular rulers, was one of many aspects of the rise of the individual. Other manifestations were the emergence of urban society and the mercantile class, the intellectual freedom enjoyed by the new universities and the development of Parliament. Even the major productive monastic craft-industry of book production was rendered redundant in the later Middle Ages by the invention of printing.

By the beginning of the sixteenth century both the conditions in which monasteries were first conceived and their original purpose had both changed out of all recognition. The sixth century world had been wild, lawless and turbulent: monasteries offered a safe haven that set an example of how Christian life could be lived. They became the only providers of education, charity and pastoral care. By the sixteenth century the rule of law prevailed and safe havens were anachronistic. Grammar schools and universities provided an alternative source of education, while the parish system increasingly provided pastoral care. The relevance of monasteries to secular society waned.

---

[98] David Knowles: *The Religious Houses of Medieval England*.

9

The St Albans Monastery

St Albans is, in comparison with the other monasteries of the Realm, over-slenderly endowed.

An extract of a 1395 letter from King Richard II to Pope Boniface IX in support of Abbot Thomas' financial negotiations.

Historical overview of the monastery

The century following the consecration of the Norman abbey saw a steady growth of both the number of monks and the abbey's reputation as a centre of spiritual excellence and integrity, both reaching their peak in the abbacy of the saintly Abbot John de Cella (1195–1214). This century saw the establishment of the dependent cells and the growth of the abbey as a centre of learning. It also saw an increase in the popularity of St Albans as a pilgrimage destination, to the extent that a westward extension to the nave of the abbey church, lengthy though it was, was planned to accommodate the pilgrims. The fact that Nicholas Breakspear, the only Englishman ever to be elected pope, as Adrian IV (1154–59), was educated at St Albans, only further enhanced the abbey's prestige and supported its claim as the premier monastery of England.

In the early thirteenth century arts and letters flourished in the abbey, and the 'St Albans school of history', inspired by the work of the chronicler-monk Matthew Paris, achieved international renown.

However, as St Albans Abbey was growing in reputation and wealth, so was the papacy growing in power and ambition, culminating in the papacy of Innocent IV (1198–1216). He convened the fourth Lateran Council, which lead to extensive reforms and interference in monastic affairs. A variety of external factors combined to make life difficult for the monastery: the decline in agricultural income and corresponding inflation: predatory taxation from both the papacy and the monarchy, 'acts of God' such as the 1250 earthquake, which irreparably damaged the presbytery, and the climatic disaster of 1315, which caused severe famine. Despite this adverse headwind, the presbytery was rebuilt by 1290. There followed a succession of three weaker and short-lived abbots in nineteen years (1290, 1302 and 1309) increasing the financial burden of seeking papal confirmation of their appointment, which pushed the monastery's debt, by the time of the St Albans revolt in 1327 (discussed later) to some £3,000, twice its annual income.

This period of decline, which is likely to have been accompanied by the decline in observance that was recorded throughout the Benedictine Order, was arrested and repaired a by a succession of three outstanding abbots – Richard of Wallingford (1327–1336), Michael de Mentmore (1336–1349) and Thomas de la Mare (1349–1396). Under these abbots monastic observance was at least partially restored, the finances recovered and the abbey's reputation salvaged – all this despite the collapse and rebuilding of five bays of the south arcade of the nave, the ravages of the Black Death, in which forty-seven monks and Abbot Michael de Mentmore lost their lives, the turbulence created by the St Albans revolt of 1327 and the Peasants' Revolt in 1381. Thomas de la Mare was undoubtedly the greatest of all the St Albans abbots, and also the most widely respected. He held the presidency of the Benedictine general chapter, raised the standard and administration of all the St Albans houses and was subsequently invited by King Edward III to visit and advise on the reform of other Benedictine houses.

His successors, who continued and revived the tradition of St Albans chroniclers with great distinction, confined their reforms to improving observance and monastic management. They did not acknowledge the growing movement, as advocated by Wyclif, for more fundamental reform to counter the steady acquisition of wealth and power of the Benedictine monasteries.

Abbot Thomas de La Mare as depicted in a fourteenth century brass memorial in St Albans Abbey.

This movement of reform, driven underground at the suppression of the Peasants' Revolt, resurfaced in the 1420s when disaffected monks (referred to as 'false brethren' by Walsingham)[99] appealed to King Henry V for a return 'to the pristine religion of our ancestors'. Henry reacted energetically, making a tour of monasteries and calling council at Westminster (1421), where he proposed more fundamental reforms to be discussed with six delegates, one of whom was the Abbot of St Albans, John of Wheathampstead. The reforms, which in any case only called for a more rigorous return to the Benedictine Rule, were inevitably kicked by the delegates into the long grass[100]. Henry died the following year and thus a great opportunity of reform was lost. Henry, if he had lived, possessed the energy and commitment to insist on a thorough reform that would have blunted humanist criticism of monasticism (see Chapter 11) and so may have made Cromwell's programme of suppression of the monasteries far more difficult than it eventually was.

Abbot John Wheathampstead; a digital reconstruction from his skeleton exhumed in 2017 in preparation of building works on the site of the former chapter house. (By kind permission of University of Liverpool, John Moore University/FaceLab.)

---

[99] Preest and Clark: *The Chronica Maiora of Thomas Walsingham.*
[100] David Knowles: *The Religious Orders in England.*

The rest of the fifteenth century was relatively uneventful, with standards of management set by Abbot Thomas being maintained by the two abbacies of John of Wheathampstead (1420–1440 and 1452–1465). The exception to this period of calm were the two battles of the Wars of the Roses that took place in St Albans, in which the sanctity of the abbey was violated in the second battle (1461) by the victors, the Lancastrian troops. Steady decline set in towards the end of the century – a decline in monastic discipline and levels of observance.

Description of St Albans monastery – the mother house

In terms of prestige, St Albans, on account of its dedication to St Alban the British proto-martyr and also to the size of its abbey church – the largest monastic church in England – was regarded as the premier monastery in England, although this rank was from time to time hotly contested by both Westminster and Canterbury. In terms of both its endowment and population of monks it was certainly large, but not as large as Canterbury, Peterborough and Bury St Edmunds. Accurate numbers of monks are unavailable but the consensus is that it was about fifty on dedication in 1115, rising to a peak of nearly 100 in the early 1200s. In the event this expansion proved to be financially unsustainable, the result being that the number of monks declined to about sixty in the early fourteenth century. The Black Death (1349), in which forty-seven monks died, reduced the number to less than thirty. By the end of the century the monk population had recovered to about sixty. In the final decades of the monastery the numbers declined further. At the Dissolution thirty-nine monks signed the surrender document.

Of course the abbey was populated by many people beside the monks: artisans, servants and pensioners, all of whom would be lay people. RH Snape[101] has collated plenty of evidence that the number of artisans and servants in large Benedictine monasteries equalled the number of monks. This ratio of 1:1 perhaps increased with time so that in the fifteenth century it may have been as high as 1:1.5. The fluctuating number of pensioners – known as corrodiers – is not known but could have been several dozen (by comparison with the known numbers at Croyland Abbey). On this basis the total population of St Albans Abbey could have risen from about 100 soon after its consecration in 1115 to a peak of well

---

[101] RH Snape: *English Monastic Finances in the Later Middle Ages*.

over 150 a hundred years later, declining to about sixty following the Black Death and about eighty before its dissolution. These estimates of the population of St Albans monastery are for the mother house: that of the twelve daughter houses, which are briefly described below, would increase the estimates by about 30 per cent, so that at the peak the abbot would have been responsible for over 200 monks.

The daughter houses

Daughter houses – also known as priories or dependent cells – were small bodies of monks – or nuns – dependent on the mother house, the abbey, and bound to obey the abbot or his deputy the prior as much as were the monks based in the abbey. St Albans was the mother house to twelve priories and one nunnery with a peak population of some seventy monks. Although St Albans may have been emulating the example set by the monastery of Cluny in France, the acquisition of the daughter houses by St Albans appears to have been opportunistic rather than planned, Archbishop Lanfranc playing a leading role as a broker. St Albans was not alone in this respect but had more than any other monastery, Gloucester Abbey and Durham cathedral being its nearest rivals. The endowment represented by the acquisition of the new daughter houses transformed the finances of the abbey and made it one of the richest monasteries in England.[102]

The benefits to the mother house were many and various: enhanced prestige, additional reach, additional income, but above all it provided the mother house with an enlarged pool of talented monks who could be considered as suitable candidates for election to the abbacy when this situation was vacant. Thus the abbey's greatest abbots, John de Cella, Richard of Wallingford and Thomas de la Mare came from the Wallingford and Tynemouth priories respectively. Conversely the priories provided remote retirement homes especially suitable for banished awkward or troublesome monks. The daughter houses are briefly described.

---

[102] PA Hayward: *The Cult of St Albans, Anglorum Protomartyr, in Anglo Saxon and Anglo Norman England.*

Priory	County	Dates	Founder/Main benefactor	No. of monks (nuns)
Belvoir	Leicestershire	1076	Robert of Todeni	<10
			William d'Albini	
			William d'Albini	
Wallingford	Oxfordshire	1077	Nicholas d'Albini	<10
Redbourn	Hertfordshire	1078	Abbot Simon	<5
Binham	Norfolk	1093	Peter de Valognes	about 15
Tynemouth	Northumberland	1093	Richard de Mowbray	about 20
Hatfield	Hertfordshire	1093	Ralph de Limesi	12
Hatfield Peverel	Essex	1095	William Peverel	<10
Wymondham*	Norfolk	1110	William d'Albini	20
Sopwell**	Hertfordshire	1140	Geoffrey de Gorham	(12)
Beaulieu	Leicestershire	1140	Robert d'Albini	about 5
Markyate***	Bedfordshire	1145	Geoffrey de Gorham	about (5)
Pembroke	Pembrokeshire	1443	Humphrey Duke of Gloucester	About 10

*Wymondham gained its independence from St Albans in 1440 and thereafter became an abbey in its own right.
** Sopwell was a house of Benedictine nuns.
*** Markyate, a house of Benedictine nuns, was strictly not a daughter house as it was owned by St Paul's Cathedral.

Wallingford Priory[103]

The Priory of the Holy Trinity in Wallingford, although far from the biggest of the daughter houses was the oldest and perhaps the most successful, supplying four of the twenty-six medieval abbots, including John de Cella and Richard of Wallingford. The Church of the Holy

---

[103] Katherine Keats-Rohan: *The Origins of Wallingford Priory*.

Trinity, formerly part of a Saxon college for the training of secular (non-monastic) priests, was granted to St Albans in the late eleventh century by Nicholas d'Albini, the brother of Richard d'Albini, who succeeded Paul de Caen as abbot in 1097. Unfortunately nothing remains of the priory, which was completely demolished in the Reformation and its stone used to repair Wallingford bridge. Only the seal remains.

Belvoir Priory[104]

Belvoir Priory, in Leicestershire, and the smallest of St Albans' daughter houses, was founded in 1076 by Robert of Todeni, Lord of Belvoir. Originally intended as a monastery, Robert was unable to complete the construction of the work and was advised by Archbishop Lanfranc to confer the foundation to St Albans. William d'Albini, a benefactor, was buried in the chapter house. Roger of Wendover, a prior in the thirteenth century – reputedly a rather dissipated one – was transferred to the mother house as the first chronicler. The monastery was totally demolished in the Reformation. The priory was staffed by four monks, declining to just two in its final years.

Tynemouth Priory[105]

The origin of Tynemouth Priory is both obscure and colourful. It was originally founded by King Edwin of Deira in the early seventh century, but destroyed by the Danes in the ninth. It was rebuilt by Robert de Mowbray, Earl of Northumberland, late in the eleventh century and dedicated to St Oswin, whose relics were translated to the new priory. Mowbray was in dispute with the Bishop of Durham, in whose diocese Tynemouth was situated, which led to the Archbishop of Canterbury,

---

[104] Victoria County History: *Houses of Benedictine Monks: Belvoir Priory.*
[105] D Lumley: *The Story of Tynemouth Priory and Castle.*

THE ST ALBANS MONASTERY

Lanfranc, recommending that the priory should be granted to St Albans. On his first visit to Tynemouth, Paul de Caen, the Abbot of St Albans, was prevented from entry by a hostile Bishop of Durham. Shortly after this episode, in 1095, Robert de Mowbray led a rebellion against William II in favour of William's brother, the eventual King Henry I. This uprising was put down by a force commanded by William d'Albini, nephew of the future St Albans abbot. Mowbray was subsequently captured, accused of treason, convicted and imprisoned in Windsor castle – maybe avoiding the death penalty on account of his re-founding of Tynemouth? We finally hear of him as a monk at St Albans, presumably pardoned by King Henry I on his accession. It is said that the then Bishop of Durham, Ranulf Flambard (more of whom in Chapter 11), re –translated St Oswin's relics to St Albans in 1103.

In many ways the history of the priory mirrors that of the mother house: it grew prosperous in the twelfth century and embarked on substantial expansions of the priory church, with an eastward extension to provide a grander presbytery, a chapel dedicated to St Oswin and a westward extension of the nave. The priory probably overreached itself with this project and fell into debt, made worse by the repeated incursions of the Scots, a struggle with English military leaders (jealous of its superbly strategic site) and interference by the bishops of Durham. Thomas de la Mare, as Prior of Tynemouth, was successful in asserting

A conjectural depiction of Tynemouth Priory after the thirteenth century extensions, from the south east, as presented in Gibson's Guide to Tynemouth.

the priory's independence and his own primacy and supervised the extensive repairs and restoration after such turbulent times. Following further raids by the Scots the fortifications were once more strengthened by the construction of a new gatehouse, by Prior John of Wheathampstead (1390–1419 and subsequently Abbot of St Albans).

The ruins of the presbytery of Tynemouth Priory as they exist today.

Binham Priory, Norfolk

Binham Priory was founded in 1093 by Peter de Valognes, William the Conqueror's nephew, who had extensive landholdings in Norfolk as well as his main residence in Hertfordshire. The new priory, based on the Saxon church of St Mary, was intended for the shared use of the village people and the Benedictine community, which initially comprised six monks from St Albans. At the Dissolution the priory was demolished, sparing only the nave of the priory church which was retained as the parish church.

An aerial view of the remains of Binham Priory, showing the nave.

Hertford Priory

Construction of this priory started in 1087 by Ralph de Limesi, another nephew of William the Conqueror. Hertford priory was large with a complement of twelve monks and was entirely demolished in the Dissolution.

Hatfield Peverel Priory, Essex

This priory, like Wallingford, was originally a Saxon secular, or canonical, college that was converted to a Benedictine house by William Peverel in 1100 and subordinated to St Albans Abbey.

Wymondham Priory, Norfolk

By contrast, Wymondham Priory – later Abbey – was the largest and most magnificent of the daughter houses. It was founded in 1107 by William d'Albini as a dependency of St Albans, where William's uncle was abbot. The foundation was unusual in that the priory church was jointly used by townspeople as well as the Benedictine community, an arrangement which led to disputes: in 1249 these were referred to Pope Innocent IV,

The surviving nave of Wymondham abbey church from the south.

the nave, the north aisle and the north-east tower, leaving the rest to the priory. This arrangement meant that at least the nave was spared destruction in the Dissolution. It seems that the community resented their dependency status, manifested in their change of the priory's dedication, in 1170, from 'St Mary and St Alban the Martyr', to 'St Mary and St Thomas Becket'. Relations worsened until the priory was granted its independence from St Albans by the pope in 1448, in response to a Priory petition.

Beaulieu Priory, Bedfordshire

This small priory was founded by Robert d'Albini on the site of a hermitage established by his father Henry. Since it was always too poor to be viable, Abbot John of Wheathampstead merged the priory with the abbey, the annual income being assigned to providing scholarships to support St Albans monks studying at Oxford.

The Priory of Sopwell, St Albans

Sopwell Priory, a house for Benedictine nuns, situated just to the south east of the abbey, was founded in 1140 by Abbot Geoffrey de Gorham to accommodate the few nuns surviving from the original Saxon convent. An early benefactor was Henry d'Albini and his son Robert when his sister Amica joined the priory as a nun. The initial complement of nuns was twelve.

Pembroke Priory

Pembroke Priory was built in 1098 by the Earl of Pembroke as a dependent cell of St Martin of Séez, Normandy. It was dissolved in 1441, as part of a policy of the dissolution of all alien, or foreign-owned, houses, and assigned to St Albans by Humphrey Duke of Gloucester.

The Priory of Markyate

Markyate Priory, a house for Benedictine nuns, was founded in 1145 by Abbot Geoffrey de Gorham. Strictly speaking it was a dependency of St Paul's Cathedral rather than St Albans, having been built on land owned by St Paul's.

Abbots, kings and popes

Appointment of the abbots

In the Benedictine Order it was up to the monks of a monastery to elect their own abbot when this position fell vacant, but with the growth in the importance and wealth of monasteries kings felt the choice of abbots was too important to be left to the monks and required royal ratification. One of the consequences of the Papal Revolution was that the selection of senior clergy – bishops and abbots – was arrogated by the pope, so that in reality both royal and papal approval was required for the appointment of new abbots. Such approvals, which were by no means a formality, had to be sought by the elected abbot in person, which involved considerable expense and effort. One of the implications of the feudal system was that on the death of an abbot the income of a monastery reverted to the monarchy until a new abbot was in post so there was every incentive for a cash-strapped king to linger over his approval, after which the papal approval involved a lengthy journey to Rome or Avignon. Once an audience had been granted, the appellant abbot found himself thrown to the mercy of the papal legal bureaucracy, which involved the maximum humiliation and extortion. An example of this Kafkaesque procedure, described by a twelfth-century abbot as 'a journey into the land of the insatiate sons of the horse leech, ever athirst for money', is provided by the experience of Abbot Richard of Wallingford at the hands of Pope John XXII in 1328, of which a full account is available[106]. Richard was lucky in that the papacy at that time had removed to Avignon with a travel time from St Albans of just six weeks each way. Richard was an extremely thrifty churchman, acutely aware that his new abbey was heavily in debt, but even with the greatest economy the cost of the whole procedure was £953 10s 11d – Richard kept good accounts – about half the annual income of the abbey at that time. This level of expenditure for every new abbot was unsupportable, especially when there was a rapid turnover of new abbots, as happened between 1290 and 1309, when three new abbots were obliged to make the journey to Avignon. This practice was brought to an end when Abbot Thomas de la Mare negotiated with Pope Boniface IX a modest annual payment of £14 in place of visits by future abbots.

---

[106] John North: *God's Clockmaker – Richard of Wallingford and the Invention of Time*.

I Am Called Alban

Papal privileges

Great importance was attached by St Albans, as well as by other major monasteries, of independence from episcopal control by the bishop of the diocese in which it was situated – Lincoln in the case of St Albans. This independence was naturally rejected by successive bishops with as much vehemence as it was asserted by successive abbots, who maintained that these privileges had been originally granted to St Albans at the time of its supposed foundation by King Offa in 793. The dispute was resolved by the happy circumstance of a St Albans man, Nicholas Breakspear, being elected pope in 1154 – taking the name Adrian IV – just before the visit to Rome by a new Abbot of St Albans, Robert de Gorham, to receive papal confirmation of his appointment. This would have been a far more congenial meeting than that experienced by Richard de Wallingford described previously. Pope Adrian IV confirmed – and indeed extended – the privileges: St Albans was granted freedom from jurisdiction of any bishop and of visitation by anyone other than a papal legate. The question of precedence was also settled in St Albans' favour by his ruling: 'For just as the Blessed Alban is known to be the protomartyr of the English, so also the abbot of his monastery should be held out as first among abbots of England in order of dignity …'[107]

"Pope Adrian IV from a 19th century painting by G Fracisci, by courtesy of Hertfordshire County Council."

Nicholas Breakspear, who became Pope Adrian IV, was the son of a tenant of St Albans Abbey at Abbots Langley, Hertfordshire, and later in life a monk at St Albans. According to Matthew Paris (who was not above elaboration for the greater glory of the Abbey), Nicholas was educated at the abbey school but was rejected as a monk by St Albans on account of his inadequate education. However, far from bearing any resentment, as Pope he remembered St Albans with great fondness.

---

[107] Paul Hayward: *The Cult of St Alban, Anglorum Protomartyr*, in Anglo-Saxon and Anglo-Norman England.

Duties of the abbot

The main duty of the abbot was of course to lead the monastery and act as father figure to the monks, the lay brothers, artisans and servants of both St Albans Abbey and the daughter houses. Within this remit the abbot was also responsible for maintaining and indeed enhancing the dignity of the house, home as it was to the relics of England's proto-martyr, in order to sustain the income derived from the alms of pilgrims and gifts from wealthy benefactors. This core responsibility tended to be crowded out by more temporal duties: those of a feudal lord of the liberty of St Albans, as a senior member of Parliament, as a visitor to other monasteries, and by no means least the important task of dispensing appropriate hospitality. This last task was especially onerous because of the abbey's proximity – just one day's ride – from London and a convenient first stopover en route to the north. The term hospitality does not quite convey the scale – it certainly wasn't a question of the odd traveller popping in for lunch. Matthew Paris, the great abbey chronicler, records that the abbey provided stabling for 300 horses, necessary, for instance, when Humphrey, Duke of Gloucester, visited with 300 men and stayed a fortnight.

Management of the monastery

Albanstowe

The majority of the thirty-two manors owned by St Albans Abbey were situated in the area around the monastery, which became known as Albanstowe, or the liberty of St Albans. As we have seen, it was not subject to the religious control of the Lincoln diocese and neither was it under the political control of Hertfordshire, the county in which it was situated. In effect it was an autonomous independent area answerable only to the king and the pope. The area covered by Albanstowe in Hertfordshire was approximately 200km^2 or 20,000 hectares in extent, as shown in blue in the map below, and comprised 24 parishes. In feudal terms the Abbot of St Albans was the 'tenant in chief' who pledged fealty to the king in return for the use of the land. The abbot sub-leased the land to sub-tenants, who in turn pledged fealty to the abbot: it was the rental income from this land, both in terms of money, produce or labour that provided the base income of the monastery.

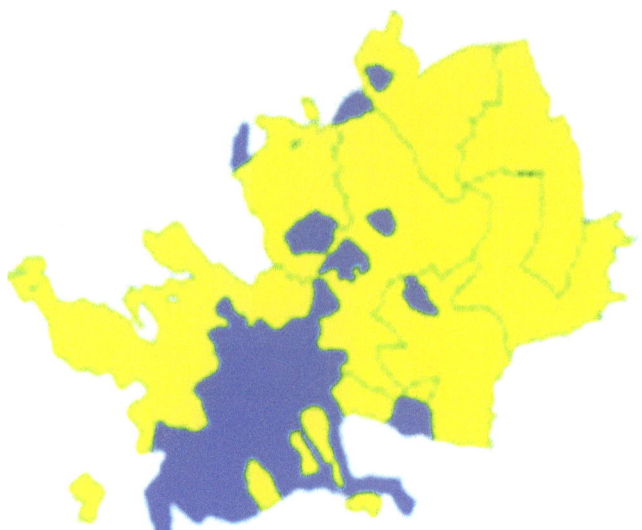

A map of Hertfordshire showing in blue the extent of Albanstowe or the Liberty of St Albans, of which the abbot was tenant-in-chief.

Monastic management

As we have seen, the Benedictine Rule requiring monks to contribute to food production by their manual labour had long been abandoned, which gave rise to the need to find – or invent – jobs for monks (known as obedientiaries) to keep them occupied. In 1380 the category I obedientiary positions were the abbot, the prior, the sub prior, the precentor, the succentor, the keeper of the shrine and the archdeacon. Category II positions included scrutators, the cellarer and his assistant, the chamberlain, the almoner, the kitchener, the refectorer and his assistant, the infirmater, the forestarius, the guest master and the warden of St Mary's Chapel[108].

Thus there were twenty-four official positions for a house of, initially at least, fifty-six monks; the rest – those without official positions – would have been musicians, writers, retired. The duties of many of these obedientiaries are reasonably obvious: those in category I provided the management team, those in category II were responsible for the abbey church and the services and also the preservation of order (the scrutator).

---

[108] Dugdale: *Monasticon Anglicanum*.

The obedientiaries of the third category were responsible for housekeeping and although not specifically identified, the care of the garden and maintenance of the fabric. The management system may seem bizarre compared with modern management practice: specific sources of revenue, manor rentals, mill royalties, Church tithes etc., were assigned to each money-spending department, whose obedientiary would have been at least nominally responsible for collecting the income, and the good management of those sources of revenue. This system, while inefficient and inflexible, at least prevented the risk of all financial responsibility being invested in one person, the abbot.

Abbey finances

Income

There were two main sources of revenue for the abbey: spiritual and temporal. Spiritual sources comprised tithes from appropriated churches, alms and benefactions, while temporal sources included rental income, mill royalties and proceeds from the sale of home produce surplus to the needs of the house, including timber production and fishing. It would also include the fees and fines from feudal courts and market dues.

Because of this diversity of revenue source and of the lack of any central accounting control in monasteries, it is very difficult to estimate the income of the abbey with any confidence. The only data available, apart from the *Valor Ecclesiasticus* drawn up at the time of the Dissolution, is the *Taxatio Nicholai* prepared in 1288 on the order of Pope Nicholas IV as a basis of granting Edward I one tenth – a tithe – of all Church revenues for six years to fund Edward's contribution to the cost of the Tenth Crusade. However, this evaluation of ecclesiastical revenue is not considered to even approximately correspond with the actual income. The next guide available is a more accurate valuation of French Benedictine houses, carried out in 1388 on the order of Pope Benedict XII. This evaluation, only available for 104 monasteries in the province of Rouen, shows the average income to have been £15 per monk[109]. On this basis the revenue of St Albans Abbey, at its peak population of about 100 monks, would have been £1,500. This figure compares reasonably well with the statement that the cost of Richard of Wallingford's confirmation by the pope in 1327 – £953 – was said to be about half the abbey's annual income. The income per head in the twelfth century, before the period of

---

[109] RH Snape: *English Monastic Finances in the Later Middle Ages*.

inflation (see previously) would have been half this value, so that the annual income of St Albans Abbey with a population of just fifty monks may then have been in the range £300–£400.

After the depredations of the Black Death, both the abbey's population and revenue would have declined, although it's difficult to say which was the cause and which the effect. The abbey would have been badly affected by the shortage of labour and the national economic slump – rental income was relatively inelastic while wages increased markedly in the second half of the fourteenth century. Moreover, the revenue from alms had been in decline throughout the thirteenth century as a result of the spectacular growth in the cult of St Thomas Becket, which resulted in Canterbury taking over from St Albans as the prime pilgrimage destination. In summary, it is fair to say that the abbey's annual revenue grew substantially throughout the middle ages, very approximately as follows:

Estimate based on Rouen data for 50-monk monastery	£300–£400
Taxatio Nicholai (1291)	£850
Estimate based on Rouen data for 100-monk monastery	£1,500
Estimate based on Abbot Richards data (1327)	£1,900
Royal Audit on the death of Abbot Thomas de la Mare (1396)	£1,053
Valor Ecclesiasticus of 1535	£2,102

Expenditure

The main heads of expenditure were, in descending order of their approximate magnitude:
- Architectural developments and major repairs.
- Papal exactions for confirmation of a new abbot.
- Expropriation by the king of monastic revenues between the death/retirement of one abbot and the appointment of a successor.
- Taxation.
- Supplies of food and drink.
- Artisan and servant salaries. As we have seen the secular population of the abbey was equal to or exceeded the clerical population so that by the early fifteenth century the annual wage bill could have been in the range £20–£30.
- Alms, hospitality, entertainment and gifts.
- Interest on loans.
- Visitation fees.

The cost of architectural developments and rebuilds
There were three major campaigns of architectural development, described in more detail in a following section
- The westward extension of the nave and the reconstruction of the west front in the late twelfth century.
- The reconstruction of the presbytery in the second half of the thirteenth century.
- Collapse and reconstruction of the south arcade of the nave and the construction of the lady chapel.

In the absence of any accounts, it is extremely difficult to estimate the cost of building works so we have to look to data from other contemporaneous building projects. We know that the cost of building Salisbury Cathedral in the early thirteenth century was £28,000, while detailed accounts of Henry III's rebuilding of Westminster Abbey shows that the building costs in 1253 were £1,652, 70 per cent of which was for labour and 30 per cent for materials.[110] By comparison, the construction cost of the Caernavon, Conway and Harlech castles was £14,000[111]. With such data as a rough guide, it would be reasonable to hazard that each of the major building campaigns at St Albans would have cost sums equivalent to several years of the monastic income. It is likely that these building projects would have required considerable borrowing, including from Jewish money lenders before their expulsion in 1290 – Aaron of Lincoln being the most famous – incurring heavy interest payments.

Cost of papal confirmation of abbots
As we have seen, St Albans, along with other large monasteries, was keen to receive the privilege of independence from episcopal control: the price of the granting of this was that abbots, on election, were required to travel to Rome – or Avignon – for papal confirmation. This was ordained in the fourth Lateran Council in 1215 and was only relaxed in 1395, after which payment of an annual fee was agreed. A total of nine St Albans abbots were required to make the journey, either to Rome or Avignon (depending on the seat of the pope at the time), at an average cost of £1,500 per visit, giving total cost of £13,500, equivalent to an annual cost of £75 over the 180-year period. The abbey was subjected to royal expropriation of

---
[110] Richard Jones: Gleanings from the 1253 building accounts of Westminster Abbey – Aviva Forum.
[111] JL Bolton: *The Medieval English Economy 1150–1500*.

monastic revenues at each of the twenty-four changes of abbot; assuming an average change over period of three months and an average annual income of £1,500, the total thus expropriated would have been approximately £9,000, an equivalent annual cost of £25. Thus the total annual cost of a change in abbots averaged out at £100, a significant portion – about 8 per cent – of the total annual income.

Alms, hospitality and education
The direct giving of alms was always a haphazard affair, frequently associated with the journeys of the abbot or obedientiaries and never systematic. There is of course no data on the amount given, but after extensive research RH Snape concludes that the amounts were very small, typically about 3 per cent of annual income[112].

Other charitable expenditure, on the two leper hospitals at St Julians and St Mary de Pre, both founded by Abbot Geoffrey de Gorham, were paid out of their founding endowments.

The expenditure on hospitality is unknown but was undoubtedly huge, as indicated by the extent of stabling provided for visitors' horses. As reported by John Amundesham (Thomas Walsingham's successor)[113], large scale hospitality reached its peak in 1423–4 when Duke Humphrey, his wife and 300 retainers spent the Christmas season at the abbey: hospitality was provided on a similar scale in 1426. As time wore on hospitality was increasingly restricted to royalty, aristocrats and visiting Church dignitaries: lesser mortals were expected to lodge in the various inns that the town had to offer. The expectation was that the cost of hospitality for those who received it would be at least partly offset by generous benefactions. Any shortfall would have been ascribed to the cost of buying favour and influence. Evidently this system did not survive the accession of King Henry VIII.

Housekeeping
There is no data on housekeeping costs, but it is likely that the monastery was self-sufficient in terms of food and fuel. Imported foods, wine and servants' wages would have had to be paid for out of income.

Taxation
St Albans Abbey would have been taxed by both the kings of England and

---

[112] RH Snape: *English Monastic Finances in the Middle Ages*.
[113] David Knowles: *The Religious Orders of England*.

the popes, often working in collaboration. Papal taxation was introduced by Pope Innocent III in 1199, requiring a fortieth of ecclesiastical income to fund the Fourth Crusade. Where Innocent III led, his successors were not slow to follow: in 1226 Honorius III demanded an ecclesiastical tax 'for the better support of his dignity' (although this was not approved by Parliament). In 1228 King Henry III promised Pope Gregory IX a tithe (10 per cent) on both the Church and laity, with further extortions being demanded during the course of the thirteenth century until the tax of Pope Nicholas III referred to previously, in which King Edward I was awarded 10 per cent of all ecclesiastical revenue for a period of six years to fund Edward's contribution to the crusade. This contribution, to reinforce the Christian occupation of Acre, was never actually made – clever politics by Edward since the pope took all the blame and he all the money. Edward I, forever in the throes of war, was always short of money and in 1295, as a desperate measure, imposed a levy of 50 per cent of Church income.

Debt

Most Benedictine monasteries were frequently in debt in the Middle Ages, but not excessively so: the average debt was less than their annual income. St Albans was no exception, apart from the end of the last half of the thirteenth century and the first quarter of the fourteenth, when, by the end of the abbacy of Hugh de Eversden, the debt rose to about £3,500 or three times the annual income. At this point Abbot Eversden petitioned the pope for permission to appropriate churches in the liberty of St Albans to raise capital. The debt had been mounting over many years and was the culmination of a variety of causes: abbatial mismanagement and extravagance, excessive taxation, acts of God resulting in extensive repairs to the abbey fabric and a reduction in its agricultural revenue.

Commissioners were appointed by the young King Edward III to investigate the causes of the debt and their findings were highly critical. Eversden's successor Abbot Richard of Wallingford and his immediate successors were successful in reforming the financial management and recovering the financial discipline of the abbey.

Relations of the Abbey with the town[114]

The embryonic St Albans grew up next to the Saxon monastery and it was the Abbot Ulsinus who established it as a town complete with three parish

---

[114] John North: *God's Clockmaker – Richard of Wallingford and the Invention of Time.* Ch 10.

churches and a market. The Saxon abbots nurtured the town – very much the Abbey's town – and protected it against the adjacent royal Burgh of Kingsbury. The 'ownership' of St Albans by the monastery was formalised after the Norman conquest in a charter granted by King Henry II, in which the Abbot of St Albans was confirmed as the king's tenant in chief with feudal rights over the town and the surrounding manors. The town prospered, with the income associated with the inflow of pilgrims and with servicing the monastery, which towards the end of the end of the twelfth century would have employed well over a hundred artisans, servants and labourers. As the urban population of England blossomed with the growth in trade and the money economy, many new towns were created and some 170 charters granted. Such charters provided fiscal autonomy for the property-owning classes – the burgesses – and a freedom of operation in which private enterprise could flourish. Not unnaturally the citizens of St Albans grew resentful and frustrated that the feudal system, which was rigorously enforced by the abbey, denied them of the opportunities enjoyed by the charter towns. Nor were these frustrations just financial: charter towns were entitled to select the two burgesses to represent them at parliaments, a privilege denied to the unfree feudal towns such as St Albans, where the selection was in the hands of the abbot. Furthermore, all milling in the town, both for grain and fulling cloth, was required to be carried out, for a fee, by mills owned and operated by the abbey.

The first expression of trouble we hear of occurred in 1275 when Abbot Roger of Norton accused one Michael Bryd of building a hand mill in violation of the privileges of the abbot, and Henry de la Porte of using a mill not owned by the abbey. Both were fined one mark (13s 4d or 67p). In another contravention, the following year, the guilty party settled out of court offering five tuns of wine in compensation.

Tensions between the town and the abbey built up in the last decades of the thirteenth century and the first quarter of the fourteenth, exacerbated by the reign of Edward II, which lurched from disaster to disaster: the ongoing conflict with his barons; a disastrous marriage ending in separation and rebellion; the calamitous defeat by the Scots at Bannockburn; the Great Famine in which some 10 per cent of the population lost their lives; and brutal taxation, corruption and maladministration. Not surprisingly there was an increase in poaching at this time. Edward's reign ended in the autumn of 1326 when his wife Queen Isabella, together with her lover Roger Mortimer, invaded England, at which point Edward fled to Wales, where he was eventually imprisoned and murdered in September 1327.

The St Albans Monastery

It was in this febrile atmosphere that the leading burgesses of St Albans, as those of two other monastic towns, Abingdon and Bury St Edmonds, were emboldened by the examples set by uprisings in the big towns, to rise in revolt in early 1327. The uprising at St Albans was well timed by the townsmen: they would have been aware that Abbot Eversden (1309–1327) was well regarded by King Edward II, who had made seven visits to the abbey during this time, and would have been correct in thinking that Queen Isabella, on behalf of the fifteen-year-old Edward III, would take the contrary view: she would inevitably support the town where her husband would have automatically sided with the abbey. The trouble at St Albans was triggered, in early January 1327, by an attack on an abbey servant in the town, in the course of which one of the attackers lost his life. This incident was followed the next day by a deputation of twelve townsmen who called on Abbot Eversden with a petition asking for what they thought was a restoration of ancient rights and liberties, which included self-governance, the right to choose their own representatives for Parliament, independence from monastic justice and freedom to own hand mills. After some prevarication, Eversden gave his verbal assent, but this did not satisfy the townsmen: they attacked the main gate of the abbey but were repelled by abbey security forces, after which the townsmen besieged the abbey for ten days. Meanwhile the abbey obtained a royal writ authorising the county sheriff to relieve the abbey, together with all its inhabitants. The townsmen withdrew while the matter was referred to the royal court, which infuriated the mob and provoked another attack, in which one rioter was captured and imprisoned. Subsequently the court issued a writ stating that the abbey had indeed deprived the townspeople of their rights and liberties, contrary to the provisions of the Magna Carta. However, this writ was conditional on a requirement for the abbey treasurer and chamberlain to inspect the Domesday Book to find out whether St Albans was originally a free borough or not. The inspection showed that St Albans belonged to the abbey, nullifying the first writ. The town's claim was eventually settled by a conference of arbitrators, meeting in St Paul's Cathedral churchyard, the outcome of which was a recommendation substantially in favour of the town. A detailed agreement was prepared, which received royal assent on 19 April 1327. This agreement granted St Albans the status of a borough and all its inhabitants burgesses, although they would still be subject to the abbot's justice and would still not be allowed to own their own hand mills. This agreement was bitterly opposed by the monks, but eventually conceded by Abbot Eversden under pressure exerted by Queen Isabella, who visited St Albans at this time.

There the matter may have rested, but for the death of Abbot Eversden and the indiscipline on the part of the burgesses, who totally ignored the handmill requirement in the agreement and set up some eighty handmills of their own. It is not known whether Eversden death was precipitated by the humiliation of both backing down over the dispute with the townsmen and the severely critical report into the abbey finances by the royal commission of inquiry.

Hugh Eversden's successor, Richard of Wallingford (1327–1336), was determined to revoke the liberties unjustly wrested from Abbot Hugh. Although regarded by the townsmen as a 'class traitor', coming as he did from artisan stock, it was not only a point of honour for him, as abbot, but a practical necessity because the abbey finances, precarious at the best of times, could ill afford the loss of revenue associated with the granting of the liberties. Richard, a consummate strategist, played a long and subtle game: he would attack on the spiritual front. He alleged there had been a serious slackening of moral standards since the granting of the liberties. Accordingly he indicted a prominent burgess, one John Taverner, on a charge of adultery and excommunicated four others for moral laxity and contempt of his authority. The summons were served on Taverner by Richard's marshal, who was assaulted by Taverner. In the melee that followed Taverner was killed, whereupon the mob turned on the marshal and he, too, was killed. The town coroner accused Abbot Richard, two clerks and the archdeacon of murder and ordered their arrest. The trial eventually took place in the Hertford Priory before two visiting judges. Richard's tactics were shocking: he launched a counter indictment against the townsmen for the death of his marshal and a servant and against the coroner for maliciously conspiring against him; he challenged the selection of every jury nominee from St Albans; he canvassed support from the great and good of the establishment and liberally wined and dined the judges on the eve of the trial. Unsurprisingly the court found in favour of the abbot and against the coroner and townsmen, who were variously fined or imprisoned. More importantly they agreed to surrender their royal charter of liberties, their silver seal, their common chest and their hand mills. They also provided a surety of good behaviour.

So the Abbey won, but the underlying problems and ill-will were not resolved, and lingered during the following decades to re-surface at the time of the Peasants' Revolt (1381). This uprising was the manifestation of deep discontent, not just of the peasantry, and was precipitated by the deteriorating living conditions of the wider working class, resulting from the greed of landowners and the attempt by Parliament to curb the increase in wages caused by the shortage of labour in the aftermath of the Black Death. A poll tax to pay for the unpopular and unsuccessful French wars made matters even worse.

As recounted in Thomas Walsingham's *Chronica Maiora*,[115] in June of 1381 a party of some 500 townsmen of St Albans, led by the splendidly named William Grindcobbe, seized the opportunity of the revolt to regain the short-lived freedoms they had won in 1327 by congregating in London, where they colluded with the revolt leader Wat Tyler. He sent them back to St Albans promising his support in the realisation of their plans to take over various pastures, fish ponds and woodland, to kill the prior and various monks (who managed to escape to the Priory of Tynemouth) and indeed to destroy the monastery should this be necessary. Grindcobbe also managed to petition King Richard II for a letter to the abbot saying that the freedoms granted in previous charters should be renewed. The townsmen, suitably emboldened, returned to St Albans and besieged the abbey and forced Abbot Thomas de la Mare to negotiate. Meanwhile their ardour was cooled by the death of Wat Tyler and by a royal proclamation defending the abbey and its abbot. In the following weeks the rebellion was put down and Grindcobbe, together with the more prominent of his supporters, were arrested, tried and hanged. Subsequently the Kentish preacher John Ball, a priest of radical sympathies, was arrested in St Albans and received the same punishment. Otherwise the authorities, fearful of provoking further disturbances, dealt with the bulk of the rioters relatively gently. Overall, it has to be said that the rioters achieved most of their objectives: no further attempt was made to proceed with the poll tax, the demise of feudalism was hastened and the lives of working people began, slowly, to improve.

---

[115] Preest and Clark: *The Chronica Maiora of Thomas Walsingham.*

10

The Fruits of Their Labours

For if heuene be on this erthe and ese to any soule
It is in cloistere or in scole be many skilles I find
For in cloistere cometh ne man to chide ne to fighte
But alle is buxumnesse there and bokes to rede and to lerne

From William Langland's *Piers Plowman*, Chapter X.

The prime purpose of Benedictine monasteries was to lead the battle of Christendom against the devil through prayer and by creating, in microcosm, an example of a just, godly and meritorious society. Reading and learning were strongly encouraged but apart from that there was no specific pressure on, or encouragement of, monks to indulge in any form of self-expression. However, this is just what they did, at St Albans and elsewhere, primarily to beautify and adorn their abbey church.

Christina of Markyate[116] and the St Albans Psalter

One of the most arresting figures to emerge in the story of St Alban is Christina of Markyate. Born in Huntingdon into a prosperous Anglo-Scandinavian family in about 1096, she was marked out for sanctity while still in the womb: her mother saw a dove 'whiter than snow fly from Huntingdon Priory straight towards her where, in the sleeve of her tunic, the bird rested for seven days.' This happened over the Feast of the Annunciation and it was taken to signify that the child would be inspired by the Holy Spirit and nurtured and protected by the Virgin Mary. At the age of fifteen, having grown to be a girl of 'uncommon beauty and holiness', her parents took her to St Albans Abbey – then not fully complete – and this visit made such a deep impression on her that she vowed to remain a virgin and to devote her life to the service of God. One

---

[116] Anon: *The Life of Christina of Markyate*, translated by CR Talbot.

The Fruits of Their Labours

of the canons of Huntingdon Priory, Sueno, provided great spiritual support and she confirmed with him the vows she had made after the St Albans visit: it was at this time when she changed her name from Theodora, her baptismal name, to Christina. When she was seventeen and still living at home with her parents, the Bishop of Durham, Ranulf Flambard, who happened to be Christina's aunt's lover, tried unsuccessfully to seduce her – but was foiled by Christina's quick-wittedness. (Flambard was subsequently imprisoned, for unrelated offences, by King Henry I in 1122.)[117] After this episode Christina came under great pressure from her parents – and the bishop – to marry a local young nobleman, which she eventually did, unwillingly, only to refuse to consummate the marriage on the wedding night. A local hermit, Edwin, on hearing of this situation, helped her flee her parents' house, disguised in male clothing, to take refuge with a female recluse, Alfwen, who lived at Flamstead, a village some 5 miles north of St Albans. After two years of lying in hiding with Alfwen, Christina moved in with Edwin's brother, Roger, a St Albans monk and hermit whose cell was at Markyate, a neighbouring village, but remaining, so the *Life of Christina* assures us, chaste. Roger became her spiritual mentor and protector, but she had to remain hidden until her husband gave up all claims on Christina, who was granted an annulment by the Archbishop of York. On Roger's death in 1121 Christina, with great misgiving about her inadequacy, took over Roger's hermitage and although not officially a dependant cell of St Albans, this situation brought her into close contact with the new abbot, Geoffrey. Here we must briefly divert the story to introduce Geoffrey.

Richard d'Essai (1097–1119), the second Norman abbot, took a close interest in the abbey school, which, although closely associated with the abbey, was not part of it, and was under lay management. When a vacancy in the mastership of the school occurred Richard invited Geoffrey de Gorham, a scholar from the province of Maine in France (it is likely that the contact was through Geoffrey's uncle, a bishop of Bec) to take up the position. Geoffrey accepted this offer, but by the time he arrived at St Albans the post had been filled by another. Undeterred, Geoffrey took up the mastership of a school in Dunstable, a town 10 miles up Watling Street, not far from Roger's hermitage. While there he wrote and produced a mystery play on the life of St Catherine of Alexandria to be performed by the boys. For this production he borrowed some ecclesiastical vestments from the abbey – rather valuable vestments as it

---

[117] D Lumley: *The Story of Tynemouth Priory and Castle*.

turned out. Unfortunately a fire broke out in Geoffrey's house after the first night, a fire in which the vestments were destroyed. Geoffrey was so mortified by the loss that he begged Abbot Richard to admit him as a monk so he could do penance for the rest of his life. As a monk he would have met – and probably become friends with – Roger the Hermit and may have heard about Christina. Geoffrey, clearly a man of intellect and charisma, rose rapidly through the monastic ranks, becoming prior. On the death of Abbot Richard in 1119 he was elected abbot by the monks. He is portrayed in the *Life of Christina* as rigorous but arrogant: in the words of the *Life*, 'God decided to provide for the needs of his virgin through this man and through her to bring him back to the fullness of his vocation'. Geoffrey developed 'a very deep respect for the maiden and saw in her something divine and extraordinary. From that time forward he sought her company with great assiduity, thinking little of the fatigue of travelling in comparison with the profit gained from the journey'.

Thus Christina and Geoffrey formed an intimate lifelong relationship in which they both benefited: Christina exerted a beneficial influence on Geoffrey's spiritual development and Geoffrey provided her with his enduring protection and the security of a new Markyate Priory, of which she was the first prioress. It has to be said, however, that Geoffrey's devotion to – infatuation with? – Christina attracted the suspicions and hostility of the St Albans monks. Under her influence Geoffrey's focus became more philanthropic – he founded, or re-founded, Sopwell Nunnery and two hospitals for lepers, one for monks at St Julians, the other for nuns at St Mary de Pré. But perhaps his greatest gift, a gift of love, was the psalter.

The psalter – St Albans Psalter as it has become known – was written in the St Albans scriptorium in the 1130s and is of sublime beauty. It's more than a book of psalms, as it includes a liturgical calendar, the 'Chanson of St Alexis', forty full-page paintings illustrating the life of Christ and a diptych showing the martyrdom of St Alban and of King David, the author of the psalms. It was initially intended as a psalm-book for liturgical use in the abbey, but at some stage, most probably when the scribes had reached psalm 105, it is evident that the purpose changed: it was to be specifically for Christina.

Customarily, the initial letter of each psalm was illuminated to illustrate the essential meaning of that psalm. The initial for psalm 105, the letter C, shows a nun – Christina – on behalf of a group of monks imploring Christ for mercy and forgiveness. Christina and the monks, on the left, are given a green background, while Christ on the right a heavenly blue. The two worlds, the earthly and heavenly, are divided by a thin white line which the hand of Christina, through her sanctity, can penetrate. After this psalm, it is noticeable that the emphasis of the illuminated initials changes.

The illuminated initial letter C of Psalm 105 of the St Albans Psalter.

The *Chanson de St Alexis* was included by Geoffrey as an allusion to Christina's identification with St Alexis, who was similarly bullied into a marriage by pushy and wealthy parents in sixth-century Rome. Like Christina, and for the same reasons, he refused to consummate the marriage and fled for a life of devotion to Christ. He subsequently became the patron saint of beggars and pilgrims, as Christina would have known because there was a chapel in the abbey dedicated to St Alexis.

It is clear from the very different style of the illustrations in the *Chanson* that it was a standalone booklet and not necessarily the product of the St Albans scriptorium[118]. The opening illustration of the *Chanson* shows, in the left hand panel, Alexis giving his newly married wife a parting gift of a ring and his sword, signs of his fidelity, with an undisturbed marriage-bed in the foreground. The central panel shows the wife, unusually in almost full face, weeping at his departure. In the right hand panel Alexis leaves the house to embark on his ship. The captions

---

[118] Kathryn Gerry: *Cult and Codex – Alexis Christina and the St Albans Psalter.*

read: 'Blessed Alexis, the chosen youth' and 'O blessed wife, forever bound to grief'.

The departure of St Alexis.

It is not entirely obvious why the inclusion of the *Chanson* in the Psalter was thought to be appropriate: a possible reason for its inclusion was that it was feared the Chanson would otherwise be lost in obscurity as the cult of St Alexis declined.

The psalter, although given to Christina, was kept in the Markyate Priory until the dissolution of the monasteries in the sixteenth century. It eventually was taken to Lamspringe monastery in Germany for safe keeping by English Benedictine monks in the seventeenth century and subsequently passed to the church of St Godehart near Hildesheim, Germany. A copy of the entire psalter is available on the Aberdeen University website.

Recent scholarship has shown that the connection between the psalter and Christina is more tenuous than traditionally thought[119]. However these connections are strong enough, together with the hagiographical style of the life of Christina, to support the supposition that it was the intention of Abbot Geoffrey to promote the cult of Christine with a view to her being made a saint. However, this was not to be: the cult of Christina never took root, possibly because of the antagonism of the St

---

[119] Kathryn Gerry: *Cult and Codex – Alexis, Christina and the St Albans Psalter.*

Albans monks, possibly due also to the enthusiasm in the later twelfth century for the canonisation of Thomas Beckett and St Albans' home-grown Amphibalus. The cult of St Alexis also declined in the second half of the twelfth century for the same reason.

The chroniclers and book production

Despite the commitment of the Benedictine Rule to literacy, it was always understood that the literacy was to be in Latin and it may be that in the early years of English monasticism monks struggled with this language. It was not until the Norman conquest, and the profound changes brought about by the replacement of nearly all the senior Saxon churchmen with Normans, familiar with Latin, that serious progress was made in the literacy of monks. This may at least partly explain the absence of written records from the Saxon St Albans monastery. The Benedictines were not confined to canonical writings but also responded to current political, social and public events. They came to see themselves and be seen as society's self-appointed historians. William of Malmesbury (1095–1143) was the first and perhaps the most highly respected of the post-conquest English chroniclers and his *Gesta Regum Anglorum* (Deeds of the English Kings), may have been both the model and the impetus for other Benedictine chroniclers, including those at St Albans.

The 'St Albans school of history', which makes a huge contribution to the historical literature now available, was initiated in the early thirteenth century by Roger of Wendover and his pupil Matthew Paris, who bequeathed a tradition of historical writing that lasted until the mid-fifteenth century. There was then a lull in literary culture immediately, during which the tradition was kept alive by a succession of lesser writers, the most prominent being William Rishanger, who updated the *Gesta Abbatum* and described the campaigns of Edward I and the second baronial war at the end of the thirteenth century. The mantle was then maintained until the appointment of Thomas Walsingham, a chronicler who bore comparison with Matthew Paris. Walsingham was followed in 1422 by John Amundesham, who was the last of the succession.

Roger Wendover

Roger Wendover's contribution, which lasted from 1219 to 1235, was to write a history of the world entitled *Flores Historiarum*, – Flowers of History – which, as he explains in his preface, was based on the sources available at the abbey at that time, 'just as flowers of various colours are gathered from various fields'. One of the sources was material written by John de Cella in the period before he became abbot in 1195. He was also influenced in the preparation of this history by Roger of Howden, who wrote his *Chronica* between 1169 to 1201. Roger worked in the St Albans scriptorium with Matthew Paris until he was appointed, in the early 1220s, as Prior of Belvoir, the smallest and least well-endowed St Albans dependency, whereupon Matthew took over the post of chronicler until his death in 1259. As a footnote, Roger was deprived of his office of prior by Abbot William de Trumpington in 1226, for 'dissipating the goods of the church in reckless prodigality', but continued his work on his chronicle until his death in 1236.

Matthew Paris[120]

Matthew Paris, a monk at St Albans and a pupil and associate of Roger, took over Roger's baton from 1219 to 1259. Matthew was a prolific writer and also an illustrator, cartographer and occasional diplomat. He was a voracious collector of news and certainly cultivated contacts in high places; he was the confidante of Henry III – whose reign covered Matthew's entire working life – and senior nobility and bishops. His output comprised two major works – the *Chronica Majora*, or Great Chronicle, and the *Gesta Abbatum*, or Deeds of the Abbots – and a number of writing on more specific subjects, including his life of St Alban, the lives of several other saints and various itineraries and maps.

Matthew was a passionate man: passionate in his love for the abbey, the defence of its liberties, the enhancement of its beauty and the increase of its revenue. He was also passionate, and only a little less so, in his love for his country and for the Benedictine Order. Correspondingly he loathed and detested foreign interference, the abuse of power, corruption and profligacy: on these criteria popes and their curia failed on all counts while the kings of England hovered on the brink of his ire. For instance, he was highly critical of King John for surrendering the sovereignty of the nation to Pope Innocent III. The Bishop of Lincoln was condemned when he tried to exercise episcopal control over St Albans but commended when he opposed papal misuse of patronage. Yet he was by no means advocating radicalism. His message was: respect the office, criticise the holder.

The Great Chronicle, which traces the history of England and the Church, inasmuch as it impacted on St Albans, from Saxon times up to

---

[120] Michael Glasby and Gail Thomas: *Matthew Paris*.

1250. Much of the first part of the chronicle, which covers the Magna Carta period, is based on Roger's *Flowers of History*, with some infilling where Roger lacked access to sufficient material, and extensions covering the second quarter of the thirteenth century. It seems that the confusion that inevitably attends dual authorship over several decades resulted in their account of the various versions of the Magna Carta being a 'complete muddle'[121]. Matthew, in his version of the chronicle, 'instilled the text with moral comments of his own, and distorted and fabricated history in an attempt to attribute his own attitude towards papal domination etc'[122]. Such excursions from an impartial account of history are consistent with his purpose in writing the *Chronica Majora*: 'for the benefit of posterity' and to assert the living presence of St Albans in his shrine in the abbey, to promote the abbey as a centre of Benedictine excellence and to provide a foundation for the abbey's status and privileges. Thus the intended readership was as much the wider community as the monks of St Albans themselves. The book itself was lavishly produced and illustrated by Matthew himself. The range of subjects and style in which they are painted is extraordinary, from the formal and devotional Virgin and Child to the curious, the most famous of which is perhaps is his drawing of an elephant given to King Henry III by King Louis IX of France.

Matthew Paris' The Virgin and Child *(left) and* King Henry III's Elephant *(right).*

---

[121] JC Holt: *The St Albans Chroniclers and Magna Carta*.
[122] VH Galbraith: *Roger of Wendover and Matthew Paris*.

Similarly, the *Gesta Abbatum* is a compilation of contributions by several authors, initially assembled by Matthew and continued after his death by a number of chroniclers, primarily targeted towards monastic readership, for the guidance of future monks, obedientiaries and abbots. The earliest contributor was Adam the Cellarer, an obedientiary of the monastery writing through his servant and amanuensis Bernard in the period 1140–1180. Although 'unlettered', Adam was single minded in his pursuit of the consolidation and improvement of existing endowments and the acquisition of new ones. Thus his contribution was devoted to the aim of enhancing the pedigree and profile of the abbey by the composition of a possibly fictional – certainly enhanced – early history of the Saxon abbots and the creative writing of the royal charters.

His biography of the two abbots, Simon and Warin, not directly known by either Adam or Matthew, are naturally brief. Matthew had direct contemporary knowledge of the next three abbots – John de Cella, William de Trumpington and John of Hertford, all of whom won Matthew's broad approval. The lives of the abbots who came after Matthew's death were written by monks working in the scriptorium, most of whom remain anonymous with the exception of William Rishanger, who died in 1312, followed by a succession of chroniclers.

Thomas Walsingham

Thomas Walsingham (c. 1340–1422) was the last prominent chronicler. Thomas spent his entire life as a monk of St Albans except for a four-year break as Prior of Wymondham, a St Albans daughter house in Norfolk, from 1394–1396. He studied at Gloucester College Oxford but left before he took his degree. At St Albans he was for a time precentor and the master of the scriptorium, in which capacity he continued in the tradition of Matthew Paris by updating both the *Chronica Majora* and the *Gesta Abbatum*. Greatly interested in current affairs, he wrote his *Chronicon Angliae* covering the period 1328–1388 and was the principal authority for the lives of three kings: Richard II, Henry IV and Henry V, as well as John Wyclif and Wat Tyler. His range of interests was considerable, and wrote in such diverse subjects as music, Latin classicism and astrology[123].

Conclusion

For all the renown for their scope and range, the St Albans chronicles were reactionary and possibly constrained by having to write, by

---

[123] JG Clark: *A Monastic Renaissance at St Albans*.

convention, in Latin. The chroniclers, following the format laid down by Roger of Wendover for nearly three centuries, showed they were quite incapable of understanding or empathising with the reasonable aspirations of their rural and urban tenants or of the socioeconomic conditions of the wider world. Their attack on the teaching of Wyclif, crude and disproportionate, even allowing for the accepted contemporary use of colourful language (Walsingham called him 'weak belief' and the 'angel of Satan' and referred to his ideas as 'ravings'), was perhaps influenced as much on the perceived threat to their financial security as to their theology – neither de la Mare nor Walsingham were theologians. The ferocity of their refutation, based on abuse and wilful misrepresentation, belied a consciousness of the weakness of their position.

Book of Benefactors

Thomas Walsingham also compiled the *Book of Benefactors*, which lists the benefactions made to St Albans, which was begun in 1380 by Abbot Thomas de la Mare. The list gives the names, portraits and details of the gifts of all benefactors, retrospective and contemporaneous, starting with King Offa and continuing up to the last days of the monastery with the portraits drawn by a lay artist Alan Strayler. Although the book is organised hierarchically, from the monarchy down to lay artisans, it's amazingly democratic in that the great range of benefactions are all included, from landed estates, to money, jewellery, manuscripts, vestments and wine.

Pride of place in the book was given to King Offa, claimed by the medieval monastery as its founder.

I Am Called Alban

Nigel the Miller: one of the more modest benefactors who gave 4 shillings annually – about £50 in today's money.

In return for their gifts, irrespective of the value, each benefactor was admitted to the confraternity with a lavish induction ceremony, with the promise of spiritual benefits and a place in the book, which was kept on the high altar of the abbey church – altogether an effective and surprisingly modern way of raising money.

The book has been digitised by the British Library[124].

Joan, Countess of Kent and Princess of Wales and Aquitaine (d. 1385), gave a gold necklace and 100 shillings.

Book production and printing

The copying of both home-produced and other texts, illumination and binding – was naturally a major activity throughout the medieval period

---

[124] Blogs.bl.uk/digitised manuscripts/2020/05/the-st-albans-benefactors-book.htms.

until the advent of printing. A printing press was set up in St Albans in 1479 – the third in the country – by an anonymous 'sometime scolemyster of Saynt Albans'[125], spelling the end of the newly rebuilt scriptorium. A total of eight books were printed in the period: the first entitled *'Rhetorica nova Fratris Laurentii Gulielmide Saona'* in 1480 and the last the *'Boke of Seynt Albans'* in 1486 attributed to 'Dam Julyans Barnes' who was the Prioress of the Sopwell Convent. This book, possibly an easier read than the *Rhetorica Nova*, was a treatise on hawking, hunting and heraldry.

Architecture[126]

Throughout the medieval period, not a century passed without some major structural modification to the abbey:
- twelfth century: the nave extension and new west front;
- thirteenth century: the rebuilding of the presbytery and shrine;
- fourteenth century: the lady chapel and collapse and rebuilding of part of the nave, the abbey gateway and the cloisters;
- fifteenth century: the new Wallingford Screen, watching loft, windows.

The nave extension

The ostensible, or at least the generally accepted reason for extending what was already the longest nave in England, and which had only recently been completed, was that it was required to accommodate the growth in the number of monks and that an extended nave would provide more space for the Benedictine speciality of ceremonial processions. But was it really necessary? After all, it only lengthened the nave by three bays: was this extra length so critical? It may also have been seen as an opportunity to emulate a similar project recently built in the new Gothic style, at Canterbury, St Albans' great rival in the pilgrim market. Furthermore it was quite natural for all abbots to want to leave their mark in a tangible way, and this was Abbot John de Cella's (1195–1214) contribution. The project required the demolition of the Norman west front and its adjacent bays followed by the construction of the new west front and the infill bays, all in the Early English style. The brutal juxtaposition of the rugged brick Norman arcade, with the architecturally

---

[125] FJ Kilvington: *A Short History of St Albans School*.
[126] This section draws heavily on Eileen Robert's *The Hill of the Martyrs – an Architectural History of St Albans Abbey*.

more sophisticated gothic arcade, built of Tottenhoe limestone, offers a stark contrast. The new design did, however, respect the geometry of the Norman arcade in terms of pier spacing and the heights of the three orders – main arches, triforium and clerestory. The design of the two arcades, Norman and Early English, are shown next to each other to facilitate comparison. The Early English architects/ masons also respected the Norman work by continuing the Norman flat timber ceiling.

The new west front was originally intended to be flanked by twin towers (the foundations were laid and the south west tower started, but they were never built, probably due to lack of funds) but only the inner arches of the three porches now survive.

The Norman and Early English designs of the nave arcade, as drawn by John Carter[127].

As with many grand projects throughout history, Abbot John's initial estimate of costs was woefully inadequate and it is known that he made

---

[127] John Carter: *Some Account of the Abbey Church of St Alban*.

stringent economies in the monastic housekeeping budget to help pay for the nave extension – to the extent that wine was banned for fifteen years. However, it is probable that such economies were insufficient and that John would have had to resort to the Jewish money-lending community for funds, especially because at that time the abbey would have been expected to make a contribution towards King Richard I's £100,000 ransom and a further £1,000 payment to King John. Abbot John was widely regarded as a saintly man who was largely responsible for the doubling increase in the monastic population. He may not have been a particularly effective project manager – certainly not a lucky one – so in the end the nave extension took about thirty years to complete and was well over budget. Matthew Paris probably had the measure of the man: he was 'ignorant of everyday affairs after the fashion of scholars'. The nave extension was completed in the abbacy of William de Trumpington, who left his mark by replacing the pyramidal Norman tower roof, which was said to be 'threatening to fall' with a much taller octagonal broached spire, constructed in timber and lead. This was felt necessary to provide more vertical balance to the extended nave. Unfortunately there is no contemporaneous drawing to show the impact this spire would have made to the overall appearance of the abbey.

The rebuilding of the presbytery

It was noticed, during the 1250s, that the condition of the central apse at the east end of the abbey church was deteriorating and by 1257 its condition was so bad as to warrant the demolition of the three easternmost bays, incorporating the central and the flanking apses. This deterioration has been ascribed to an earthquake that took place in December 1250, reported by Matthew Paris, but whether this event alone was a critical factor is open to doubt: a recent study has revealed that seven earthquakes took place in southern England in the decade 1247 to 1257 – none of them severe – so it may have been a cumulative effect[128]. Apses were more structurally vulnerable than gables because the horizontal thrust at the top of the wall, exerted by the roof, would tend to induce vertical tension cracks in the wall, leading to collapse. Certainly earthquakes would only make matters worse. To counter this an apse would require stronger buttressing than would a straight wall, yet there is no evidence that such buttresses were provided by the Norman builders: Sir Gilbert Scott's model reconstruction of the Norman abbey church

---

[128] British Geological Society: *The Seismicity of the British Isles to 1600*.

shows the apse supported only by flat pilasters similar to those still visible at the north transept.[129] Romanesque churches with apsidal east ends were common in France but not England, Canterbury and Norwich cathedrals being outstanding exceptions. Canterbury's presbytery was destroyed by fire in 1174 and was rebuilt in the new Gothic style, with an apse supported by flying buttresses. In Norwich's case the apse was modified, heavily buttressed, in the fifteenth century.

There seems to have been no discussion on the question whether to rebuild the damaged presbytery as it was, using Roman bricks and flints, or whether to build a new presbytery in the gothic style in stone: the strong impression is that the monastery felt that the case for the latter option, which provide a more impressive setting for the shrine of St Alban, was overwhelming, despite the extra expense. Thus the entire Norman presbytery was demolished, leaving only two bays of the Norman walls that provided support to the east side of the tower. East of this the Norman work was replaced by three full-height bays terminating in a square gable wall, as shown in the plan. Beyond the eastern end wall the opportunity was grasped to build a lady chapel, almost a requirement at that time, when the cult of St Mary was at its height, for every monastery and cathedral.

The choice of a reconstruction in the Gothic style brought with it the possibility of a vaulted ceiling. A stone vault would have required the walls to be supported by flying buttresses to resist the lateral load of the stone vault, which would have been unaffordable. Instead it was decided to build the vault in timber, which was much lighter, cheaper and structurally less demanding. The vault, using timber given by King Henry III, is a masterpiece of timber engineering: the structure still stands, in good condition, 750 years later.

All this work was carried out in the abbacies of John de Hertford (1235–1263) and Roger de Norton (1263–1290), although the lady chapel was not completed until the early fourteenth century under the abbacy of Hugh de Eversden. It is remarkable that this extensive building project, the cost of which would have been equivalent to at least three times the monastery's annual revenue, was carried out during the administration of five abbots and the turbulent reigns of three kings, when the abbey was facing a crisis of morale and debt. To make matters worse – much worse – part of the Norman nave collapsed.

---

[129] Eileen Roberts: *The Hill of the Martyr – an Architectural History of St Albans Abbey*, Figure 19.

The Fruits of Their Labours

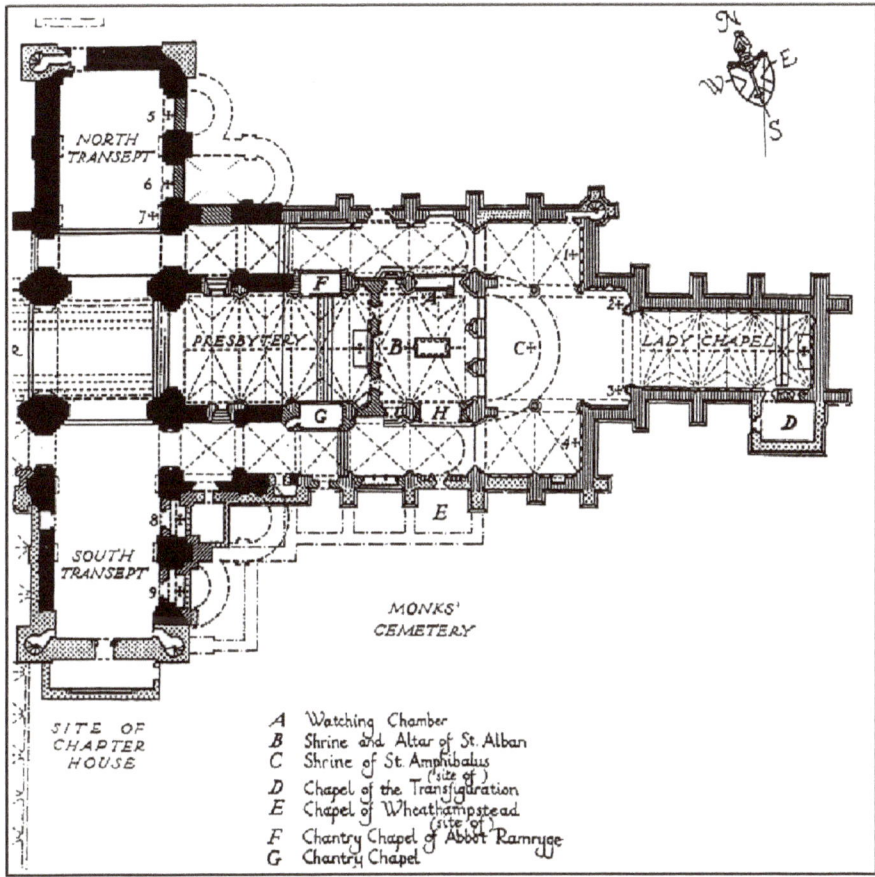

Plan of the new presbytery[130] showing the new rebuild superimposed on the Norman original.

Collapse and rebuilding of part of south arcade of the nave

On 10 October 1323 two Norman piers of the south arcade of the nave collapsed. As reported in *Gesta Abbatum*: 'suddenly two great columns of the south side of the church, giving way first from the foundation, fell successively to the ground with a terrible noise and crash... scarcely an hour had passed when, behold the whole wooden roof, which was built upon the said columns with beams rafters and ties and the aisle on the south side of the church and almost all that side of the cloister followed in the same way'.

---

[130] Harrison, McNeill, Pluummer, Simpson: *The Presbytery Vault at St Albans*.

What might have been the cause of such a localised failure of the massive columns that had been standing, by then, for some 250 years? It is clear from the eyewitness account that the collapse was caused by a foundation failure and not the failure of the column itself. One obvious possibility is the formation of a sink hole caused by the dissolution of an underlying strata of chalk – such phenomena are by no means uncommon in the Chiltern area – the most recent example being a 6m-wide 3m-deep hole in the city of St Albans in 2018. Another possibility is that the particular columns were founded on an area of made ground in a spot where previous human activity – mining or an abandoned building – had subsided. Whatever the cause, the collapse of the two columns (numbers five and six counting west from the tower) must have jeopardised the integrity of the bays either side of these so that these had to be demolished. The damaged arcade was rebuilt in the current style – Decorated – but designed to complement the Early English arcade immediately to the west. The rebuild also had to include, naturally, the damaged south aisle and new cloisters, a trace of which is still visible on the outside of the south aisle wall.

The shrine

The original Norman shrine was a stone sarcophagus located at the chord of the great apse of the Norman church. Abbot Geoffrey de Gorham (1119–1146) commissioned a new shrine comprising a highly ornate casket, made by a highly skilled metal worker/monk named Antekil, which would have contained the relics of St Alban, set on a slab of Purbeck marble supported by marble pillars. This shrine would have been placed on a platform just behind the high altar so that it would have been visible – indeed prominent – from the entire presbytery and choir. This shrine had to be moved during the reconstruction of the presbytery when it was replaced between 1302 and 1309 by a new stone shrine. This was subsequently moved a short distance east to accommodate the construction of the new Wallingford Screen in 1484 (see later) and shortly after destroyed in the Dissolution in 1539. A drawing of the reconstructed shrine is shown in the frontispiece to Part One of this book.

Other architectural contributions

After the semi-continuous building activity of the thirteenth and early fourteenth centuries the pace of changes to the abbey fabric eased off somewhat, giving way to smaller projects to beautify and modernise the abbey, mostly in the latest architectural style – the perpendicular. These comprised the watching loft, the rood screen, the replacement of Norman and Early English doors and windows, chantry chapels and the high altar screen. There was also yet one more natural disaster to be dealt with: the abbey gateway was rebuilt by Thomas de la Mare in 1346 after a great storm is said to have damaged the Norman monastery gateway beyond repair. But did it? There is no record of any other buildings suffering damage, and gateways were normally very sturdy structures – especially Norman ones. Perhaps Abbot Thomas seized the opportunity, as his predecessors had done before him, to modernise the monastic fabric, especially such a prominent structure as the gateway.

Part of the collateral damage of the 1323 nave collapse may have been the early thirteenth century timber rood screen. In any event, it was replaced later in the fourteenth century by a new screen, constructed in stone. Like the original, the new screen, which still stands, separated the lay people's nave from the monks' central and eastern part of the church and was provided with a pair of doors to allow the passage of great processions.

The early fifteenth century saw the construction of an oak watching loft, built on the north side of the saints' chapel to enable the monks to maintain a full time watch of the relics and to ensure the good behaviour of the pilgrims, indicating that despite the competition of St Thomas of Canterbury, St Alban remained an important pilgrimage destination.

One of the particular attractions for pilgrims were chantry chapels, which for reasons of prestige were situated as close to the shrine as possible. Chantry chapels were privately endowed by the rich so that prayers and masses could be said for the dead to minimise the time their souls spent in their passage through Purgatory. Four such chapels were built in the abbey, for Abbot John Wheathampstead (1429), Humphrey, Duke of Gloucester (1443), Abbot William Wallingford (1476) and Abbot Thomas Ramryge (1521). Duke Humphrey, being a royal, has the best location while Abbot Ramryge has the most exquisite. It is notable that only the abbots of the final years of the monastery were rich enough – and vain enough – to spend huge amounts of money in constructing and endowing their chantries.

Further major changes to the abbey's appearance were made by the insertion of three large perpendicular windows, one in the west front in 1447 by Abbot Wheathampstead and the other two in the north and south transept fronts by Abbot William of Wallingford later in the fifteenth century. Other modifications carried out at this time also made a huge difference to the appearance of the abbey: Thomas de la Mare's broached spire was taken down and replaced by a 'Hertfordshire spike', similar to the needle on Notre Dame Cathedral: the steep pitched roofs were replaced with typical Tudor roofs, lead covered with a very flat pitch: the tops of the walls and the tower were battlemented. As will be seen in Chapter 13, these changes were not without their long-term structural consequences.

The wealth of the last abbots is especially noteworthy: Abbot William of Wallingford personally funded the construction of the high altar screen, a massive stone reredos, built in 1484, that separates the shrine from the presbytery to the west. Thus for the first time the shrine was hidden from wider view, and seems diminished as a result. The west face of the screen was elaborately embellished with statues of saints, set in canopied niches and a central crucifix attended by the apostle John, the Virgin Mary and angels. The east face is almost entirely plain and unadorned.

Paintings

One of the consequences of the absence of stone in the construction of the abbey was that painting offered the only means of beautifying the masonry surface of plastered brick, carving not being an option. Stone carving is entirely confined to the stone extensions and repairs to the nave, the rebuilt presbytery and the screens described previously.

The first decorative work on the internal walls was applied in the twelfth century and was intended to mimic stonework: it comprised yellow dado stripe painted about 2m above the floor level throughout the abbey, imaginary masonry courses picked out in black and decorative Norman patterns of lozenges, chevrons and blocks, painted in earth colours of red and yellow on the moulding and soffits of the arches.

Shortly after Abbot Geoffrey de Gorham commissioned woven woollen tapestries to be hung in the nave to relieve the starkness of the interior. One of these tapestries depicted the life of Alban and may have been similar in style and content to the contemporaneous illustrations in the St Albans Psalter.

The first images on the flat plastered brick-built columns of the nave, hitherto left bare of decoration, were painted in the thirteenth century following the completion of the work involved in extending the nave. Whereas the upper-class monks generally considered themselves rather above such artisanal work, the man responsible for much of the nave paintings was Walter of Colchester, a monk originally from St John's Priory, Colchester. Like St Albans Abbey, St Johns Priory was built of

The Fruits of Their Labours

reused Roman bricks that were subsequently plastered, which was where he presumably developed his skills that brought him to the attention of St Albans. He was appointed sacrist by Abbot William of Trumpington and worked on decorating the abbey with his brother, nephew and lay assistants. The plan was that the west face of each Norman column was painted with a large crucifix, underneath which were painted scenes from the life of the Virgin. The space between each column therefore formed a small chapel. Of course the Norman columns have only survived on the north side of the nave, but surely the south side would also have been similarly painted.

The earliest crucifix was painted on the most western pillar of the nave in about 1215, and is one of the better preserved. What we see is the underpainting of the original, the surface layer either having flaked off or been damaged. The faces appear dark due to chemical change in the pigments.

The mural shows the cross roughly hewn and painted green to signify hope of new life with the figures of Mary and a young man, probably St John, in calm contemplation, drawn with great beauty.

The south faces of the columns were decorated with a series of saints (from west to east): St Christopher, St Thomas of Canterbury, St Zita of Lucca and St Alban and St Amphibalus. The latter mural, shown in Part One, depicts the moment when Alban and Amphibalus exchange cloaks prior to Amphibalus' escape and Alban's arrest, with Amphibalus giving Alban a cross surmounted by a disc. It is noteworthy both men are shown barefoot, which by convention was reserved for Christ and the Apostles – a promotion accorded by the St Albans monks. The mural overlooked the original location of the shrine to St Amphibalus, which was moved after the collapse of the south arcade.

The layout of paintings to the east of the nave – in the choir and presbytery – seems somewhat haphazard. Of the nineteen pictures listed by Eileen Roberts[131] just seven are figures, the best being those of St William of York and of Doubting Thomas. Both these paintings were probably executed by Master Walter of Durham, King Henry III's painter and his son and assistant Thomas of Westminster, who are thought to have moved to St Albans after the king's death in 1272.

The first, St William of York, was originally part of an altarpiece in the saints chapel and dates from the early fourteenth century, but modified in about 1390. In this mural, the best preserved in the abbey, St William is shown as a half-sized figure, and would have been flanking a crucifix. This picture, the colours of which haven't faded, is one of the Abbeys great treasures.

William held two tenures as Archbishop of York, 1141–45 and 1153–54. Both were subject of fierce opposition by Cistercian monks. He was murdered, probably by his archdeacon by a poisonous chalice. He was canonised by Pope Honorius in 1226.

How St William became the subject of this painting is unknown, but it may have come via St Albans monks at Oxford who were aware of the cult of William, who was commemorated at Balliol and Trinity colleges, both northern foundations.

---

[131] Eileen Roberts: *The Wall Paintings of Saint Albans Abbey*.

The Doubting Thomas mural is positioned in the north transept and was painted in the fourteenth century in a position to catch the eye of incoming pilgrims before reaching St Alban's shrine. It shows Christ, in a white robe, guiding Thomas' right hand to the wound in his side and saying 'Blessed are they that have not seen and yet have believed.' Thomas, dressed in dark green, has sunk to his knees, saying, 'My Lord and my God.' The setting of the mural shows, in its humanity, a strong Italian influence, similar to Giotto's work in the arena chapel in Padua, with the three-dimensional Italianate background, the dynamism of the two figures and the sensitive drawing of the hands and eyes.

Doubting Thomas. This mural was painted on a dark gesso ground – an Italianate preparation – using expensive pigments. The style of the mural, the use of expensive materials and the advanced technique required for their use supports the probability that it was executed by Westminster Court painters.

The wooden ceilings of the nave, tower and presbytery were also painted, initially when the vault was constructed in the late thirteenth century and then again, with a different design, in the fifteenth century. Recent restoration work on the presbytery vault has enabled the original thirteenth century design to be depicted.[132]

---

[132] Harrison, McNeill, Pluummer, Simpson: *The Presbytery Vault at St Albans*.

How the original painted decoration of the presbytery vault may have appeared.

This design was replaced in the fifteenth century under the direction of Abbot Wheathampstead with the ceiling we have today. This comprises, on each side of each bay, roundels displaying the symbols of his patron saints, an eagle for St John the Evangelist and the lamb for St John the Baptist, all surrounded by a pattern of formalised leafy foliage. What is more, Abbot Wheathampstead covered a thirteenth century mural of Christ in Majesty with the shields of St Oswin, the seventh-century Northumbrian saint (buried in Tynemouth Priory), St Alban and St Amphibalus.

Fifteenth-century decoration of the presbytery wooden vault.

Learning

The original purpose of Benedictine monasteries was not learning – it was to provide a refuge from which the spiritual war against evil could be mounted. They became centres of learning, which was always held in high esteem, because this 'war' required study of sacred texts and so demanded literacy in Latin. Learning, however, was not only inescapable, it was also very useful and for many centuries, until the formation of universities, cathedral and monastery schools were the only institutions providing education necessary for the creation of an administrative elite, ecclesiastical or secular. To provide this education size mattered, and it was not until the population of monks at St Albans Abbey grew in the twelfth century that its school had the resources necessary to achieve a high standard of education.

The school – grammar school – whose foundation goes back to Saxon times, reputedly to Abbot Wulsin in 948, was unusual because it was open, for a fee of 4d a quarter, to boys, from the town as well as monastic novitiates. In addition, from the end of the thirteenth century, as part of their charitable work, the abbey funded the education of sixteen poor scholars, thus widening access to the monastery and providing a measure of cultural integration of the monastery and the town. By the thirteenth century the school received an accolade from Matthew Paris, who wrote: 'there could scarcely be found in England any school better or more productive or more useful or more full of scholars'. The curriculum was limited to literacy – reading and writing in Latin – which was the minimum qualification required for admission to the monastery but with time it broadened to include arithmetic. Although the school was not part of the monastery, successive abbots took a close interest and acted as a medieval version of the chairman of governors. The school was regulated, from 1309, with Statutes of the Grammar School, which stipulated, amongst other things that 'the scholars were not allowed to wander or run about the streets without just cause, are not to bear arms or inflict injury or molestation on other scholars either within the school or without.' By the fifteenth century the school was over 100 scholars strong with at least two assistant masters and ushers[133].

The majority of the abbots, scholars in their own right, nurtured the monastic library, originally founded by Archbishop Lanfranc, and guided the monks' studies so that the abbey became a centre of learning – almost

---

[133] Frank Kilvington; A Short History of St Albans School.

a university in its own right. The library grew, slowly at first, by home-produced texts and by contributions by the abbots, each reflecting their particular interest. For example Abbot Warin (1183–1195), a Cambridge scholar, had previous studied medicine at Salerno, the renowned school of medicine in Italy, while Abbot Richard of Wallingford was a mathematician and astronomer of international standing. Concurrently with the expanding library, the scriptorium, part of the Norman monastery, was reconstructed by Abbot Thomas de la Mare reflecting the growing importance of book production. Intellectual life at St Albans attracted talented recruits through its network of daughter houses and its proximity to London, which provided opportunities for interaction with political and royal visitors.

And learning was in the air: the twelfth century saw the formation of the first universities, first in Italy (Bologna, Salerno) spreading to Paris and then to Oxford and Cambridge. The mendicant orders – Dominican and Franciscan – were quick to grasp the benefits that a university education could confer and this alarmed the Benedictine movement in England, which belatedly began to encourage suitable monks to attend a university, initially at Oxford.

However, student life in Oxford exposed young monks to formidable temptations. To counter these, soon after the founding of the first colleges, the general chapter of the southern Benedictines agreed, in 1277, to set up a specifically Benedictine college. This was to be funded by a levy (of 3 pence for every £1 income, equivalent to 1.25 per cent of income)[134] on all Benedictine houses, but this proposal was far from popular and action was delayed until 1283 when St Peter's Abbey, Gloucester, took the initiative and set up an Oxford cell for their monks. Within sixteen years all sixty of the Benedictine houses in the province of Canterbury were on board, and Gloucester College was launched. It comprised communal buildings – hall, kitchen, bakery and chapel and a number of houses, rather basic even by thirteenth century norms, each house belonging a different monastery[135]. The college was nominally under the control of a prior, but discipline was light by monastic standards. The aim of the general chapter was that one in twenty monks should attend the university, but as time progressed, St Albans, as befits the premier abbey, was sending up to one in five of its monks – and bearing a corresponding proportion of the costs, to the extent that the St Albans coat of arms was

---

[134] Seb Falk: *The Light Ages*.
[135] John North: *God's Clockmaker – Richard of Wallingford and the Invention of Time*.

carved over the college gateway. But sending monks to Oxford was an expensive business: Abbot Thomas de la Mare, in his capacity of president of the provincial chapter, ruled in 1360 that the minimum funding of a student should be £15 a year plus travel expenses, equivalent to the annual wage of a master craftsman or a lawyer. Such an investment certainly tells us a lot about the high esteem Benedictines had for a university education, as well as the wealth of the principal monasteries. Nor did enthusiasm for university education fall off as time went by: in 1420 Abbot John of Wheathampstead paid for and stocked a library building for Gloucester College.

Science and technology

There was no question, in the thirteenth century, of the twentieth-century two-cultures debate being entertained: the early medieval scientific revolution, equally profound as that of modern times, was totally mainstream and widely embraced. Indeed the word 'science' had at that time not yet not been invented but became a collective term for the liberal arts quadrivium, embracing mathematics, geometry, astronomy and music. Astronomy, in particular enjoyed a close relationship with religion and was seen as making an important contribution to glorifying God: it was not seen as a threat.

The availability of newly translated Greek and Arabic texts via Spain, made possible through the percipience of scholars such as Gerbert of Aurillac, propelled the study of these sciences to the forefront of the universities syllabus. Initially supportive – on the election of the scholar Gerbert as Pope Sylvester II (999–1003) – the papacy subsequently had misgivings about the acceptability of the recently translated natural philosophical works of Aristotle and the heretical implications of delving into the rationale of the created world. In the end, helped by Thomas Aquinas' *Summa Theologiae*, which sought to reconcile pagan science with Christianity, it acquiesced in the study of science provided it did not impinge on theology. This meant that Aristotle assumed a central place in the curriculum of the fledgling universities[136]. Thus the several hundred St Albans monks who were educated at universities in the thirteenth, fourteenth and fifteenth centuries would have had a good grounding in the sciences. But such knowledge was not limited to the

---

[136] James Hannam: *God's Philosophers – How the Medieval World Laid the Foundations of Modern Science.*

university-educated monks – learning was disseminated within the monasteries whose libraries would have acquired books on medicine and astronomy.

This joined-up approach was first exemplified by Alexander Neckam (1157–1217), born in St Albans, and who after attending St Albans school studied theology at Paris University. Whilst there he came across the newly translated Greek and Islamic scientific texts and became a passionate Aristotelian. Indeed, his stated aim was to use diverse examples from nature for religious edification. Following his studies he returned to St Albans to take up the post of master of the school, during which time he wrote two pieces, *On Instruments* and *On the Nature of Things*, the latter intended to be a manual summarising the state of scientific knowledge, as a preface to a theological commentary on Ecclesiastes. Neckam's extra theological writing was mostly devoted to nautical subjects – the importance of tides, which he deduced were governed by the phases of the moon, which could be used to predict tide times and the use of the magnetic compass as a navigational aid which led to a discussion on the nature of magnetism. He also wrote about advances in the study of medical science. From schoolmastering at St Albans his career took him to Oxford, where he lectured in theology and thence to Cirencester Abbey, where he eventually became abbot.

The next player on the scientific stage at St Albans was Matthew Paris, also a polymath with a keen interest in the natural world. His contribution as a chronicler has already been described but he also was an artist and map maker. He produced a tide table, based on the work of Neckam, of the time of the high tides at London Bridge for each day of the lunar cycle. He produced a number of drawings apart from those illustrating his books, most famously perhaps King Henry III's elephant. He also drew maps of Britain, revolutionary in that, for the first time in British cartography, north is positioned at the top of the page and south at the bottom. This map shows the constituent countries – England, Wales and Scotland – in approximately the correct relative positions, the location of the main cathedrals and monasteries, rivers and roads. At the end of his life the wide range of his interests led him to write a book of astrological predictions – astrology was a respectable science in the middle ages – largely drawn from the work of Hermann the Lame, one of the most brilliant astronomers of the eleventh century and expert in the use of the astrolabe.

The giant of St Albans science was Richard of Wallingford (1292–1336), the son of a Wallingford blacksmith who died when Richard was just ten years old – old enough to have learned a lot of the skills of blacksmithing, but too young to take over the family business. Richard was lucky enough to be adopted by Prior William of Holy Trinity Priory, a daughter cell of St Albans, 'on account of his aptitude and great promise' and was educated at the priory school. Such was his progress that Prior William sent him to Oxford at the age of sixteen, at the priory's expense. Richard was there for six years, during which time he took his bachelor's degree in the liberal arts and was well on his way to a master's degree when in 1317 the money ran out: his only recourse was to walk to St Albans and take his vows as a monk, with the intention of returning to Oxford to complete his studies. At this time the St Albans policy was that they would only fund monks who were ordained priests to study at Oxford. It took Richard just two years to become ordained, whereupon he returned to Oxford to study for the prestigious degree in theology, the key to future advancement. A secondary motive was the lure of advanced mathematics and astronomy, his great passions. Richard was a contemporary of Thomas Bradwardine, also a mathematically minded theologian destined for high office, who was at the centre of a group subsequently known as the Merton Calculators[137]. Richard must have been in this circle, which made the now obvious (but then revolutionary) step of applying mathematics to problems posed by natural philosophy. At all events Richard was sufficiently well thought of at Merton College that they later claimed him, probably fraudulently, as a Fellow. Richard finally left Oxford and returned to St Albans in 1326. After having taken his theology degree and having written a treatise on trigonometry he designed and constructed an instrument, the rectangulus, to facilitate complex three-dimensional trigonometrical calculations. He also invented an instrument he called the Albion (possibly as a thank-you to St Albans?), which enabled astronomers to make accurate predictions of the sun, moon and the planets, an instrument, together with its accompanying treatise, far in advance of other texts and techniques then available[138].

Within months of his return to St Albans the abbot, Hugh de Eversden, died and much to Richard's – and everybody else's – surprise, Richard was elected abbot as his successor. Richard was immediately overwhelmed by the work required in getting papal approval and in reforming the administration, the finances and the observance of the abbey, not to

---

[137] James Hannam: *God's Philosophers*, p. 174.
[138] John North: *God's Clockmaker – Richard Wallingford and the Invention of Time*.

mention overseeing the completion of the nave repairs. However, Richard was a workaholic and found time, in his short abbacy, to design and construct a clock. The importance of finding a better method of time keeping than was provided by astronomical observations and devices such as water clocks cannot be overstated, and much effort was being made throughout Europe to resolve the issue. Liturgical observation was of supreme importance to followers of the Rule of St Benedict, which stipulated eight daily offices, or services, the first being matins at 2 a.m. and the last, compline, at 7 p.m. The first mechanical clock to be built in England was that at Norwich cathedral, which simply sounded a bell every hour, whereas Richard's also showed the position and phases of the sun, moon and planets, predicted lunar eclipses and even the time of high tide at London Bridge, using data from Neckam's predictions, as collated by Matthew Paris. Richard employed the father and son clockmakers responsible for the Norwich clock, Laurence and Roger of Stoke. The mathematics, astronomy and engineering of the clock were Richard's own, a rare combination of intellect and practicality, the Benedictine Order providing the education and opportunity. His achievement was of course not fully appreciated at the time, the astronomical functions not being strictly required. So why did Richard build it? Perhaps because he had previously expressed regret at the time he had spent in scientific pursuits at the expense of theology and through his clock he had made amends by bringing God's universe into the Church.

Richard of Wallingford's clock as reconstructed by the St Albans Engineering Society from Richard's drawings preserved in the Bodleian Library.

Richard died at the early age of forty-four, having been in post for only nine years. He was severely afflicted by leprosy, which may have been the cause of his early death. The clock worked for 200 years, but unlike other thirteenth century clocks, housed in cathedrals, it did not survive the dissolution of the monasteries.

Richard of Wallingford, from an illuminated manuscript, complete with crozier and mitre, pointing to his clock, which was installed high in the south transept of the Abbey. The disfigurement of leprosy is clearly shown.

The last scientist associated with the abbey was a monk named John Westwyke, a mathematician and astronomer. We don't have any dates for him, but he was active in the 2nd half of the 14th century, during the abbacy of Thomas de la Mare. Born the son of a yeoman farmer on the nearby estate of Westwyke or Gorhambury, it is not certain that he received any formal education other that provided at the monastery school. What is certain is that the 1270s he had fully comprehended, annotated and illustrated Richard of Wallingford's treatises on the Rectangulus and the Albion. He moved to Tynemouth Priory in 1280 and it was here that he completed his masterwork, the design of his Equatorie an instrument for calculating, with greater accuracy than previously available, the movement of the planets, sun and moon. His manual for the use of this instrument was written Middle English rather than Latin probably influenced by Chaucer, who had used English for a guide on the use of the astrolabe for his son (see Seb Falk: *The Light Ages,* Pengiun 2021).

Music

The chanting of plainsong, in use during the lifetime of St Benedict, was an integral component of Benedictine observance. It comprised the chanting of the psalms, canticles, responsories and hymns of the daily office and the Gloria, Credo, Sanctus, Benedictus and Agnus Dei of the mass, celebrated every day. Although the chants were standard in all Benedictine houses, they were not, initially at any rate, codified, and local variations were tolerated as a means of expressing the individual character of each establishment. The chanting was sung by the monks themselves, who mostly knew the chants, and indeed the texts, by heart. Chants slowly evolved – but very slowly – with the better voices being selected for the solos of the responses and more complex versions being developed for certain texts, depending on the availability of competent singers: thus the choir was born[139].

After the Norman conquest many English cathedrals and abbeys made their own compilation of the liturgy in use in their church. That compiled at Old Sarum – the precursor to Salisbury – by the first Norman bishop, St Osmund, was based on the Roman Rite but was customised to include elements of Norman and Anglo-Saxon traditions.

An example of the processional from the Sarum Rite which was adopted throughout southern England and would undoubtedly have been used at St Albans up to the Dissolution.

---

[139] Andrew Gant: *O Sing Unto the Lord*.

But chanting plainsong, no matter how elaborate, was felt to be a constraint on individual and monastic creativity. Musical experimentation in the form of adding a second voice to the plainsong, the singing of two notes at the same time, was both natural and inevitable. Initially the second voice was sung a third or fourth above the main plainsong line, producing, with time and practice, a very pleasing result. Matthew Paris, at St Albans, was certainly enthusiastic, referring to *'voces cantatium dulcissimus'* and *'voces psallentium et dicentium in sublime'*. The next step was to add a third voice – a treble, making magical new sounds: this was the birth of polyphony, initially improvised by the singers but in time arranged and written down by individual – and increasingly professional – composers. The earliest example of English music manuscripts was found at a Catholic school at Old Hall in Hertfordshire, not that far from St Albans Abbey. How it got there is a mystery. The manuscript, compiled for the king's brother Thomas, Duke of Clarence, contains 145 compositions, mostly mass settings but also some motets, by some twenty composers, including one Roy Henry, thought to be King Henry V. It provides the best available source of information on early harmony in England at the transition from medieval to renaissance styles and it shows that the sacred music scene was thriving in the early fifteenth century.

But musical support to worship was not provided by voices alone: pipe organs were in use at a much earlier stage although the first mention of an organist at St Albans, named as Adam, who contributed to a feast given to mark the election of John de Maryns as abbot, was in 1302. The next reference to organ music is at the installation of John Moot as abbot in 1396: 'the sermon ended, the hymn *Te Deum Laudamus* was solemnly and devoutly chanted by the convent, the organs alternating.'[140] Later, in 1438, Abbot John Wheathampstead presented the abbey with a new organ, said to be the largest in England. The smaller organ that this replaced was moved to the retro-choir, where it was used for daily services. Both organs were maintained – and the organist paid – until the Dissolution.

The first named musician, after Adam, known to have been associated with St Albans was John Dunstaple, whose family would have originated in Dunstable some 10 miles north of St Albans. Born in about 1390, he was too young to be represented in the Old Hall manuscript. It is not known where he was educated but it seems that he was another polymath – a musician with a strong interest in astronomy, astrology and

---

[140] Peter Hurford: *The Organs of St Albans Abbey*.

mathematics. He spent thirteen years, in the early fifteenth century, in France as musician to John the 1st Duke of Bedford and the dowager queen Joan, King Henry V's brother and widow respectively. His legacy of this period was a European-wide reputation for the quality of his – and English – music. During this time he probably would have met another English musician, Leonel Power, also in the employ of the Duke and who was the best-represented composer in the Old Hall manuscript. Dunstaple was probably a wealthy amateur musician attached to the duke's household and a personal friend of Abbot John de Wheathampstead, for whom he composed the motet *Albanus Roseo Rutilat super Astra* (Alban glows red above the stars) to a poem by the Abbot John Wheathampstead, the first stanza of which was taken from a thirteenth century original.[141]

From 1437, following the death of the Duke of Bedford, he was employed by the youngest of the three brothers of Henry V, Humphrey, Duke of Gloucester, who was a friend of Abbot John and who was buried in the abbey. Would it be stretching conjecture too far to suggest that Dunstaple may have been educated at St Albans? After all, his interest in astronomy, astrology and mathematics suggests monastic associations. He might even have been responsible for compiling the Old Hall manuscript in the St Albans scriptorium. John Dunstaple died in 1453 and was buried in St Stephen Walbrook, London. On his death in 1453 Abbot John wrote an affectionate epitaph entitled: 'Upon John Dunstaple, an Astrologer, a Mathematician, a Musician and Whatnot'.

We are on surer ground with the most famous St Albans musician of this period, Robert Fayrfax, who was born of well-connected parents in Deeping, Lincolnshire in 1464 but was brought up in the village of Bayford in Hertfordshire. It is probable that, as a boy, he was a chorister in the St Albans Abbey choir until he was 'head hunted' to join the Chapel Royal in 1497: he remained loyal to both these institutions all his life. He took his bachelor of music at Cambridge in 1501 and his doctorate in 1504. The seventeenth century antiquarian Anthony Wood, who called him 'the prime musician of the nation,' tells us that he was appointed 'informator chori' (master of the choristers) at St Albans in 1511, happily combining this job with that of a gentleman of the Chapel Royal with the blessing of King Henry VIII, whose favourite musician he was. In this capacity he took part in the funeral of Henry VII, the coronation of Henry

---

[141] Hilary Corke: *John Dunstaple and the Alban Motet from the Fraternity & Friends of Saint Albans Abbey Occasional Paper No 1.*

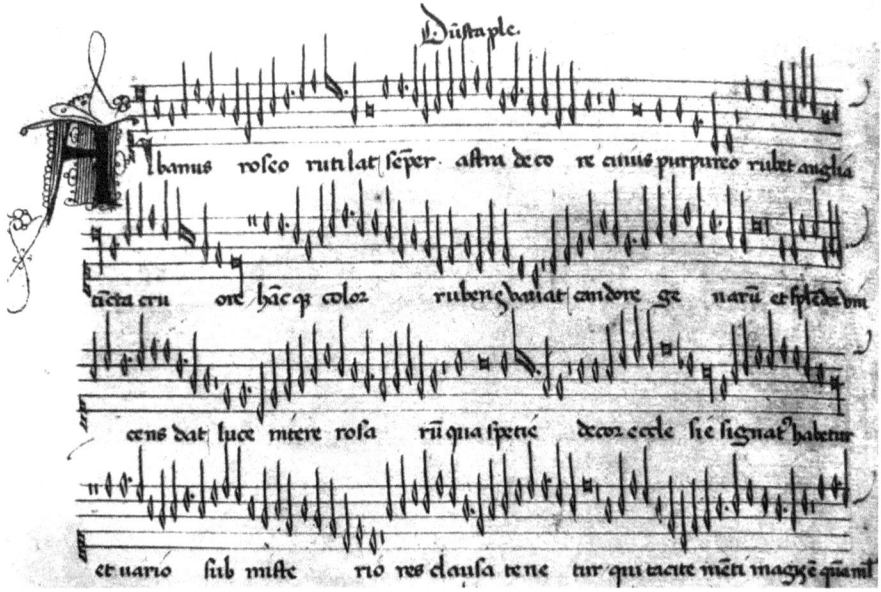

The opening lines of the manuscript of Dunstaple's motet Albanus Roseo Rutilat super Astra. (Courtesy of St Albans Cathedral.)

VIII and the extraordinary example of musical diplomacy at the Field of the Cloth of Gold in 1520.

The St Albans choir at this time comprised eight men and four to six boys, just half the size of the full complement of the Chapel Royal. Fayrfax's works were more restrained than, and avoided the vocal virtuosity of, his contemporaries, anticipating post-Reformation simplicity. Most of his masses are based on *cantus firmus* in the tenor – a slow rendering of the plainsong chant – while other voices interweave around this line in more elaborate polyphony. His compositions that have survived include six masses, two magnificats and ten votive antiphons, all of which were written for either the Chapel Royal or St Albans Abbey, or both. One of the masses, the *Missa Albanus*, together with its associated antiphon *O Maria Deo Grata* were written specifically for St Albans[142], possibly in fulfilment of a contractual obligation.

Robert Fayrfax died on 24 September 1521 and was buried in St Albans Abbey.

---

[142] David Skinner: Notes accompanying a recording of Fayrfax's works by The Cardinall's Musick.

11

The End of St Albans Monastery

I do not blame them for cherishing their Rules, but I blame those of them who think their rule more efficacious than the gospel.

Erasmus

Would for once you would remember your name and profession and take thought for the Reformation of the Church. Never was it more necessary, and never did the state of the Church need more vigorous endeavours. We are troubled with heretics, but no heresy of theirs is so fatal to us and to the people at large as the vicious and depraved lives of the clergy. That is the worst heresy of all.

From a sermon by John Colet, Dean of St Pauls
to the Convocation of Clergy, 1512.

The Reformation

Prelude

The power struggle that existed between successive popes and monarchs was exacerbated by the Papal Revolution. Despite this it was in the interests of both sides to maintain a harmonious working relationship and to this end kings acquiesced to limited papal powers, such as papal approval of the appointment of bishops and abbots and a separate judicial system for the clergy, provided their sovereignty was not jeopardised. The lawyer-popes, however, wanted more: they aspired to a theocracy in which they were supreme and to which kings pledged their fealty. The only instance of this was the subjection of King John to Pope Innocent III in 1214, which led to the Magna Carta and the baronial war. As time wore on popes became more realistic in their aspirations, but the legacy of the previous conflicts was a mutual feeling of mistrust and suspicion. This was not a sentiment confined to England: the Alps became a major cultural barrier between the northern countries that resented the vast sums they provided to the profligate south. Successive kings took steps to erode papal power in England. In 1295 Edward I initiated the seizure of foreign-owned priories, a process that was continued by his son and grandson. And it was the grandson, Edward III, whose statutes *Provisors*, which removed the right of the pope to bestow vacant benefices on non-English nationals, and *Praemunire*, which made it illegal – treasonable – to act in a way that recognised papal authority over that of the king. These statutes only codified the power that previous kings (except King John) had assumed and provided Henry VIII all the legal power he needed to implement the Reformation over 130 years later.

Royal aversion to foreign interference by popes was shared by scholars and churchmen, but for different reasons: corruption. Perhaps the earliest English scholar to articulate his opposition, attracting European attention, was the Franciscan William of Ockham (1285–1347) who stoutly defended the Franciscan Order from papal attacks over the principle of apostolic poverty. In this he went so far as to accuse Pope John XXII of holding heretical views. Ockham was not alone in this – Matthew Paris, later in the thirteenth century, frequently accused the papacy of avarice, simony, usury and other vices.

But it was the Oxford scholar John Wyclif (1324–1384), born in north Yorkshire of farming stock, who went further than Ockham by denouncing, probably in forthright Yorkshire terms, the retention of all forms of wealth and worldly power by ordained priests, including bishops and abbots. He maintained that the pope should not interfere in worldly matters but should be an example of holiness and that the king should govern the Church. The Bible was the only source of Christian orthodoxy, and therefore it should be available, translated into English, for everybody to read for themselves. In fact Wyclif adumbrated the entire Reformation programme: the Bible in English instead of Latin, consubstantiation instead of transubstantiation, the end of idolatry and the replacement of papal supremacy by royal supremacy. Initially his views on restricting the wealth and the power of the Church had the support of some of the clergy and the aristocracy, although the monasteries, especially the larger ones and especially St Albans, were appalled. But it was only when, towards the end of his life, he developed his ideas on the Eucharist, especially on transubstantiation, that he was declared a heretic.

It was Wyclif's legacy, an underground movement known as Lollardism, that nurtured a tradition of anti-clericalism already a thriving culture amongst the urban poor, unsurprisingly in the light of the wealth and power of the Church, in which a total of 50,000 clergy, half of them monks, 'served' a total population of just 3 million, and owned and controlled a third of the national wealth. This was not helped by them being set apart from the laity through their celibacy and their literacy in Latin.

All of this happened at the same time as the build-up to the Peasants' Revolt (which Wyclif did not condone) and the Great Schism (1378–1417) when there were two rival popes; the stability of society suddenly didn't feel that secure. The combination of Wyclif's ideas, the revolt and the activity of the Lollards thoroughly alarmed the establishment to the extent that orthodoxy was imposed and the pursuit of radical ideas, together with the Lollards, were driven underground. Despite this, anti-clericalism would not go away, but manifested itself in an English translation of parts of the Bible and in the works of the outstanding poets of the day, Langland and Chaucer, both contemporaries of Wyclif.

Langland, a man of deep personal faith, humble and compassionate, was as critical of the Church as Wyclif, but possessed a sense of underlying reverence that Wyclif lacked. He also retained a love for a possibly idealised vision of early medieval monasticism (see the preface to this Chapter 10) which makes his critical judgement of the contemporary Church all the more powerful. By contrast Chaucer, the urbane courtier, a man of science, made his criticism through the use of wit and satire. In the prologue of the Canterbury Tales, he presents an enduring portrait of a monk, well-bred and full-bodied, genial and worldly, who dismisses the Benedictine Rule as a code only fit for the Dark Ages. That three such disparate characters – Wyclif, Langland and Chaucer – could share such similar views may indicate that these views were widely held: the monasteries had good reason to fear for their future. None of this cut any ice with the monasteries: Thomas Walsingham, St Albans chronicler at the time, maintained his utter contempt for all calls for reform.

Wyclif's ideas found their way to Bohemia, where in 1415 they inspired Jan Hus, the dean of philosophy at Prague University, to found a reformist Church. The Hussite Church, however, never succeeded in establishing any alliances in neighbouring countries and so it remained an isolated national movement, semi-independent of Rome.

The German Reformation[143]

The causes of the German reformation lay deep in the Great Schism, a period of thirty-nine years from 1378 to 1417 when two (and briefly

---

[143] Diarmaid MacCulloch: *Reformation*.

three) rival popes, one in Rome and one in Avignon, claimed headship of the universal Church, both excommunicating the other. This situation was only resolved when a general council was convened at the German city of Constance in which both popes were persuaded to resign and a new pope, Martin V, was elected. It was originally agreed that the council would re-convene every ten years as part of a permanent reform to provide a check on papal power. However, the shock waves of the fall of Constantinople, the mother of eastern Christianity, in 1453 resulted in a general recognition that the western Church, in such turbulent times, needed strong single-point leadership. With the end of the safeguard provided by the general council, a resurgent succession of popes, energised by the Italian Renaissance and enabled by a new source of income from mining alum that was discovered in papal territory, became more assertive. Starting with Nicholas V, they conceived ambitious, hubristic and expensive plans for the remodelling of the city of Rome, the demolition of Emperor Constantine's monumental basilica on the site of Peter's crucifixion and its replacement with an even grander cathedral. Work on St Peter's had to wait for the election of the pugnacious Pope Julius II, who with his successor Leo X funded the project by taking out a huge loan from the banker Jakob Fugger, the wealth of the papacy having been dissipated by previous popes, not least by the infamous Borgia pope, Alexander VI. This loan was to be financed by a combination of taxation and on the proceeds of the sale of indulgencies.

The indulgencies, which the faithful were exhorted to buy from the Church, provided the promise of a reduction in the time that they would have to spend in Purgatory after their death. It could even work retrospectively for the already dead. To realise its full potential, the popes required the international cooperation of bankers. In the case of Germany, 'cooperation' meant an unholy three-way deal between Pope Leo X, Jakob Fugger and Albrecht of Brandenburg, the younger son of the Hohenzollern family and brother of Joachim, the Elector of Brandenburg. In this deal Fugger lent the papacy the money it needed to build the new St Peters – equivalent to many billions of pounds in today's money – and the funds necessary for Albrecht to become Archbishop of Magdeburg, at the tender age of twenty-three. To enable him to repay this loan the pope granted Albrecht the indulgencies franchise in Brandenburg and Saxony: half the proceeds of the sales would go to paying off the St Peters loan, and half to paying off Albrecht's loan. Subsequently Albrecht became the Prince Archbishop of Mainz, which carried with it the position of the primate of the German Church and elector of the Holy

Roman Empire, thus entrenching the power of the Hohenzollern dynasty.

This was altogether too much venality for Martin Luther, a young Augustinian monk who was a teacher of theology at the new university of Wittenberg. Luther's response to the sale of indulgencies, which he regarded as a heresy, was to write, in 1517, his ninety-five statements – or theses – for disputation. He sent one copy of the theses to the Archbishop of Mainz, who forwarded them to Pope Leo X, and allegedly posted another on the door of the Wittenberg university church. Printed copies, in Latin and German, then circulated throughout Germany. Thus started the Protestant Reformation. There followed several years of scholarly debate, during which Luther developed his ideas in three key books, which culminated in an accusation of heresy.

The Reformation in England[144]

By the fifteenth century the struggle between the monarchy and the papacy had largely been won (by the monarchy), partly due to the weakened state of the papacy following the Great Schism and the series of corrupt popes that followed it. King Henry VIII, vainglorious and idle as he was, had ambitions as a statesman on the European stage and to this end indulged in ruinously expensive – and futile – wars with the French. In furtherance of his aims he fostered good relations with Pope Clement VII to help him achieve this. As a traditional conservative Catholic, who identified his dynastic stability with that of the papacy, Henry conceived a deep loathing of Luther and burned his copy of the books. He went further in writing, surely with the help of his theologians, a rebuttal called *The Assertion of the Seven Sacraments* which so delighted Pope Leo X that he conferred the title 'Defender of the Faith' on Henry. But by this time Henry had delegated the ruling of his kingdom to the all-powerful Wolsey, who had become chancellor of the king's council, a cardinal (through Henry's influence) and the pope's legate in England, all of which gave him supreme temporal and ecclesiastical power in England.

Meanwhile, Henry was becoming increasingly frustrated of his wife's inability (as he saw it) to provide him with a male heir and successor, to the extent that he planned a divorce. This required a papal annulment and the task of obtaining this fell to Cardinal Wolsey. Catherine, however, was the aunt of Charles V, the Holy Roman Emperor, who had become increasingly disillusioned by Henry on account of the latter's inability, through lack of funds, to respond positively to the pope's call to arms for

---

[144] GR Elton: *Reform and Reformation – England 1509–1558.*

The End of St Albans Monastery

the defence of the Turkish attacks on Hungary. By this time the pope was virtually the prisoner of Charles, the most powerful man in Europe, who saw Henry's divorce of his aunt as an insult to his family's honour and obliged the pope to refuse an annulment. He also withdrew from his betrothal to Henry's daughter Mary, doubtless realising the full horror of having Henry as a father-in-law.

For Henry the birth of a son and heir was a matter of the future stability of the realm. Henry also came to believe that his marriage to his deceased older brother Arthur's widow, Catherine, was illegal, so the lack of an heir by Catherine could be seen as God's vengeance. A divorce, enabling him to marry Anne Boleyn, was therefore imperative. The pope denied this interpretation of the consanguinity laws and refused to sanction an annulment. If the pope would not oblige, Henry's only recourse was to break with Rome, assume the headship of the English Church and give himself an annulment. Henry, at this stage at any rate, didn't really want an all-out reformation, he just wanted a cooperative pope. Like other temporal monarchs he identified his survival as a monarch with that of the pope as a spiritual monarch – it was a case of monarchical solidarity. However, events moved rapidly out of his hands when he delegated the necessary legislation to his new chief minister, Thomas Cromwell, who relied heavily on his knowledge and mastery of Parliament, with its long tradition of anti-clericalism, to pass the Act of Supremacy (1534). This act established the monarch as the head of the English Church, whereupon his newly appointed Archbishop of Canterbury, Thomas Cranmer, quickly annulled Henry's marriage to Catherine. Henry's visceral hatred of radical change in general and of Luther in particular, enthusiastically supported by Sir Thomas More, the arch-remainer of his day, polarised the spectrum of opinion on reform, so that the voice of the moderates, based on the ideas of Erasmus, who recognised the need for reform but were opposed to radical theological change, was obliterated in the cross-fire between the extremes: the choice became either no change at all or full-on Protestantism. As Henry's mental state deteriorated and Cromwell entrenched his position the result was inevitable.

The final century of the monastery

The European-wide decline in the relevance of the Benedictine Order to contemporary society, outlined in Chapter 8, proceeded at a different rate in different countries and in different monasteries. England, slow to develop monastic orders to their full extent, may have also been slow to follow the European lead in decline. Larger monasteries like St Albans had the resources to weather the adverse climate in the fourteenth century better than could smaller, less well-endowed houses. St Albans, under the inspirational abbacy of Thomas de la Mare, enjoyed a late flowering – a renaissance or possibly an Indian summer – lasting into the early part of the 15th century.[145] Abbot Thomas was by common consent St Albans' greatest abbot, and this was recognised by his presidency of the Benedictine Chapter in England. His advice was sought by the most powerful in the land, yet his first commitment remained to his monks, for whom he was a father figure.

Abbot Thomas' legacy was continued by the chronicler Thomas Walsingham and Abbot John of Wheathampstead, under whom the standards at St Albans were broadly maintained until later in the fifteenth century. Wheathampstead, unique amongst abbots by having two terms of office, was well educated and literary. Following in the footsteps of his predecessors Mentmore and De La Mare, he presided over the Benedictine Chapter for twelve years. He reformed the abbey's finances and appointed a master of works to take charge of the fabric of the abbey, together with a separately funded chest. But he was something of a dilettante and failed to provide constancy, firm leadership or commitment – indicated by his resignation from his first period of abbacy for no discernible reason. Abbot Wheathampstead cultivated close relationships with royalty and nobility, especially Humphrey, Duke of Gloucester, whose retirement from public life may have been a factor in Wheathampstead's decision to resign in 1441. It was this retirement that initiated the beginning of the long and slow and ultimate decline of the abbey. His successor, John Stoke, was weak and Wheathampstead's second abbacy was marked by the two battles of the Wars of the Roses that took place in St Albans, after which royal favour grew more tenuous and the political climate more insecure. Under these pressures, and the weak leadership provided by Abbot William Albon, Wheathampstead's successor, internal rumour and dissent threatened to overwhelm Albon's energetic prior and archdeacon, William Wallingford, who was accused of perjury, theft and corruption – unsubstantiated accusations which nevertheless split the community in two. Despite this, he eventually succeeded Albon as abbot, but became the object of a vendetta prosecuted by Cardinal Morton, Archbishop of Canterbury and King Henry VII's

---

[145] James Clark: A Monastic Renaissance at St Albans: Thomas Walsingham and his Circle

lord chancellor, who was jealous of St Albans' exemption from his power of visitation. This privilege was challenged and counter-challenged in the Curia in Rome, the upshot of which was the granting of a bull by Pope Innocent VIII in 1490:

> It has come the ear of the Pontiff that some monasteries in England have greatly deviated from rectitude. He therefore urges the archbishop that he should visit every superior monastery in his province and bring them back to conformity.[146]

This bull gave Morton the right to carry out a one-off visitation of St Albans. Whether this took place is not clear but such a detail didn't deter Morton from serving an admonition on Abbot William, which lists the usual defects: the dilapidated condition of the abbey, the relaxed discipline of the monks and neglected hospitality. In particular:

> The brethren of St Albans, some of whom, as it is reported are given over to all the evil things of the world, neglect the service of God. They live publicly and continuously with harlots and mistresses within the precincts of the monastery and without.[147]

No action was taken as a result of this episode, but the damage had been done: St Albans was now vulnerable. Decline there certainly was, but not on this scale. On the face of it, all remained well until the end of the fifteenth century. The monastic revenue held up and relations with the townspeople recovered somewhat from the nadir of the fourteenth century. The abbey continued to produce books in the scriptorium, at least until a printing press was set up in the school in 1479 and promising young monks continued to be sent to study at Oxford until the end of the fifteenth century. The standard of the music of divine office improved, with the advent of polyphony, the introduction of organs and the contribution of professional musicians of the standing of Dunstaple and Fayrfax.

But maybe there was a change in mood. The vehemence with which Thomas Walsingham, William Binham and Nicholas Radcliffe had attacked the ideas of John Wyclif belied a deeper insecurity and suggests a

---

[146] Nicholson: *The Abbey of St Albans – Some extracts from its early history and a description of its conventual church.*
[147] Rushbrook Williams: *A History of St. Albans Abbey.*

personal animosity: similar ideas, in respect of vernacular scripture and opposing clerical wealth, put forward 120 years later by Erasmus were politely, if not enthusiastically, received.

The increase in per capita income, with the fall in monastic population and the rise in its gross income, resulted in monastic life diverging evermore sharply from the Benedictine Rule and the abandonment of austerity. With papal sanction,[148] meat was eaten and wine drunk as a matter of routine. The ideal of communality was abandoned, with monks routinely sleeping and eating in their private rooms. Manual labour had long been abandoned, but after many centuries in which the feudal system and the abbey estate had been doggedly maintained – long after it had been relaxed in secular estates – the tied villeins were granted manumission in the fifteenth century so that monasteries' tenants paid their rents in cash rather than goods and services. This had the effect of further removing monastic communities from any involvement in the management of the rural economy: the rents were collected by agents and the former obedientiaries became unemployed. This in turn led to the accrual of more power in the hands of the abbot and a removal of incentives to young monks. In the case of St Albans, however, additional power accrued instead to the archdeacon, William Wallingford, who in 1445 became the cellarer, bursar, forester and sub-cellarer. Little wonder, then, that later, as Abbot, he could afford to build the great screen in the abbey at his own expense. Monks received a wage to cover the cost of clothes and luxuries, a dividend of monastic profits and fees for the performance of chantry services. Annual payments ranged from 9 marks for a junior monk to £40 for the Prior.

With the death of Thomas Walsingham no chronicler of any renown continued his work. Whereas St Albans sent more monks to study at Oxford than any other monastery in the fourteenth century, in the period 1500–1535 St Albans monks comprised less than 5 per cent of the total: six other monasteries did better[149]. With the second battle of St Albans in the Wars of the Roses, when the victorious Lancastrians took King Henry VI prisoner and devastated St Albans and the Abbey estates, the age of close relations between monarchs and abbots came to an end.

Architectural activity, a bell weather of spiritual confidence, continued in the fifteenth century but the projects undertaken seem not quite

---

[148] David Knowles: *The Religious Orders in England*.
[149] Peter Cunich: *Benedictine Monks at the University of Oxford and the Dissolution of the Monasteries*.

essential to the functioning of the abbey: chantry chapels for wealthy individuals; the high altar screen that, although magnificent and built to enhance the celebration of the mass, also obscured the shrine of St Alban; the construction of perpendicular windows that provided more light than the Norman windows they replaced at the expense of architectural coherence and the sense of mystery.

An analysis of late fifteenth-century wills of St Albans residents[150] shows a class divide: only the wealthy left money to the monastery, and that to cover the expenses of the monks to pray for the souls of their departed. The poor left their money to one of the four parish churches of the town: St Andrews, St Peters, St Stephens or St Michaels.

Somehow, it feels as if the abbey had lost its soul. Its pastoral role had been taken over by parish priests, its scholarly role by the universities and its spiritual power had ebbed away. That Cardinal Morton was able to issue his admonition on Abbot Wheathampstead shows how vulnerable St Albans was in the absence of royal support and in the face of an equivocal papacy. St Albans became fair game, not helped by the falling off in the calibre of the last abbots[151]. The last abbot elected by the monks themselves, independent of royal influence, was Thomas Ramridge (1492–1521). Little is known about Ramridge, historical writing having ceased, except that the abbey sunk further into debt and that in the last five years of his abbacy, due to his declining mental powers, the administration was devolved to two assistants, the prior and the cellarer, under the supervision of Cardinal Wolsey. From this time onwards the abbey lost its independence. Thomas Wolsey contrived to have himself appointed abbot in *commendam*, a position in which he had control of the monastic revenues without having to fulfil the duties of abbot. Wolsey held this position for nine years, during which time he siphoned off all its income, driving it to bankruptcy. This was a purely cynical appointment – Wolsey was driven entirely by greed and hardly ever visited St Albans. On the deprivation of his abbacy in 1530 the St Albans monks proposed their prior, Andrew Ramridge, as abbot but were overruled by Henry, who imposed Robert Catton, Prior of Norwich. Catton's references were not, however, exactly glowing: a visitation of Norwich Priory had found him guilty of corruption, laxity and indiscipline. He was also an ardent social climber and proved to be the worst abbot that St Albans ever had

---

[150] Rebecca Toepfer: *The Abbey of St Albans and Its Relationship with Its Lordship in the Late Middle Ages*.
[151] JG Clark: *Reformation and Reaction at St Albans Abbey, 1530–58*.

since its Norman refoundation. At St Albans he cultivated his royal connections and a friendship with Cromwell and facilitated the transfer of several manors in the liberty to the crown. This incensed the monks to the extent that they submitted two petitions calling for the removal of Catton, or at least the appointment of a co-adjudicator to limit his freedom of action. Ultimately the monks were successful and Catton was deprived of the abbacy in 1538. The king reluctantly approved the monks' choice of their prior, Richard Boreman, as his successor – reluctantly because Boreman made no secret of his opposition to the demise of traditional religion. As Prior he was a patron of a polemical treatise known as *The Confutacyon* written by John Gwynneth, a musician associated with St Albans and a friend of Boreman. *The Confutacyon* was a defence of the theology of the Eucharist against the ideas of John Frith, a prominent protestant theologian.

The extent of governmental disapproval of Boreman is shown by his confinement – house arrest – soon after his election for the non-payment of various debts or bribes.

Dissolution of the monasteries

If the Reformation was almost an accident, so too was the Dissolution – accidental in that it was not initially a fully formed plan. It was not inconceivable that a reformed English Catholic Church, with the king as its supreme governor, could not include reformed religious houses, Benedictine or otherwise, providing they acknowledged Henry as the supreme head. On the other hand, dissolution or suppression of the monasteries was not seen by the secular Church as an heretical act – it was one that Erasmus strongly supported. While suppression was certainly envisaged, it was initially thought to be limited to unviable or irremediably corrupt houses, which would have certainly included those devoted to the cult of saints – as at St Albans.

Royal interference in monasticism was hardly new. During the Hundred Years War some seventy alien religious houses – French owned – had been closed down, without any perceptible protest, and the assets redistributed: St Albans itself had been a beneficiary by the acquisition of Pembroke Priory. Subsequently Cardinal Wolsey appropriated some minor religious houses to fund his Cardinal College in Oxford and his school in Ipswich. Once this was accomplished, through the efforts of his secretary Thomas Cromwell, unopposed by either the ecclesiastical establishment or popular reaction, a precedent had been set; the piecemeal dissolution of first the priories and then the monasteries was able to proceed. However, there was a world of difference in the closure of failing houses in order to redeploy their assets to a new more effective use, as Wolsey had done and the closure of houses to enrich the monarch. This problem was, however, eased by the suppression of monasteries in Germany and Scandinavia carried out for just this purpose[152].

Cromwell set about his reforms by commissioning an audit of Church assets – the *Valor Ecclesiasticus*, primarily for tax purposes – followed by visitations, mostly confined to religious houses, by a commission comprising a small team of lawyers, led by Dr Richard Layton and Dr Thomas Leigh. Every member of the team had received a humanist education and had graduated in canon law, but only Layton was an ordained priest. Their first task in 1535 was the visitation of all monasteries with an annual income of less than £200. Their visitations, necessarily rushed, and their reports, predictably negative, provided Cromwell all the ammunition he needed for the suppression of about two-thirds of the smaller monasteries in the First Suppression Act of 1536. This act, which was not drafted by Cromwell and not seen by Henry until the day he gave it royal assent, was disingenuous in its purpose: *'lytel and small monasteries showing lytel or no amendment are to be utterly suppressed'*. But the commissioners, acting up to or perhaps beyond the limits of their brief, did not give the monasteries much opportunity for 'amendment' so that many monasteries surrendered voluntarily.

The suppression of the minor religious houses, which included all the St Albans dependent houses, together with Henry's break with Rome, and wider economic grievances, all focussed on the perceived autocratic behaviour of Thomas Cromwell, provoking a series of rebellions in the north of England. The first of these, involving about 10,000 men, took place in Lincolnshire and was swiftly suppressed. It was followed a much larger rebellion, known as 'the Pilgrimage of Grace' which spread from Yorkshire to all of northern England and which posed a much greater challenge to the Tudor monarchy. This was dealt with by the granting of limited concessions which, when these were subsequently rescinded, provoked a third rebellion. That the rebellions were limited to the north can be explained by the relative doctrinal conservatism and the higher proportion of minor houses in the north than in the more affluent south. Nevertheless, the Dissolution programme was put on hold for a year until the northern rebellions were completely quelled, and when it did resume

---

[152] James Clark: *The Dissolution of the Monasteries*.

with the suppression of all the major monasteries, it was carried out with much greater haste. However, to minimise the number of discontented out-of-work monks ready and willing to protest, the monks were offered far more generous compensation terms than had been the case with the monks of the minor houses.

This second wave of suppressions was preceded, as before, by visitations asking a similar range of questions as previously, that explored the degree of observance and the state of the house, but the visits were carried out with great haste and the visitors' reports were clinical and objective, with all departures from strict observance – of which there were many – itemised.

The visitation of St Albans took place from 5 to the 12 December 1538 by Dr Leigh and William Petre. On their arrival, and in the absence of Abbot Boreman, the commission found 'just cause' for closing the monastery down. The Abbot was summoned and on his return he put up a stout resistance, saying he would rather choose to beg his bread rather than consent to surrender. The commissioners appealed to Dr Layton who, it appears, subsequently convinced the abbot and monks that they would have to surrender, although this was delayed by a year. An extract from William Petre's letter to Cromwell, echoing Cardinal Morton's admonition of 1490, reads:[153]

> Please it your Lordship to be advertised:
> At our coming to St Albons on Thursdaye last, we beganne a visitacion among the monkes, the Abbot being then in London. And because we wolde the more fully knowe the whole state of all things, tarred the longer in the examinacion of theym. And upon Fridaye last we sent a monicion for the Abbot to appere before us, who came hether on Saturday before none: whom we have likewise as fully examined upon all things as we might. And although, as well by the examination of the monkes, as by confession of the Abbot himself, there doth appere confessed and fully proved, just cause of deprivacion against the Abbot, not only for breking the King's injunctions, but also, for manifest dilapidations, making of giftes, negligent administracion, and sundry other causes; yet by waht meanes we know not, in all communications or motions made concerning any surrendre, he sheweth hymselfe so stiff, that as he saith he wold rather choyse to begge his bredde all the days of his life, than consent to any surrender. We have everich of us

---

[153] DW Barrett: *Sketches of Church Life – Diocese of St Albans*.

severally and also together, communed with hym and also used all suche motions as we thought might most further that purpose; but he contynueth allweys one man, and waxeth hourly more obstinate, and less conformable: whether he so doo upon trust and confidence of any friendshippe, we know not ...

This report led directly to the suppression of the St Albans monastery. Richard Boreman, the last Abbot, surrendered the ancient monastic seal on 5 December 1539. By a charter dated 14 December 1539 the abbot was granted a pension of £266 13s 4d while the prior received £33 6s 8d. The thirty-seven monks were given smaller amounts.

Thus the verse in Langland's *Piers Plowman* appears to have been prophetic:

Ac there shal come a kyng and confesse yow religouses,
And here yow, as the bible telleth for brekyng of yowre reule
...
And thane shal the abbot of Abyngdoun and all his issu for euere
Have a knokke of a kyng and incurable the wounde

Twelve days after the surrender all moveable treasure, comprising the jewels adorning the shrine, some 100 ounces of gold and several thousand ounces of silver-gilt, was carted away for the king's use by government officials. The books – several hundred of them – were dispersed but eventually found their way to what became the British Library. The monastery buildings were mostly sold to Sir Richard Lee, a military engineer and architect who demolished them to provide building materials. The land was sold or granted to friends of the king and the gentry which, on a national scale, ensured widespread involvement in and support for the Dissolution. The abbey church – perhaps too big for Sir Richard to handle, was eventually sold to the town to serve as their parish church. The abbey gateway was retained to serve as a town prison and stabling for government use.

There were few protests from the Church against the suppression, with just three abbots, of Colchester, Reading and Glastonbury, refusing to surrender their monasteries and suffering the death penalty as a consequence. There was no widespread monastic protest, although low-level resistance at St Albans had been sustained and vocal in the 1530s[154].

---

[154] JG Clark: *Reformation and Reaction at St Albans 1530–56*.

Prominent in this were the secular priests of St Albans, in particular Thomas King who, as chaplain, preached in the chapel of St Andrews, attached to the abbey, against King Henry and in favour of returning to Rome. Only one monk is known to have spoken out, William Ashwell: both he and king had been questioned by the authorities and defended by the then Prior Boreman.

To what extent was this Dissolution the policy of the king and his ministers, and if so was the motive financial or social? It seems most unlikely that the dissolution of the monasteries resulted from the implementation from a planned policy. The Benedictine Order was acutely aware of the interest of the crown and potential interference ever since the 1421 Council of Westminster and the subsequent intervention of Henry VII, which led to Archbishop Morton's visitation of St Albans Abbey[155] in 1490. The Benedictines, who were early enthusiasts of Erasmus, thus expected reform and were aware of the changing climate of opinion, with Lollardism, supported by a substratum of anti-clericalism, morphing into Lutherism. Certainly, monasticism was not popular or even widely respected. Humanist opinion in the Church, informed by Erasmus, felt that monasteries had had their day. The bishops resented the privileged wealth, the power and above all the independence of monasteries. The population regarded them – especially the richer ones – as largely irrelevant, the universities rather indifferent. So, what started as reform quickly transformed into opportunist suppression, the crown, being financially broke, needing to realise the wealth of the monasteries.

Conclusion

Thus ended the 750-year history of the monastery of St Alban – so ancient and so proud as it was. Through its antiquity, its sanctity and prestige it was acknowledged as the premier monastery of England, many of its abbots becoming national figures. But although the Dissolution spelled the end of the monastery, it was by no means the end of the abbey church, built to the glory of God and St Alban, and which, after recovering from such a severe blow – the 'knokke of a kyng' in Langland's words – eventually entered a new and equally distinguished future which will be recounted in the final part of this book.

---

[155] James G Clark: *The Benedictines in the Middle Ages*.

Timeline of relevant events: part two

Century	Year	Event	Abbot
Twelfth	1119	The St Albans Psalter written for Christina of Markyate	De Gorham
	1141	The Empress Matilda entertained en route for London coronation	
	1195	Westward extension of the nave commenced	De Cella
Thirteenth	1214	Magna Carta drafted at St Albans and signed at Runnymeade	
	1215	The French Dauphin occupied St Albans	
	1215	Papal confirmation of abbots appointment starts. Painting of nave murals starts	
	1217	Matthew Paris enters St Albans Abbey	
	1219	Roger of Wendover writes the *Flowers of History*	Trumpington
	1250	Earthquake caused irreparable damage to the Abbey Presbytery	
	1254	Nicholas Breakspear of St Albans appointed Pope Adrian IV	
	1257	Norman Presbytery demolished: work starts on new presbytery	
	1259	Matthew Paris dies	
	1283	Gloucester College, Oxford inaugurated	De Norton
Fourteenth	1302	New presbytery completed and new shrine constructed	De Berkhamstead
	1315	Start of six years of famine, killing nearly 1 million	De Eversden
	1323	Collapse and rebuild of s. arcade of nave	
	1327	St Albans Revolt. Creation of the astronomical clock	De Wallingford
	1345	Black Death: forty-seven monks and Abbot Mentmore died	De Mentmore
	1346	Abbey gateway rebuilt	
	1377	Wyclif tried for heresy	
	1378	Great Papal Schism	De la Mare
	1381	Peasants' Revolt	
	1395	End of papal confirmation of abbot appointments	

Fifteenth	1420	Start of construction of the watching loft	Wheathampstead
	1421	Council of Westminster	
	1453	Fall of Constantinople	Wheathampstead
	1455	First Battle of St Albans	
	1461	Second Battle of St Albans	Albon
	1479	Printing press set up at St Albans	Wallingford
	1484	High altar screen constructed	
	1491	Cardinal Morton served an admonition on St Albans	
Sixteenth	1517	Martin Luther writes ninety-five statements	Ramryge
	1521	Henry VIII writes 'The Assertion of the Seven Sacraments' and is awarded the title 'Defender of the Faith by Pope'	Wolsey
	1529	Turks overwhelm Hungary	
	1534	Act of Supremacy	Boreman
	1536	First Act of Suppression: St Albans daughter houses dissolved	
	1539	Abbey surrendered	

PART THREE

From Parish Church to Cathedral

12

The Parish Church of St Alban in a Period of Religious Turmoil

And if there cannot be an end of our disputing and contending one against another, yet let there be a moderation in our affections...because God hath so placed us Englishmen here in one commonwealth, also in one Church, as in one ship together, let us not mangle and divide the ship, which being divided, perisheth.

George Foxe – *Book of Martyrs*

Bare ruin'd choirs where late the sweet birds sang.

William Shakespeare – Sonnet 73

Aftermath: 1540 to 1547

During this period, which covers the remaining years of King Henry VIII's reign, the abbey church would have remained locked and empty, although parish services would have been held in the Chapel of St Andrew. Within a few weeks of the surrender of the monastery the movable treasure was carted away from the abbey for the king's use. Other assets were kept in the hands of the Court of Augmentation, a body set up by Cromwell for their safe keeping and eventual disposal. The land and buildings were granted or acquired by a small number of gentry, mostly with local connections, who were associated in some way with either the king or Cromwell. The individual who gained most was one Ralph Rowlatt, a wealthy merchant, reputed to have informed on anti-Cromwellian sermons preached by Thomas King in the abbey – or perhaps in St Andrews Chapel, contiguous to the north-west wall of the nave – in the 1530s. Rowlatt was granted the manors of Gorhambury, the Pré, the site of the former monastic hospital, Westwick and possibly other manors and properties: in any event at his inquest in 1542 he was discovered to own a total of ten manors and three houses in the town. Another local beneficiary was Henry Gape, a former abbey official who had leased a property from Abbot Boreman in 1538: he was granted the contiguous manor of St Michael.

More significantly, all the monastic buildings, with the exception of the abbey church itself, the abbey gateway and the great court, were acquired – either granted or sold, it is not clear which – to Richard Lee, a military engineer in the service of the crown. Lee was an interesting but rapacious character: energetic, ruthless, litigious and deeply ambitious. He became a friend of Cromwell when, as a twenty-year-old surveyor, he was commended for successfully supervising Cromwell's building works on his country house in Hackney. He was subsequently appointed as surveyor of Calais and soon after surveyor of the king's works, which led to a knighthood for his surveys of Edinburgh. As his surveyor Lee would have been known to Henry, which helped him survive the demise of Cromwell in 1540 – a survival helped by his wife, who Henry held 'in no small favour'[156]. During the course of this activity, he rented Sopwell Priory after its surrender in 1537 and subsequently acquired its freehold. Through this association with St Albans he acquired, after the Dissolution, possibly in lieu of arrears of salary, the immediate precincts of the abbey church. He proceeded to demolish Sopwell Priory and all the conventual buildings, using the materials from both to build a new country seat, named Lee House. It is tempting to conjecture that these transactions would have been encouraged by the Court of Augmentation, as the demolition of both the monastic buildings and Sopwell Priory would make any subsequent attempt to re-found the monastery very much more difficult.

What was the immediate religious legacy? James Clark makes a strong case for some continuity of devotion on the part of the monks, with three remaining, unbeneficed, in the town, and seven finding livings in parishes within the archdeaconry[157]. Of these, two became vicars of St Stephens and St Michaels, parishes in the town, while a third, William East, was appointed archdeacon and rector of the abbey church. As for the former abbot, Richard Boreman, he returned to Oxford after the Dissolution to complete his doctorate of theology, after which he lived in London.

The momentous Reformation and Dissolution had repercussions beyond the closure of the monasteries. With the surrender of the St

---

[156] Peter Newcome: History of the Abbey of St Albans.
[157] JG Clark: *Reformation and Reaction at St Albans 1530–58*.

Albans monastery, the archdeaconry was without an archdeacon until 1542, when it was transferred to the diocese of Lincoln. Similarly, the liberty of St Albans, in the absence of an abbot, reverted to the control of Hertfordshire. More immediately the governance of the town of St Albans, previously under a bailiff answering to the abbot, was in the absence of a town charter, leaderless. In this power vacuum the leading burgesses and landowners – including those identified previously – formed an unofficial town corporation. With the surrender of the monastery came the closure of the school, which, although not an integral part of the monastery, the headmaster being secular, was housed in a monastic building and was so closely associated with the monastery that its closure, temporary as it turned out, was inevitable.

The abbey church was retained by the crown throughout this period, probably because it was Henry's project that some of the income from the Dissolution would be used to endow the creation of thirteen new sees, to be based on former abbeys, of which St Albans was to have been one. In the end there were insufficient funds and only six of the thirteen were created: Oxford, Gloucester, Chester, Peterborough, Bristol and Westminster, the latter see only surviving until 1556. It is likely, however, that the abbey was in continuous use as the parish church during the remainder of this period as St Andrews Chapel, which had served as the parish church, was demolished by Lee. Furthermore, Henry, in search of a middle way between traditional Catholicism and extreme Protestantism, may have begun to regret Cromwell's reform programme, which he may have felt had gone too far, too fast. Henry was a traditionalist, attached to Catholicism[158], (the Abbot of St Albans officiated at the christening of two of King Henry's children, Edward and Elizabeth, in 1537)[159] and for him to sanction the sale, inevitably leading to the destruction of the abbey church, which was believed to have been founded by his predecessor Offa 750 years earlier and dedicated to Alban, Britain's proto-martyr, was unthinkable.

Church reform was very much on the backburner during the closing years of Henry's reign, partly because of his religious conservatism and declining health, and partly because of a fear of military interference by Charles V, the Holy Roman Emperor, which England was in no position to repel, such was the parlous state of the national finances.

---

[158] Eamon Duffy: *The Stripping of the Altars*.
[159] James Clark: *The Dissolution of the Monasteries*.

Edward VI: 1547–1553

Henry's only son, Edward VI, who inherited the throne as a nine-year-old boy in 1547, had been educated by reform-minded tutors despite his father's religious conservatism with the result that, on his accession, the reforming faction of the Church felt freed from the restraints that had been imposed by the former king. Despite Archbishop Cranmer's concern that too much haste in reform would provoke a backlash and would appear manipulative of the boy king, he ordered the destruction of religious imagery and chantry chapels, with compliance ensured by a nationwide royal visitation. A new collection of homilies or sermons, written by Cranmer, were promulgated to outline the new evangelical theology. At St Albans any images surviving the dissolution were destroyed: wall paintings whitewashed, statues smashed, shrines demolished, stained glass removed. Processions were banned – ironically for St Albans Abbey church, which was almost designed to accommodate processions. The four chantry chapels in the abbey church survived this storm of iconoclasm probably because any endowments they may have had been in possession of had already been sold off or given away. Cranmer issued a new prayer book in 1549, in which he tried to plot a middle way between traditional Catholicism and Puritanism by drawing extensively from the liturgical changes in Lutheran Germany while retaining elements of the Catholic missal. This was not a success and provoked civil unrest in the pro-traditional west country and opposition in the more protestant east. A second, more radical edition of the prayer book was issued three years later influenced by the views of a significant influx into the country of more extreme, non-Lutheran reformers fleeing from the European Counter-Reformation. Both prayer books were legally imposed by the Act of Uniformity.

Institutional change was also taking place: in 1549 the last Abbot of St Albans, Richard Boreman, sought and obtained permission from King Edward to revive the school and in 1551 he was able to purchase the Lady Chapel of the Abbey Church for the sum of £536. In 1550 the St Albans archdeaconry was transferred from the Lincoln diocese to that of London, while on 12 May 1553, the year of King Edward's death, the town of St Albans was granted its first charter, which as a new borough then bought the abbey church for the sum of £400*. This giveaway price (there were

---

* However, the price of £400 appears rather expensive compared with the £100 the 'four guardians' of Romsey paid King Henry for their abbey.

some 580 taxpayers in the new borough)[160] may reflect both that the condition of the church, after nearly fifty years of little or no maintenance, was in a poor state and also the desire of the crown to shed responsibility for its future survival. It is not known how the £400 was raised – surely not from local taxation because the borough had only just been created – so it was probably found by contributions from the local great and good, including those already identified who benefited financially from the dissolution of the monastery.

Queen Mary I: 1553–1558

On Edward's death in 1553, Mary, Henry's eldest daughter by Catherine of Aragon, and Edward's half-sister, assumed the throne. Mary was a staunch Catholic whose overriding aim was to return England to the Roman fold.[161] To achieve this her short-term objective was to seek reconciliation with the pope and to receive absolution for the sin of schism. The longer-term objective was to provide an heir to ensure a Catholic succession. As she was already thirty-seven years old finding a suitable husband was the highest priority. In this she was successful and duly married Phillip, the son of Charles V and heir to the Spanish throne, just six months after her coronation. This aroused the grave suspicions of even Mary's Catholic supporters, who made it very clear that while they were happy to go back to the Latin Mass, there could be no question of them giving up monastic land they had been granted or had bought following the Dissolution[162]. Thus the refoundation of monasteries was ruled out from the very start. It was on these terms that Pope Julius III sent Cardinal Pole as his legate to work out the details. Pole, a cousin of Henry VIII, had lived for twenty years in Italy, during which time he had developed reformist, almost Lutheran leanings. The actual mechanics of the return to Roman obedience were problematic because in the twenty years since Henry's Act of Supremacy Protestantism had put down surprisingly deep roots. Although Parliament eventually repealed Edward's reformation legislation, including the Act of Uniformity, and re-instated the old pre-Reformation heresy laws, they were not willing to repeal Henry's Act of Supremacy. This put Mary in an invidious position in which as a Catholic she was bound to obedience to the pope while as monarch she was the supreme governor of the English Church. This

---

[160] Mark Freeman: *St Albans – A History*.
[161] GR Elton: *Reform and Reformation – England 1509–1558*.
[162] GR Elton: *Reform and Reformation – England 1509–1558*.

dilemma was made worse by the accession of a new pope, Paul IV, six months after Cardinal Pole's appointment. Pope Paul IV was hysterically opposed to the Holy Roman Empire and to the Kingdom of Spain and ordered the return of Pole, whom he regarded as a Lutheran heretic, to face the Inquisition. Mary refused to allow this, which only heightened the equivocation of her position.

Meanwhile she did what was within her powers as supreme governor to reverse the reform: she caused the separation of some 2,000 parish priests from their wives and in time replaced all Protestant-inclined bishops with Catholics. Cardinal Pole also worked diligently, though rather legalistically and without any passion or imagination, in the restoration of traditional worship, although this return was tempered by his Lutheran sympathies – he allowed an English translation of the New Testament to be used. He arranged for Cranmer and other senior churchmen to be prosecuted for treason and burned, which allowed Pole to appoint himself Archbishop of Canterbury. Once the heresy laws were reinstated, Mary and Pole embarked on a programme of heresy trials that resulted in some 300 deaths by burning.

The majority of these executions were in the south-east of England with the London diocese, of which the archdeaconry of St Albans was now part, leading the way with 112. There was only one burning in the archdeaconry of St Albans, and this disparity may reflect that St Albans had not yet been fully integrated with the rest of the diocese. The single burning, at Romeland, adjacent to the abbey church, was of one George Tankerfield, a cook from Barnet, who seems to typify the profile of the majority of the victims – the artisan class[163] – and also their astonishing steadfastness: before the flames took hold Tankerfield is said to have sung

> Be the day weary, or be the day long
> At last it ringeth to Evensong.[164]

Such fortitude is why the persecution was such a disastrous policy that succeeded only in hardening anti-Catholic sentiments amongst the artisan classes.

Queen Mary did, however, confirm the town charter and the use of the lady chapel for the re-founded school. Mary's short and unhappy reign ended with her death, childless, in 1558.

---

[163] GR Elton: *Reform and Reformation England 1509–1558*.
[164] DW Barrett: Scenes of Church Life – St Albans.

Refoundation of the St Albans monastery?

The refusal of Parliament to contemplate a return to monasticism didn't deter the last abbot, Richard Boreman, a man of resource and imagination, from campaigning and planning the refoundation of the monastery at St Albans. Perhaps he was driven by the remorse of giving up the monastery seal and surrendering the monastery after his bold words refusing to do so, and accepting a handsome pension that enabled him to buy the site of the monastery, to the south of the abbey church, from Sir Richard Lee. But refoundation would have required re-endowment and this was all but impossible, so if St Albans monastery had been re-founded it would have been a shadow of its former self. Doubtless encouraged by the example of the monastery of Westminster, which was re-founded in 1556, he must have hoped that with the support of Queen Mary it could also happen at St Albans. These hopes were dashed with the death of Queen Mary: a near-contemporary account by Robert Shrimpton describes how, when the news came of the queen's death, 'the Abbot for grief took to his chamber and dyed in a fortnight'[165]. Robert Shrimpton is said to have recounted this memoir at the age of 103 and for him the senior priest at the abbey must always have been 'the Abbot'. The newly re-founded Westminster monastery was closed in 1558 with the accession of Elizabeth.

The Elizabethan Settlement

On Mary's death, her half-sister, the twenty-five-year-old Elizabeth succeeded to the throne with the firm intention of stabilising the violent oscillations of religious observance that were fostered by her half-siblings Edward and Mary. She herself was protestant but more importantly she wanted to achieve social harmony by de-politicising religion, and in this endeavour she acceded to the throne with her settlement already drafted by William Cecil and Nicholas Bacon, who was, incidentally, an indirect beneficiary of the dissolution of St Albans monastery, having been granted the manor of Gorhambury. Based on King Edward's legislation, the settlement comprised an Act of Supremacy, which included the thirty-nine articles based on Cranmer's forty-two articles and the Book of Common Prayer based on the 1552 version, but with some small but significant changes to appease Lutheran feelings. The legislation was

---

[165] John Shrimpton: The antiquities of Verulam and St Albans.

supported by the Commons but opposed by the twenty bishops, all of whom were Mary's appointees, in the House of Lords – the legislation passed by a tiny majority, after two Catholic bishops were arrested on spurious charges.

An early impact of her reign on religious life was the inscribing in large black lettering on the walls of all parish churches the Ten Commandments, the Nicene Creed and the Lord's Prayer. These are no longer visible at St Albans, but the remnants of similar lettering of other texts visible on the piers supporting the western arch of the tower give an idea what they would have looked like. The town charter was reconfirmed by Elizabeth, who also granted a new charter, called the Wine Charter, which empowered the corporation to license two people to sell wine, the proceeds of which were to fund the school, which was re-born in its new premises, the former lady chapel. To underline the separation of the school from the abbey church a new north/south public right of way was created between the saints chapel, using the stone from the destroyed shrine to build a wall to fill the space between the three arches. As the century wore on the town corporation, the new owners of the abbey, began to find other uses of the abbey in addition to worship: in 1588, at the height of the Spanish Armada, lead was stripped from the roof to make bullets, while in 1589 and 1594 the abbey was used as an alternative to the Hertford Assize Court and the Westminster High Court because of outbreaks of plague. As a thank-you, Queen Elizabeth authorised a brief to allow money to be collected at church services throughout the London diocese for the benefit of the abbey, to be spent on repairs and upkeep. It is not known how much money was raised or how it was spent.

The Stuart dynasty

To the general surprise of the nation – and dismay of the Scots – James I was enthusiastically supportive of the Elizabethan Settlement and endeavoured to maintain its inclusivity by the judicious balancing of the Catholic and Puritan extremes that fell within the Church of England. All shades of ecclesiastical opinion attended the Hampton Court Conference, called early in his reign in 1604. This conference resulted in the confounding of Puritan hopes of some sort of recognition, their only recompense being the promise a new English translation of the Bible in 1611, the so-called Authorised Version. This, together with the improvement of clerical education and various legal modifications ensuring the independence of Church estates, resulted in what Diarmaid

MacCulloch has called the Golden Age of the Church of England[166]. In the following year, 1612, King James visited St Albans and was so impressed that he authorised a brief to be served nationwide to raise funds for much needed repairs 'out of pious inclination to preserve so ancient a monument.'[167] Was this the first recorded instance of a monarch recognising the importance of the Abbey as a national asset? The brief was very successful, providing about £2,000 which was spent, most probably, on the presbytery roof, and was memorialised in an inscription over the cedar tree door (unfortunately not surviving the nineteenth-century restoration) which included the following lines:

> In zeal to Heav'n where Holy Alban bones
> Were buried, Offa raised this heap of stones
> Which, after devouring parts had life infused
> By James the First of England to become
> The glory of Alban's Proto martyrdom.

The repairs were completed in 1623.

However, despite these good intentions on the part of King James I, the fundamentalist or puritanical wing of the Church became increasingly alarmed at a perceived drift, despite the exposure 1605 Gunpowder Plot, towards Rome with the appointment of Catholic-inclined bishops and James' marriage to the only nominally Protestant Princess Anne of Denmark. This tendency was even more pronounced with the succession of Charles I and his appointment of Laud as archbishop of Canterbury. Laud was not a Catholic (although the pope offered him a cardinal's hat) but had no time for the puritanical wing of the Church, for whom he made life as difficult as he could. This resulted in the migration of Puritans, initially to Holland and subsequently, as the Pilgrim Fathers, to North America. Where they led many others followed, including a party of sixty-seven St Albans residents who fled to Massachusetts in 1637.

Civil War and Interregnum

The Elizabethan Settlement served religious life in England well, containing in its big tent the complete range of religious observance from puritanical to Catholic. But this meta-stable situation was

---

[166] Diarmaid MacCulloch: *Reformation – Coda: a British Legacy*.
[167] HO Cavalier: *King James I and St Albans Abbey*.

increasingly imperilled by the Roman Catholic leanings of Charles I to the extent that the settlement was effectively broken. The political implications of the drift towards Catholicism were just as profound as the religious ones. Both James and Charles had little time – and even less respect – for Parliament, which in turn retaliated by refusing to approve any fundraising taxation. This estrangement resulted in the Grand Remonstrance (1641), a document drawn up by the House of Commons comprehensively itemising the many failings of the monarch (without explicitly criticising him) and the Root and Branch Bill. One of the key requirements of this was the expulsion of bishops from the House of Lords and the convening in 1643 of a General Synod to advise Parliament on the reform of the Church in England. The Westminster Assembly of Divines, as the synod became known, was composed of two representatives from each county – one of the Hertfordshire delegates being Dr Thomas Westfield, the Archdeacon of St Albans. The assembly proposed sweeping changes – a Presbyterian form of Church government, on the Scottish model, and in 1646 a new confession of faith, a statement of belief which was Calvinist and Presbyterian in form. But Presbyterians, although reflecting the majority view in Parliament, were opposed by the Independents whose power base was the army. The Independents favoured a far looser Church system than the Presbyterians' centralist structure and with the increasing success and prestige of the army the Presbyterian leadership in Parliament was ousted from power. Many priests, thirty-three in Hertfordshire, were unwilling to forsake their previous vows based on the Elizabethan Act of Settlement, and were consequently divested of their livings.

Topographically and historically St Albans was in the Parliamentary camp: Parliamentary forces under the Earl of Essex arrived in St Albans in 1642 en route for Edgehill and subsequently the earl made St Albans the headquarters of his army of 15,000 men, defending the northern approaches to London. In 1648 Fairfax used the abbey for a convention of a council of senior officers to draft the Army Deed of Remonstrance, which led directly to the trial and execution of King Charles I in 1649.

Under the guidance of Cromwell as the Lord Protector, the English Church became more widely based than it had ever been. Catholicism was tolerated, Anglicans were left alone as an upper-class sect, the prohibition of Jews was lifted and the parishes left to their own devices. Dissenters were tolerated and even John Bunyan, with the publication of his popular seminal book *The Pilgrim's Progress*, eventually became a national treasure. Nevertheless, popular resentment against the interregnum governments, their imposition of high levels of taxation, the closure of theatres, the abolition of Christmas and a broad revulsion of Puritan austerity led to the restoration of the monarchy and the re-establishment of the Church of England.

Restoration of the monarchy

Towards the end of the Protectorate, Richard Cromwell, Oliver's son and successor as Lord Protector, lost control of the army, Parliament and the nation's finances. In an increasingly anarchic situation Richard called for fresh elections for a new protectorate Parliament that was dominated by Presbyterians. This provoked the overweening puritanical faction within the army, led by General Lambert, to dissolve Parliament and force Richard to resign. This action prompted the moderate Presbyterian George Monck, the commander of the army in Scotland, to march south to London, causing all opposition from Lambert to evaporate. On arrival in London Monck restored the expelled Presbyterian MPs to Parliament and set about elections for a new Parliament, which he called a 'Convention' on the grounds that only the monarch could call for a new Parliament. In response to a growing popular support in favour of restoration of the monarchy, he encouraged Charles II, in exile in Holland, to declare his position on a possible return. This Charles did in the form of the Declaration of Breda in which he indicated, in very broad terms, conciliatory policies towards former republicans and tolerance of religious differences: 'a liberty to tender consciences, and that no man shall be disquieted or called in question for differences of opinion in matter of religion which do not disturb the peace of the kingdom'.

This approach by Charles was sufficient for the Convention parliament to proclaim him as the lawful sovereign. Charles landed at Dover, where he was greeted, in the words of Samuel Pepys, an eye witness: 'and so got on shore when the King did, who was received by General Monke with all imaginable love and respect ... Infinite the Croud of people and the gallantry of the Horsemen, Citizens, Noblemen of all sorts. The Shouting and joy expressed by all is past imagination'.

Although the Presbyterians had hoped that the new king would restore the Church on Scottish Presbyterian lines, and had supported his return on that basis, it was immediately apparent that restoration of the monarchy went hand-in-hand with the restoration of the episcopy. Within a year of Charles accession, the doubtless poor relations between the Anglican and Presbyterian wings of the Church of England were further strained by the Conference of Savoy, at which twelve bishops and twelve Presbyterians were tasked to review the Book of Common Prayer: no agreement between the two parties was possible, the Anglicans willing to accept only minor changes to Cranmer's 1559 version, which was fundamentally unacceptable to the Presbyterians. This hard-line attitude in the Church was in tune with the feeling in the country: fresh parliamentary elections in 1661 returned a royalist majority, the so-called Cavalier Parliament. In the subsequent 1662 Act of Uniformity the use of the lightly edited Book of Common Prayer was made obligatory and required all holders of public office to conform. Nearly 3,000 ministers felt unable to do so and were ejected from office. Charles' undertaking in the Declaration of Breda that no man would be 'disquieted' on account of religious differences was ignored by the triumphant episcopy and the Cavalier Parliament. The persecution, though low-level, continued and was legalised by the Conventicle Act of 1664, which banned all Nonconformist gatherings of more than five people and the Five Mile Act, which required Nonconformist ministers to live at least 5 miles distant from their previous parish. Both acts were designed to impede the growth of nonconformism and both failed, to the extent that by 1669 in St Albans there were conventicles (congregations) of over 150.

The only area where all protestants – Anglican, Presbyterian and Puritan – could agree was the overwhelming necessity of replacing the Catholic King James II with Charles' son-in-law, the staunchly Calvinist William of Orange. With the vacuum caused by the flight of James another Convention was called to consider the constitutional position. After William's coronation, one of the first measures this Whig-led Convention, now converted to a parliament, to pass was a toleration act, which gave Nonconformists the right to worship legally, but still denied them full civil rights. Incomplete though the freedom was this act effectively marked the end of the period of turmoil that the country had endured since the dissolution of the monasteries in 1539.

13

The Long Eighteenth Century: The Great Slumber

The illustrious House of Hanover and Protestant Succession
To these I do allegiance swear – while they can hold possession.
For in my faith and loyalty I never more will falter,
And my lawful king shall be – until the times do alter.

(Chorus)
And this be law, that I'll maintain until my dying day, sir
That whatsoever king may reign, Still I'll be the Vicar of Bray, sir.

Song: *The Vicar of Bray*, last verse.

Background

The overall outcome of the turmoil described in the previous chapter was a rift in the national culture which left the Church of England shorn of both its Catholic and Puritanical wings. The Elizabethan Settlement, designed to create an inclusive Church in which the whole range of Christian devotional practice could feel at home, was intended to de-politicise religion in England. This strategy was supported by James I, Elizabeth's successor, to the disappointment of the Scottish Presbyterians who had great hopes that a Scottish king would impose a Scottish system of Church governance on England. Despite James' best efforts the internal tensions were too great for this accommodation to survive, so that by the time that William and Mary acceded to the throne, and with the passing of the Tolerance Act, both the Catholics and the many and various shades of Puritans, known collectively as Nonconformists, broke away from the national Church. Partly because the law required all holders of public office to be communicant members of the Church of England. The squirearchy – the landowners and the mercantile classes, collectively known as Anglicans – provided the bulk of the membership of the Church of England. Far from de-politicising religion, the Anglicans and the Nonconformists became closely associated with the Tories and the Whigs, respectively – an association that was to last for several hundred years, popularly codified as church or chapel.

The Sleeping Congregation by William Hogarth (1736). The congregation dozes (or dreams of lunch) through an interminable sermon while the clerk's thoughts are obviously elsewhere. (Courtesy of the Art Institute of Chicago)

Both the Catholic and the Nonconformist wings of the former national Church tended to take their religion more seriously than did the majority of Anglicans, many of whom attended church out of necessity. The Church of England, therefore, bereft of the devotional zeal of the Noncomformists, inevitably sank deeper into a state of atrophy: no developments of any significance took place in the Church of England during the eighteenth century. This somnolence is all the more remarkable by comparison with the almost frantic pace of change in wider society – the scientific revolution, triggered in England by the foundation of the Royal Society in 1660 and the publication of Newton's *Principia Mathematica* in 1687; the technological revolution kick-started by Newcomen's invention of a steam engine to power mine water pumps in 1702; the financial and commercial revolution initiated by the founding of the Bank of England in 1694 and the formation of the Stock Exchange soon after. Above all there was the overarching revolution of ideas known as the Enlightenment. While none of these developments were overtly anti-religious, they were, being founded on reason, strongly opposed to religious mysticism.

The contrast between the torpor of the Church of England and the energy of other aspects of national life if anything grew as the eighteenth century wore on. England became richer and more materialistic. The Hanoverian monarchy, irrespective of the personal faith of its individual monarchs, took less and less interest in the health of the Church. Trade usurped religion as the national preoccupation. Nonconformism received an enormous boost from the activities of John Wesley, the founder of Methodism, who was originally a frustrated Anglican minister. This further reduced the membership of the Church: in St Albans the number of communicants dropped by nearly 20 per cent.[168]

While it is easy to indulge in the fun poked by Hogarth of the eighteenth century Church of England, it has to be acknowledged that the Church played an important role at parish level as an agent of the state responsible, to a considerable extent, for education and the administration of charity. Staffed, for the most part, by good clergy and conscientious squires, it formed the backbone of primary education and poor relief: practical Christianity, which was seen as important as Christian piety. However, this key role began to fall short of what was required as the century wore on because of the strain imposed on the parish structure by the rapid expansion in the urban population. For example, the population of London rose from 600,000 in 1701 to about one million at the end of the century and in the absence of either any significant church-building or any state support the secular contribution of the Church inevitably fell short of what was required.

---

[168] Mark Freeman: *The Story of St Albans*.

The abbey church

Parish activities

Throughout this period the parish of St Albans, in common with its archdeaconry, was part of the diocese of London, an enormous diocese which included all of Essex as well as the city itself. It must have felt, in St Albans, that they were something of an outlier – there was no historical background to foster any closeness and no Bishop of London is recorded as ever visiting the Abbey: the four centuries of St Albans monastic supremacy was not so easily to be forgotten or forgiven. The eighteenth-century bishops of London did not share, on the whole, the enthusiasm and piety that characterised the Methodists. This relaxed attitude is nicely illustrated by a bishop describing his see, on his inauguration, as the 'Mare Pacificum'[169].

The population of St Albans in this period was about 3,000, distributed amongst the four parishes of which the abbey church was one. Bearing in mind that Nonconformists made up to 20 per cent of the total, the Abbey's congregation could not have been much more than 600, barely large enough to support the stipend of the rector. However, the abbey was a source of great pride to the mayor and corporation who were obliged to attend the Sunday service every week, fully robed. All services were held in the crossing – the choir, presbytery and the transepts – partly because the relatively small numbers of the congregation, partly because the extraordinary length of the nave had originally been designed to accommodate monastic processions, which were now very much out of favour, and partly because of the increasingly derelict state of the nave.

The crossing was gradually customised to suit its new role as parish church, centred round the construction of a grand pulpit required for the delivery of sermons, which were seen as a key element in the Protestant church. At St Albans this was located adjacent to the south-west tower pier. Provision was also made of upholstered box pews for the sole use of the mayor and corporation. Inevitably the gentry of the parish followed suit, their location and luxury denoting the owner's position in the social hierarchy. Eventually the only space left for the poor was benches at the back of the transepts. Crucially the lower part of the two eastern piers supporting the tower were cut back to create a more circular space, thereby improving sightlines: this was to have serious structural consequences. Galleries were constructed in the choir to the west of the

---

[169] DW Barrett: *Sketches of Church Life in the Counties of Essex and Hertfordshire*.

tower and in the north transept to accommodate the schoolboys. The floors were levelled and repaved.

Services were conducted, in the seventeenth and eighteenth centuries, without any musical accompaniment from either an organ or choir although some informal music making may have emerged as the eighteenth century wore on.

In addition to this customisation, other alterations were made, prompted by the baroque style that Christopher Wren had used for the fifty-one replacement churches he designed following the Fire of London in 1666. The overall aim of the alterations was to de-Gothicise as much of the early English and decorated work in the abbey as possible. Thus the Gothic tracery of the great west doors were encased in pine planks, the floor level raised where necessary to avoid steps and repaved, the tower windows partially blocked up to create circular windows (as at St Stephen Walbrook) and a shallow 'saucer dome' erected in the tower lantern (possibly emulating that in St Mary Abchurch, London).

Public interest in the Abbey

Despite official neglect – there was no visit by royalty at all in the eighteenth century, for instance – interest in the Abbey from a topographical and antiquarian point of view slowly gathered momentum throughout this period. The first record we have of such interest is a visit by the Dutch artist Jan Lievens in the early 1630s. His sketch of the Abbey

An engraving of Jan Lievens' painting of the Abbey church from the south west showing the flat roofs and the perpendicular windows of the west front and the south transept together with the Hertfordshire spike on top of the tower. (Courtesy of St Albans Cathedral.)

shows the remains of some of the monastic buildings as well as landscape features such as cattle and people.

Soon after this visit, one of the first and best known antiquaries, Sir William Dugdale, produced a description of English religious houses called the *Monasticon Anglicanum*, which contained an engraving of the abbey by Daniel King (1655). Subsequent visitors – or tourists – included a Thomas Baskerville who visited St Albans in 1677, which he dismissed as 'an ancient old fabric and now much decayed.' This view was endorsed by Celia Fiennes, who toured the whole country on horseback and visited St Albans in 1697 en route from Coventry to London and noted: 'it is now much out of repair … the whole Church is so worn away it mourns for some charitable person to help repair it'.

One of the legacies of the work of Sir William Dugdale and his associates was the foundation, in 1717, of the Society of Antiquaries, which was subsequently responsible for kindling interest in Gothic architecture and in ancient buildings. The society's first secretary, William Stukeley, visited the Abbey in 1720 and published several drawings of the interior: that of the Wallingford Screen is reproduced.

Sir William Stukeley's drawing of the Wallingford Screen at St Albans as it appeared in 1723, after the removal of the central crucifix, the high altar and all statuary. (Courtesy of St Albans Cathedral.)

Possibly as a result of this publicity Nicholas Hawkesmoor, the Hertfordshire-born architect of Blenheim Palace, visited St Albans at the time when he was busy with the design of the twin towers at the west end of Westminster Abbey. He produced a view of the north elevation of the Abbey as seen from the top of the clocktower in order to raise funds for the Abbey's repair and maintenance, with the plea: 'Support this venerable pile from being martyred by the neglect of a Slouthfull generation'.

A succession of artists and antiquarians visited the Abbey thereafter. In 1742 the Buck brothers published a book entitled *Antiquities and Venerable Remains* which included the engraving of another elevation of the Abbey, this time from the south west.

Nathaniel Buck's engraving of the south elevation of the abbey (1737). (Courtesy of St Albans Cathedral.)

The last artist to visit and paint the Abbey – and by far the most accomplished – was Thomas Girtin: his painting of the crossing and presbytery of 1795 gives a convincing impression of its appearance shortly before the restorers got to work.

An engraving from the Girtin painting. (Courtesy of St Albans Cathedral.)

The Abbey fabric

While the Church of England, and its congregations, slumbered, so the state of the fabric of the abbey church deteriorated. The story of the fabric of the abbey church, following the Dissolution, was one of steady decline, interrupted only by isolated and inadequate campaigns of repair. This decline was unsurprising considering the small population of the parish relative to the size of its church – by some margin the largest parish church in the country. The Abbey had no endowments and its maintenance was the responsibility of the town corporation whose only source of funding dedicated to the abbey was the income derived from renting the moot hall – perhaps £10 a year. To raise money from a wider population – regional or national – required the issue of a brief authorised by the monarch. The process of securing a brief was initiated by a petition from the mayor and corporation supported by the local gentry and parishioners. The strong impression, from the wording of the briefs, is that the laity cared very much about the abbey fabric.

In the period between Dissolution and the 1662 Settlement this funding was augmented by two briefs allowing nationwide church collections to be donated to St Albans. The first authorised by Queen Elizabeth I in 1596 and the second by King James I in 1613 are described in the previous chapter. Together they brought in £3,000 – £4,000 so that the average annual spend on maintenance in this 120-year period would have been in the order of £30, equivalent to £9,000 today. No money is recorded as having been spent on maintenance and repair during the reign of King Charles I or the Protectorate. This level of expenditure, significantly less than that in monastic times, was clearly inadequate for such a huge and ancient building, even though the money was well spent on essential structural repairs to the saints chapel and its roof.

In the 170-year period following the 1662 Settlement three further briefs were authorised, by King Charles II (1681), King George I (1723) and King George III (1766). These, together with other donations, brought in a total of about £10,000 – an average annual budget of about £60 or £12,000 in today's money.

The case for funding made in King Charles 1683 Brief, stated

> that this great Parish Church in the Borough of St Alban, having had the continued favour in and since the first foundation thereof of divers our worthy progenitors, more particularly of our grandfather King James of blessed memory, is now in so great decay that the ruins thereof are dangerous and offensive to divers our loving subjects who resort thither

to the service of Almighty God; and the cost of repairing the same, moderately computed, will amount to at least 6000l.[170]

Funds raised by this brief were supplemented by a grant from an ecclesiastical fund by William and Mary and the total money raised was nearly £3,000. This sum was further increased by substantial donations from Sir Harbottle Grimston, a prominent St Albans citizen, interested aristocracy, the Bishops of Winchester and Norwich and several Cambridge colleges. The most generous donation was made by John Cole, the Archdeacon of St Albans, who gave £40 a year for seven years between 1692 and 1717[171]. Most of this money was spent on structural repairs – roof leadwork, window stonework and glazing brought about by the ravages of time and also by the Great Storm of 1703[172], which blew out the magnificent perpendicular window installed by Abbot William Wallingford in the fifteenth century. A local joiner was commissioned to replace this traceried window with a timber framed window, which given its size, about 8m wide and 10m high, was a rather optimistic venture that illustrates the severe shortage of funds. However, not all the available funds were spent on structural repairs or on routine maintenance: a considerable portion was spent on non-essential alterations to the interior such as the pulpit, the levelling and re-paving the floor, box pews and other changes required to conform with contemporary taste.

The next fundraising campaign was associated with the 1725 brief authorised by King George I. This brief, which referred to the Abbey as a 'beautiful and ancient fabric' had been issued 'in order to preserve so venerable a building, which had been repaired by the Parishioners according to the best of their abilities but notwithstanding their constant care and expense there now appears a very great crack quite through to the bottom of the south wall. The north wall is gone 18 inches from the upright with many cracks and flaws and the timber of the roof greatly decayed. The whole is, by length of time and want of large repairs in so dangerous a condition …'[173] The brief, which appealed for the (rather precise) sum of £5,750, was in response to the appearance of the crack in

---

[170] Robert Clutterbuck: *The History and Antiquities of the County of Hertfordshire Vol I (courtesy of SAHAAS Library)*.
[171] Earnest Gape: *St Albans Abbey in the Seventeenth and Eighteenth Centuries*.
[172] The great storm destroyed the Eddystone Lighthouse, sank twelve naval ships, tore down 17,000 trees and caused widespread flooding.
[173] AE Gibbs: *Two Briefs for Repairing the Abbey Church of St Albans from Middlesex and Hertfordshire 'Notes and Queries' Vol I (Courtesy of SAHAAS Library)*.

the south wall of the nave together with a pronounced lean. It is not clear how much money was actually raised nor the nature and extent of the repairs. However, subsequent nineteenth-century restoration showed that iron tie rods and S plates had been inserted to resist the outward thrust of the roof.

The last brief was authorised by King George III in 1764 to appeal for funds for more repairs to the presbytery roof and also for the wooden window frame of the south transept, which had only lasted sixty years since it was built. More seriously the gothic window arch that had been cut into the original Norman wall had pushed the transept walls and the corner turrets 30cm out of vertical. This was the first occasion that the Abbey had employed a professional architect, Robert Mylne, to carry out a survey and design the repairs. However, the poor response to the brief meant that only the repairs to the window itself could be afforded: the structural problems of the masonry went unaddressed.

And still disasters afflicted the Abbey: in 1797 runoff from a severe rainstorm flooded into the abbey through the north door, the drains being blocked. This resulted in differential settlements in the floor and of the north transept arch supporting the north east pillar of the tower: no action was taken. Thus, at the turn of the century collapse of the entire building began to look like a possible outcome, but with no clear plan or leadership available to tackle the deep-seated problems.

14

Rebirth

Can these bones live?

Ezekiel ch37 v3
The text for the sermon preached by the Archbishop
of Canterbury at the enthronement of Thomas Claughton
as the first Bishop of St Albans 1877.

The end of the great slumber

The Church of England slowly woke from its slumbers early in the nineteenth century in response to a combination of a variety of stimulants.

As we have seen, the Nonconformist community, always populous and prominent, grew throughout the eighteenth century, especially through the Wesleyan movement. Methodists were particularly strong in the north and west of England but also in the south east outside London, including St Albans. In 1828 government reforms removed the restriction that only members of the established Church were eligible for public office. This relaxation was extended, in 1829, to Catholics in an effort to appease Irish discontent. These changes may also have had the effect of shaking the established church out of its eighteenth-century complacency.

The Church of England felt it had to respond to these challenges, more especially in the 1830s when the Oxford Movement provided fresh competition from the other wing of the religious spectrum – high Church Anglicanism. The potency of this development was enhanced by the Tractarians love of ceremony, which coincided with the growing interest and appreciation by the laity in church architecture and the need for sensitive restoration.

Politics also played its part, if only indirectly. The victorious end of the Napoleonic war left Britain more self-confident. The government, nervous about social and cultural cohesion in the aftermath of the American and the French revolutions, reacted by paying more attention to religious affairs: the churches were seen, through their social and educational work, as a bulwark against revolutionary sentiments. Thus in 1818, under the Churches Building Act, a new authority, the Church Building Commission, was set up to enable the construction of some 600 new churches in London and in other newly industrialised conurbations.

Funds were also made available for church restoration and to this end an eminent architect, Lewis Wyatt, the nephew of the James Wyatt (of Fonthill fame) was appointed by the Commission to carry out a detailed survey of St Albans Abbey. His report, dated July 1818, gave a dismal description of the state of the Abbey, although he commented that 'the brick walls of the rudest Norman architecture were the strongest part of the fabric and appeared to be in tolerably sound state.' He recommended extensive repairs, which he estimated to cost £16,085. The chief areas of concern were the tower, the transepts and the western end of the nave. The tower had been weakened by the cutting away of the tower piers to provide more space in the early eighteenth century), the internal timber structure supporting the bells, the roof and the spire was rotten and imposed lateral forces which the tower could not indefinitely resist. The transept roofs were in a terminal and dangerous state, as was the south window of the south transept and the transept wall that supported it. As for the western five bays of the nave Wyatt recommended either the reconstruction or the buttressing of the upper south wall.

Nothing was done in response to this report, but Wyatt's warnings and recommendations were not entirely forgotten: nine years later the then rector, Henry Small, engaged Wyatt to return to carry out a review of his previous findings. He found that the state of the southwestern nave walls, which he described as being 'crippled', had deteriorated. But still nothing was done.

The 1832 collapse

Wyatt's warning was realised in February 1832 when a portion of the upper south wall of the nave, which had a pronounced outward lean, collapsed at clerestory level. Following this event Cottingham, a rising star in the architectural firmament and recently engaged to restore Rochester Cathedral, was appointed to carry out a structural survey of the abbey and report on recommended remedial measures and costs. There is no record of any further involvement by Lewis Wyatt, whose speciality was in country houses. Cottingham's survey was professional and thorough. His general comment was that the Norman brickwork of the towers and adjoining walls were in better condition than the more recent stonework.

Concerning the nave, he identified that the fifteenth-century replacement of the original pitched aisle roofs by nearly flat lead-covered roofs had exposed the ashlar of the external face, which had previously been protected by the original pitched roofs of the aisles, had since been subjected to nearly 300 years of exposure to the elements. This, he concluded, had penetrated the inadequately pointed walls thus exposed and was responsible for the lean of the triforium walls. This outward movement of the walls had shifted support to the roof trusses from the wall plates to the inner ashlar facing – a very dangerous situation. He found that the repairs effected in the 1720s had included the insertion of iron tie rods to prevent any further leaning but these tie rods themselves needed replacing. The ends of some of the massive transverse beams had rotted and had become detached from the wall plates, so transferring their share of the load to the inner ashlar wall facing and to other, sounder beams which resulted in distortion of the structure and the ingress of rainwater. Other fifteenth-century architectural modifications had also resulted in structural problems: the large perpendicular windows at the west front of the nave (replacing Early English windows) and at the south front of the south transept (replacing Norman windows) had imposed lateral forces on the walls for which they had not been designed, resulting in a pronounced lean at these locations. There were also the usual problems associated with poor or non-existent maintenance – blocked drainage, rising damp, rusting glazing bars, eroded pointing – which although not dramatic, were equally serious.

Cottingham recommended extensive repairs, the cost of which he estimated at £14,000[174].

In response a public meeting was called by the 1st Earl of Verulam in his capacity as the Lord Lieutenant of Hertfordshire. The meeting, which was chaired by the earl (thus beginning a lifelong commitment to the abbey) raised £4,000 by public conscription. Of this £1,700 was incurred in expenses, which presumably included the temporary shoring required immediately after the collapse, so the net amount was well short of the £14,000 required. Repairs were carried out under the management of a committee comprising the earl, the archdeacon, a banker, the earl's son Viscount Grimston and the rector. L N Cottingham was appointed as architect The money was spent on the rebuilding of the collapsed section of the south clerestory wall, by extending the rotted ends of the nave roof beams with cast iron caps and the repair of the damaged south aisle roof.

---

[174] Cottingham: *Report of Survey and Estimate for the Repairs*.

Yet again there were insufficient funds for the fundamentals of the problem to be tackled, although the tower spire was also removed to reduce the load on the timber structure inside the tower and work was also carried out on the windows with the rebuilding of the south-facing south transept window and the reglazing of some of the clerestory windows. Other work, less necessary for structural safety, was also carried out, including the removal of the saucer dome at the crossing and the restoration of the lantern windows in the tower which had been partially blocked in the seventeenth century to make them appear circular. All the available funds had been spent by the end of 1834 – luckily the available funds didn't stretch to Cottingham's more wayward recommendation of rebuilding the nave roof with a mansard roof and plastering the external faces of the tower with a dark-stained render.

The Abbey church, which had been closed since 1832, was reopened to the public with the Bishop of London, Charles Blomfield, officiating: at last some notice of St Albans was being taken.

Dr Henry Nicholson

On the 13 February 1835, a few months after the re-opening of the church, Dr Henry Nicholson was appointed rector of St Albans. This was to be the corporation's last appointment, as later that year the Municipal Corporations Act disqualified municipal authorities from owning an advowson, which had given them the privilege of recommending the appointment of their rectors. In the case of St Albans this was rather ironic, because Nicholson turned out to be their best rectoral appointment in the 280 years the corporation had owned the advowson. It also meant that the corporation, or the town council as it became, no longer had any direct responsibility for maintenance and repair of the fabric of the abbey. Nicholson, who promptly bought the advowson, was on his own, answerable only to his bishop, who at that time continued to show little interest in St Albans.

Fortunately Nicholson was the right man for the job – young (forty years old when appointed), well connected and, as a fellow of the Society of Antiquaries, passionate about the conservation of medieval buildings. It was Nicholson, working with sparse resources, who kept the flame of restoration alight, and to this end, in 1845 and on the prompting of his archdeacon, he initiated the founding of the St Albans Society, the forerunner of the present St Albans and Hertfordshire Architectural and Archaeological Society (SAHAAS) and chaired its opening meeting in his rectory. From this initiative sprung the formation of a restoration committee to guide and champion future restoration work of the abbey. As the funds raised by the appeal following the 1832 collapse had been spent, money for further works was tight: to help raise funds Nicholson closed the abbey except for services and charged visitors sixpence per visit, equivalent to £2.50 in today's money. Funds were also raised by the time-honoured means of charity balls (the local press noted that at one such event the earl himself acted as an usher) and bazaars. The money available was well spent on relatively low-cost high-profile projects such as the restoration of the brass of Abbot De la Mare, the exposure of the thirteenth century murals on the nave piers, the *St William of York* mural and *The Incredulity of St Thomas* by the removal of the whitewash and the opening up of the triple arches at the east end of the Saints chapel. His passion and enthusiasm was infectious – he published an authoritative guide book, *Extracts from the History of the Abbey of St Alban and a Description of the Church*, and through his connections – his brother-in-law was a distinguished professor and a founder of the Royal Institute of British Architects, for instance – made sure the restoration project was widely publicised.

Towards a new diocese[175]

Despite Rector Nicholson's energy and commitment, it is likely that in time the restoration movement began to lose some of its momentum while at the same time the deep-seated structural defects of the abbey were getting worse. At the same time the Bishop of London, Charles Blomfield, wished to rationalise the highly irrational diocese boundaries that had evolved over the centuries. The situation that had pertained in the early nineteenth century was that determined following the dissolution of the monasteries: most of Hertfordshire was included in the diocese of Lincoln while Essex, together with the remainder of Hertfordshire – the archdeaconry of St Albans and the deanery of Braughing in the north of the county – was part of the diocese of London. This latter diocese only included the part of the city that lay on the north bank of the River Thames: south-west London was included in the diocese of Winchester while south-east London was claimed by Rochester. Blomfield's grand plan was to swap the Essex and

---

[175] Owen Chadwick: The Victorian Diocese of St Albans in Cathedral and City ed Robert Runcie.

Hertfordshire part of his diocese with the south-east London part of the Rochester diocese and to take south-west London from the Winchester diocese, so that the London diocese would include the entire city. In the event the Rochester part of the swap was realised in 1846, when all of Hertfordshire was transferred to the diocese of Rochester. Unfortunately, other deaneries in the Rochester diocese – Malling and Shoreham – were transferred to Canterbury, at the same time leaving Rochester with a diocese that comprised just a small area of Kent: the Rochester Deanery together with the whole of Essex and Hertfordshire, separated by the Thames estuary. Clearly such an arrangement could not work – the original concept of dioceses was that they should share the same boundaries as counties – and it became apparent that what was really needed was a new bishopric north of the Thames. At the very least it was agreed that the Bishop of Rochester could not live in and operate from Rochester and should move his palace and centre of operations to Essex. A suitable house was purchased – Danbury Place near Chelmsford.

By mid-century the London population had grown to about 2.7 million, more than double its number in 1800, and some 240 churches had been built. A new cathedral in Essex or Hertfordshire was widely believed to be necessary, although there was a persistent strain of opinion that the Church needed more priests, not bishops. There were several candidates for a new cathedral: St Albans, on account of its historical foundation, Colchester or Chelmsford, obviously the Essex preference, and the compromise candidate of Bishops Stortford on account of its central position. The *Times* carried a report (15 November 1846) that St Albans had been selected. Prime Minister Lord John Russell, in a fruitless effort to ingratiate himself with the established Church after his support for Catholic emancipation, also proposed St Albans, but later withdrew the plan. In 1852 the government appointed the Cathedral and Collegiate Churches Commission to inquire into the state of these churches and, amongst other things, to consider how their revenues might be made available for the establishment of new sees. Under the chairmanship of Archbishop Sumner of Canterbury, the commissioners agreed in their final report (1856) that a new see north of London was indeed desirable but made no recommendation as to where such a see might be sited. The great and good of St Albans, led by the 2nd Earl of Verulam, had lobbied hard in favour of the Abbey, but to no avail, perhaps because at that time the structure of the abbey was far from secure and the commission may have been wary about taking on the liability of choosing for its new cathedral an abbey in such an advanced state of decay.

George Gilbert Scott

In April of 1856, shortly before the final and inconclusive report of the commission was published, the 2nd Earl of Verulam, following in his father's footsteps, called another public meeting in the town hall with the dual purpose of the further restoration of the abbey and its candidacy as the new cathedral. The meeting resolved to set up a committee to manage restoration – the 'Reparation Committee' – and to coordinate fundraising. The usual personages were appointed to the committee: the archdeacon, the rector, a local worthy, with the earl as chairman. Also present at the meeting, by chance, was a wealthy barrister named Mr Edmund Beckett Denison who fancied himself as an amateur architect: of him more later in the chapter.

Unfortunately many donors had qualified their support with the condition that it was subject to St Albans Abbey being selected as the new cathedral, and as time wore on with no decision, these donors demanded their money back. Nevertheless there were enough funds to resume some work and Mr Gilbert Scott was appointed architect, Cottingham having died in 1847. In all £14,000 was donated in the period 1856–1870.[176]

Gilbert Scott, one of the best known architects of the Gothic Revival school, had long held a fascination for St Albans Abbey perhaps initiated by a memory of hearing his aunt Gilbert sing a nursery rhyme, 'When Verulam stood/St Albans was a wood/Now St Albans is a town/ Verulam's thrown down.' This fascination was intensified by a promise, never fulfilled, from his uncle to visit the abbey, but it wasn't until he turned to architecture that he 'almost dreamed of St Albans'. It was then, when he was articled to a London firm of architects, that he managed a visit, which he recalled 'with intense delight' as part of a walking tour with his brother John[177]. He steadily grew in architectural experience and reputation so that by the time he was appointed as the architect of St Albans he was perhaps the pre-eminent ecclesiastical architect of his time, a fact that can only have boosted the St Albans campaign.

However, the funds at the disposal of the Reparation Committee were insufficient to carry out the programme of work deemed necessary by Gilbert Scott: as previously only relatively inexpensive restoration works could be afforded. These included the removal of substantial quantities of earth from the interior of the nave and transepts to restore the original

---

[176] Charles Jones FSA: Restoration of the abbey church.
[177] Sir George Gilbert Scott: Personal and Professional Recollections.

medieval floor levels, which were subsequently repaved, the construction of drains to relieve the problem of rising damp, and the opening up of partially blocked west-facing windows in the south transept. The restoration work in this period was the result of a fruitful cooperation between Scott and the rector, Dr Nicholson, who died in 1866: Scott evidently had a good working relationship with the rector, to whom he paid the tribute: 'No man has been more zealous for the conservation of the church than he. He not only preserved the church from increasing dilapidation but carried out many efficient reparations and restorations out of the scantiest resources.'

On the 1 August 1870, while attending divine service, John Chapple, Scott's clerk of works, heard a loud cracking noise: an immediate investigation after the service showed that the north-east pier supporting the tower showed signs of severe distress[178]. In consultation with Scott, who was unwell in Chester, a system of timber shoring was erected to support the weight of the massive tower and so inhibit further movement. Detailed inspections showed that strength of both the two eastern piers had been severely compromised by the seventeenth century cutting away of the base of the piers to create a more open – and less medieval – space at the crossing. In places almost 2m of brickwork had been removed. These massive piers had been constructed by the Normans with the construction of an outer shell, about 1m thick, of coursed brickwork which encased a rubble core. Cutting away, in places, the entire thickness of the outer case effectively removed restraint on the inner rubble, which was unable to resist the loading. To make matters worse the integrity of the pier foundations had also been compromised. It had been noted that the flooding of the north transept in 1797 (see Chapter 13) had caused the transept arch supporting the north-east pier to subside, which indicated the friable nature of the foundations, due partly, in Scott's opinion, to the numerous graves dug in the vicinity. The base of the pier was underpinned with concrete and the missing brickwork replaced. The foundations of the south-east pier were even worse: investigations revealed a cavern nearly 2m in diameter had been excavated under the pier foundations, which was supported simply by a forest of timber struts. Gilbert Scott conjectured that this work had been done immediately after the Dissolution with the intention of destroying the building by setting fire to the struts, but that this process had been countermanded in time – no attempt having subsequently been made to fill in the cavern. The

---

[178] John Chapple: The Restoration of St Albans Abbey, 1874.

restoration of the tower base, which comprised filling the cavities and rebuilding the outer case of the piers where it had been cut away, lasted several years, during which time all services were held in the nave.

Such a muscular approach was not required for restoration work carried out at the same time at the east end of the abbey. A major advance here was made possible in 1867 by the replacement of the abbey gateway as the town prison by a new purpose-built prison elsewhere in the town. This enabled the school to purchase the gateway – at a cost of £1,100 – and thus vacate the lady chapel, once the gateway itself had been refurbished in 1871. In his report to the Marchioness of Salisbury on the condition of the lady chapel and its ante-chapel Scott wrote, 'When we come to consider the present condition of these chapels which were once of resplendent architectural beauty, how melancholy is the contrast.' This led to a committee comprising the Ladies Salisbury, Verulam, Essex and Cowper to initiate the necessary restoration[179]. At about this time (1872), as a result of the restoration work, considerable quantities of finely carved stone fragments were recovered: it became apparent that these pieces were from the two medieval shrines, smashed at the time of the Dissolution in the sixteenth century. By dint of patient and painstaking effort, the clerk of works, John Chapple, and the foreman succeeded in reconstructing the shrine, which was placed in its original position in the Saints chapel. This work was a great psychological boost: the need for a focus for pilgrimage had not much diminished in the centuries since the destruction of the shrine in 1540 and its re-creation enhanced the St Albans campaign.

However, it was not possible to close the track through the church between the saints chapel and the lady chapel, which Scott described as 'a monstrous piece of vandalism' until the land east of the lady chapel could be bought so a diversion could be provided. This took a lot of time and money and wasn't accomplished until 1878.

Once the tower had been stabilised, the only major structural challenge remaining was the condition of the nave. Here the five westernmost bays of the south wall leaned out of the vertical. This had first been noted in the eighteenth century but nothing had been done to correct this lean, which had got steadily worse: by the 1870s it was as much as 70cm out of plumb. To correct this, Scott (by now Sir Gilbert) devised an ambitious system of jacking to push the entire wall – over 30m long and 20m high – back to verticality. To do this he braced and stiffened the north wall, which only had a modest outward lean, and built a

---

[179] J Chapple: The Restoration of the abbey church of St Alban.

framework of scaffolding to relieve the south wall of the weight of the roof: this work, which involved the use of some 600 tonnes of timber, was paid for by E. B. Denison, who also claimed to contribute to the design of the operation. He was, however, highly dismissive of Scott's plan, 'A vast deal of absurd fuss was made about this really simple and easy work... his (Scott's) design for the machinery was quite wrong as anybody could see who understood mechanics'[180]. This tells us more about Dennison than it does about Scott. The actual jacking was performed by hydraulic jacks pushing on the outside of the south wall and screw ties pulling the wall from the north. Once vertical, the foundations of the south wall were underpinned while the upper wall was supported at triforium level by brick-built flying buttresses, which were concealed in the south aisle roof space, and which were in turn supported by massive buttresses.

It is thanks to Scott that the abbey was saved from collapse.

Jacking the south wall of the nave back to verticality. The success of this remarkable operation, which even today would present a considerable engineering challenge, demonstrates the extent of Scott's engineering skills. The brick-built flying buttresses are clearly visible amongst the jacks and scaffolding. (Courtesy of St Albans Cathedral.)

---

[180] Sir Edmund Beckett: *St Albans Cathedral and its Restoration*.

The realisation of the dream

Although Archbishop Sumner's report of 1856 on the reorganisation of the diocese of London, Rochester and Winchester was inconclusive, the need for a new bishopric north of the Thames had been recognised and this need became ever more acute as the London population continued its rapid growth – from 2.7 to 3.9 million between 1851 and 1871 – and the unworkability of the revised Rochester diocese became more apparent. To add to these demographic pressures bishops began to modify the way they carried out their ministry: they discovered railways and instead of infrequent mass ordinations and confirmations in their cathedrals, railways facilitated confirmations and ordinations in parish churches, which was pastorally more effective but less efficient, necessitating more bishops and the introduction of suffragans. The Bishop of Winchester, Samuel Wilberforce, a member of the Churches Commission, championed this trend by taking his ministry to the people and did more than anybody to make new bishops necessary.[181] Now Wilberforce was a close friend of Thomas Claughton[182], who had been consecrated Bishop Rochester in 1867. Surely the two friends must have discussed the need for a rationalisation and the means by which one could be achieved. Certainly Claughton, living in his palace of Danbury in Essex, regarded himself as the Bishop of Hertfordshire and Essex and the fact that his cathedral was situated in Kent was but an inconvenience. He was determined that one day St Albans Abbey would be his cathedral.

The lack of enthusiasm for selecting St Albans as the new cathedral in the 1856 report was due, in large measure, to the ruinous state of the abbey and the lack of funds available to establish its endowment. The heroic achievements of the Restoration Committee since 1856, funded by public donations, well publicised and carried out under the supervision of Sir Gilbert Scott, the most prestigious church architect of the day, must have reassured the church on the first reservation. The re-launch of the restoration fund in 1871, together with heavyweight but discreet lobbying by the Marquis of Salisbury (whose wife was deeply involved with the restoration of the lady chapel) would have provided further reassurance. On the second reservation, the Claughton-Wilberforce friendship led to the offer by Wilberforce's successor as Bishop of Winchester, Harold Browne, of Winchester House, an enormous house used as the London

---

[181] Owen Chadwick: The Victorian Diocese of St Albans – in Cathedral and City, edited by Robert Runcie.
[182] DNB

residence of the bishops of Winchester. The house was valued at £70,000. On this basis the finances were deemed to be sufficient to present the Bishopric of Saint Albans Bill to Parliament on 12 March 1875. To ease its passage through the two readings against some opposition the home secretary, promoting the bill, remarked 'it must not be held to be a necessity in the Church of England that every Bishop who might be created in the future should have an income of £5,000 a year'[183] – £3,000 to £4,000 was considered more appropriate. This olive branch appeased enough – but not all – of the parliamentary opposition and the second reading was carried by 273 votes to 212 and the act received royal assent in June 1875.

There never seemed any doubt that Thomas Claughton would become the first bishop, although a 30 per cent pay cut may have tempered his delight. However, when it came to auction, Winchester House twice failed to reach its reserve price and was eventually sold to the government for £45,000, which was not enough on its own to endow the new bishopric. To make up the shortfall, £500 a year was transferred from both the Rochester and Winchester dioceses in respect of the parts of their dioceses transferred to St Albans. Following an appeal, public subscriptions provided a further £11,500[184] so that the new see at last became a reality by an order in council on 30 April 1877.

Bishop Claughton was enthroned in his new cathedral on 12 June 1877 by the Archbishop of Canterbury, who took Ezekiel 37 as the text for his sermon: 'shall these bones live; yea Lord thou knowest'. The enthronement was suitably magnificent, with 270 clergy in the procession. One year later he delivered his 'primary charge', a *tour d'horizon* or a summary of the state of the diocese and his hopes for its future starting with a plea for the two counties of Essex and Hertfordshire 'to unite for the promotion of the Christian faith in the diocese bearing the name of England' proto-martyr.' He goes on to acknowledge that there was much to do:

> the condition of the building itself is such that grudging, envious eyes would regard its renewal as a hopeless task, but surely what has been done is an earnest of what may be done. The beautiful Lady Chapel was a school ten years back. The process of ruin and decay had gone on for three centuries; earth lay piled against its walls, many feet thick. No man

---

[183] Hansard, Volume 222.
[184] DW Barrett: Sketches of Church Life – Diocese of St Albans.

> that entered it could have felt the slightest hope that it could ever be restored. Its beauty was a thing of the past. Look at it now: can any man look at it with any other feeling than that of thankfulness and hope?... One day an alarm was given, only too well founded, that the great tower was in danger of falling. Nothing but the promptness of those on the spot could have saved it from ruin. But saved it has been – is it too much to say by God's mercy? – for its fall would have entailed the loss of all we are now rejoicing in. If the establishment of the see of St Albans be a benefit and a blessing, as we all hope it may be, the fall of that tower, which was imminent, would have rendered it almost impossible. When all this had been done, by vigorous effort and great liberality, the ruinous condition of the nave, at its western end, called for no less prompt and vigorous effort... that too has been accomplished.

The address moves on to outline his ambitions for the future, to place St Albans on a level with other cathedrals through the creation of its chapter and a choral foundation: it was said that a bishop without a dean and chapter was like a general without a staff, although in reality it was the archdeacons who really mattered[185].

His most pressing challenge, however, was how to enhance the unity of his new diocese and in particular how to integrate the parishes of north-east London that it now included. Although Hertfordshire and Essex had been part of the same diocese – Rochester – since 1846 it didn't really feel united. The exchange of St Albans for Rochester as the diocese capital changed little: St Albans, situated in the south west of Hertfordshire, was about 100 miles from, say, Harwich in the north east of Essex. Moreover the new bishop lived at Danbury near Chelmsford in Essex, an inconveniently long journey from his new cathedral, so Bishop Claughton faced a daunting challenge. To help him he appointed a suffragan, Alfred Blomfield, as Bishop of Colchester, thus reviving a Henrician provision, in 1882.

The inclusion of the north-eastern suburbs of London in the diocese, for all its challenges, was a good thing as it lent respectability to the diocese, which was otherwise predominantly rural, liable to attack for being too Barchester-like. The area in question, mostly marshland in the early nineteenth century, grew rapidly with construction of the London Docks and the Beckton gas works, the largest in the world at that time. By the time of the formation of the St Albans diocese the population of this

---

[185] Keith Jones: personal communication.

London enclave had reached some 200,000 people, roughly the same as that of the whole of Hertfordshire. Claughton set up his Bishop of St Albans Fund to raise money from the diocese exclusively for his ministry in the area, which was liberally supported by the Marquis of Salisbury. This effort led to the appointment of a second suffragan, as Bishop of Barking.

Bishop Claughton retired in 1889, twelve years after his enthronement, eleven years before the creation by Queen Victoria of a dean and chapter for St Albans in 1900. Walter Lawrance, rector since 1868, was appointed the first dean.

Sir Edmund Beckett[186]

In 1877 a faculty was granted to an executive committee of restoration, authorising them 'to restore, repair and refit the Abbey Church as a Cathedral.' The committee comprised the Earl of Verulam, Sir Edmund Beckett, the Venerable Anthony Grant, Archdeacon of Rochester and St Albans, Walter Lawrance, Rector of St Albans, Owen Davys, Rector of Wheathampstead, the three churchwardens and three prominent citizens of St Albans, Henry Toulmin, John Evans and Robert Pryor. Sir Gilbert Scott was still retained as the architect, but the only restoration activity current was the preparation for the stabilisation of the south wall of the nave, which was accomplished a few months after Sir Gilbert's death in 1878, under the direction of his son J. Oldrid Scott.

Beckett had been loosely involved with St Albans Abbey since 1856, when he was invited to the second public meeting called by the Earl of Verulam to re-launch the Restoration Committee. It was Beckett, at that time known as Mr E. B. Denison, who called for Gilbert Scott to be appointed the architect. As the best known and most respected ecclesiastical architect in the country, he was the obvious choice but it is interesting to note that Scott was acquainted with Denison through their collaboration in the reconstruction of Doncaster parish church after its destruction by fire in 1853. It was this project that fired Denison's interest in Gothic architecture to the extent that he was responsible for the design of the new east window at Doncaster, regarding himself as an amateur architect, not shy of giving Scott a few architectural tips: he clearly was not over-burdened by self-doubt.

---

[186] Peter Ferriday: *Lord Grimthorpe 1816–1905*.

However, at this time Denison's wide and varied interests – his own highly successful career as a barrister and his interference as an amateur horologist in the design of Big Ben (the bell) and its associated clock – prevented his close involvement in the restoration of St Albans Abbey. But at some stage, probably around 1874 when he succeeded to his uncle's baronetcy, Sir Edmund Beckett, as he now was, bought the estate of Batch Wood just to the north of St Albans where he built himself a mansion, the better to keep an eye on restoration progress. Although not a member of the Restoration Committee, he is on record as becoming closely involved with the restoration of the presbytery vault and yet more temporary shoring of the south nave wall[187].

The great roof debate

Once the lean of the south nave wall had finally been corrected and stabilised, the Restoration Committee turned its attention to the nave roof. Scott, in his 1871 report to the Earl of Verulam[188], referred to the architectural changes made in the fifteenth century – flat roofs and large perpendicular windows – as 'a deterioration of design arising from a decay in taste and artistic sentiment. Nothing could tend more than these alterations to the reduction of the dignity of the external aspect of the building... unfortunately the correction of this defect seems so formidable that one scarcely feels the courage to propose it'. Shortly before his death he had considered the fifteenth-century roof structure to be restorable, once the walls were secure, although Beckett claimed that Scott never made a proper inspection. After his death the committee began to consider rebuilding the nave roof at a steeper pitch (more impressive in the eyes of Gothic revivalists). The question of roof pitch developed into an almost national debate encompassing a spectrum of opinion. To paraphrase Gilbert Scott[189]: on one extreme, the anti-restorers, led by Ruskin and William Morris claiming for ancient buildings 'so intense a veneration as to almost forbid anything approaching reparation'; on the other, the utilitarians, led by Beckett, who considered it justifiable to make such alterations as 'deemed necessary to suit buildings to contemporary "convenience and even taste".' Scott was a conservator occupying the middle ground. The debate was acrimonious and bad tempered, conducted through the correspondence pages of the *Times*

---

[187] Chapple: *The Restoration of St Albans Abbey, 1874.*
[188] Sir Gilbert Scott: *Report to the Earl of Verulam, 1871.*
[189] Sir Gilbert Scott: *Recollections.*

between Beckett, an ardent high roofian and Archdeacon Grant, the Society for the Protection of Ancient Buildings and the Society of Antiquaries opposing. Beckett did not pull his punches: 'I should like to know what the Society of Antiquaries, even if they were unanimous, have to do with the matter. We are not spending their money, but our own, in restoring our own church to as much of the ancient beauty of its best days (ie medieval) as we can.' Even *Punch* magazine weighed in: 'surely it would be possible to conduct the controversy between high pitch and low pitch roof at St Albans without getting into such a high pitch of temper and a low pitch of courtesy; in short without such a flinging of pitch by the advocates of either style of roof at those of the other.'[190] The Restoration Committee was divided with Lord Verulam and Archdeacon Grant opposing: nevertheless the proposal was passed by a majority of a single vote. The question was further confused by the fact that both parties could claim to be 'restorers' – originally the roofs of the entire abbey, including the nave, had been pitched as can be seen in pre-Victorian engravings of the abbey. In the event the pitch of the raised roof was steeper than that of the medieval abbey, on the Gothic Revival tendency that associated steepness with holiness: certainly Beckett associated the fifteenth-century flat roof with the 'depravity of the monks before the fall'[191].

A meeting was convened in August 1878 of all those who had pledged more than £100 to the restoration fund at which Beckett moved a resolution, 'That the roof of the nave having become ruinous it is desirable to retore it to its original pitch indicated on the tower keeping as much of the pointed and panelled ceiling as may be in sound condition, restoring the rest in a similar style'. This motion, which was carried, was disingenuous at best: Scott had considered the flat roof restorable and the roof was not restored to its original pitch, but considerably steeper. Nevertheless the committee signed a contract for the replacement of the flat roof with a new lead-covered pitched roof, despite the fact that they had no funds. The bad-tempered wrangling continued unabated, but despite a desperate rear-guard action mounted by the antiquaries, which involved JS Neale making an accurate survey of the marks of the original roof line on the tower, the go-ahead for the new roof was given to the builders in December 1878.

---

[190] Charles Jones: *Restoration of the Abbey*.
[191] Peter Ferriday: *Lord Grimthorpe*.

Detail from Jan Lievon's seventeenth century drawing of the abbey tower showing the marks made on the tower by the medieval roof.

The as-built roof pitch was as steep as it could be without impinging on the tower's lantern windows. As envisaged by the Society of Antiquaries, the high roof robbed the tower of a certain dignity and would require a modification of the west front.

The abbey church before (above) and after (opposite) the raising of the nave roof. The western end of new steep pitched roof terminates in a temporary gable that clearly requires modifications to the perpendicular style west front. (Courtesy of St Albans Cathedral.)

The Beckett faculty

The completion of the new roof left the Restoration Committee some £4,000 in debt with a great deal of work still to be done: the west front of the nave, the north and south transepts and the presbytery. Beckett offered to pay, as a committee member, his share of the debt, which would have obliged his fellows to follow suit, which of course they couldn't afford to do. He had, effectively, ran the committee into debt[192]. Alternatively, he intimated he would pay the entire debt if he were given total freedom by a new faculty to complete the restoration at his own expense and to his own design. This was a lifeline that most committee members grasped with great relief – most, but not all: Archdeacon Grant, the rector, Walter Lawrance (Grant's son-in-law) and his churchwardens were not at all happy with the total loss of control that this offer implied. Bishop Claughton then put his rector in a difficult position by suggesting to the committee that the existing rectory did not provide enough space for the rector's study and necessary hospitality: Beckett promptly offered to pay for a new rectory[193]. In the event, only Archdeacon Grant, Earl Cowper and John Evans formally objected to the chancellor of the diocese despite a warning given by John Chapple, who had a shrewd grasp of Beckett's character, that objection was futile because of 'Beckett's untiring energy, subtle knowledge of the ins and outs of law, backed by the power of capital.' Moreover, Bishop Claughton

---

[192] Peter Ferriday: *Lord Grimthorpe*, p. 108.
[193] Gillian Harvey: *Lord Grimthorpe and Other Dragons: The Career of Walter Lawrance*.

supported Beckett's faculty: 'the Abbey will never be finished in my lifetime or any of my successors unless we avail ourselves of the offer, of that I am positive.' A town meeting, organised by the mayor, John Chapple, voted overwhelmingly to support the faculty, which was subsequently granted (1880), containing the key words:

> 'We, as Bishop of St Albans do give and grant the said Sir Edmund Beckett our leave, license and faculty to restore, repair and refit the said Cathedral': no ecclesiastical oversight, no committee control, a totally free hand for Beckett.

The west front

The first contentious work carried out under the new faculty was a new west front, contentious in that repair and modification with the retention of the magnificent Wheathampstead window would have been the least cost and most conservation-minded solution. However, once the scaffolding was erected Beckett declared that the window was beyond repair and that an entirely new west front was required. (It should be noted that Beckett, a low churchman, loathed the perpendicular style, which he associated with ecclesiastical depravity.) Three designs were prepared for the bishop's consideration and, not without an element of skulduggery on Beckett's part, the bishop selected Beckett's[194]. This elicited much local opposition, particularly from the rector, Walter Lawrance. In a letter to the bishop he said, 'to destroy the west window will be the first time in the work that has been carried out throughout our restoration work of retaining all that was architecturally valuable.' Beckett appointed John Chapple, who had previously been in Scott's employment, as his clerk of works. Chapple was probably Beckett's equal when it came to stubbornness and force of character, which may explain why they worked well together.

Predictably, the new west front was met by hostility from the architectural press, which Beckett assigned to sour grapes on the part of the architectural establishment, Royal Institute of British Architects, as it had been designed by an amateur. The *Builder* magazine's thorough review concluded with: 'The general look of the whole front may, perhaps, be indicated by saying that it is very much the sort of Gothic which one sometimes meets with in competition designs for the larger class of Dissenting Chapels – effective, in a showy way, but totally devoid of

---

[194] Eileen Roberts: *The Hill of the Martyr*, p. 216.

refinement'[195]. A critique of its architecture is also given by Eileen Roberts, who comments that it looks 'machine-made and mass produced'[196].

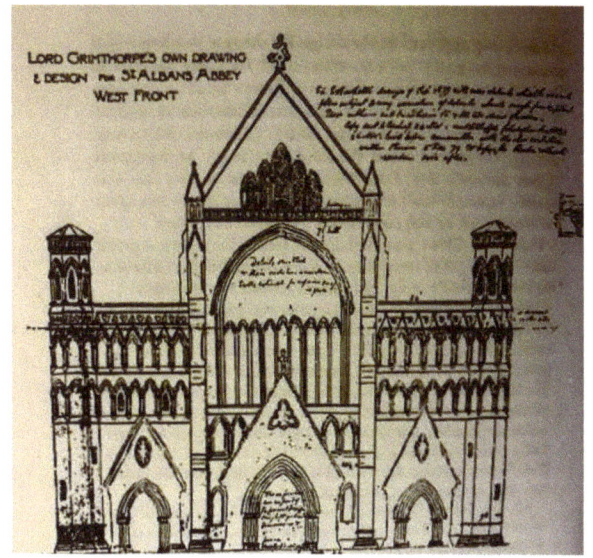

Beckett's sketch for the new west front of St Albans Abbey, which at least incorporated the triple thirteenth century porches[197]. The details would have been worked up by John Chapple, the clerk of works.

Beckett's west front as realised by John Chapple, 1880.

---

[195] Peter Ferriday: *Lord Grimthorpe*, p. 135.
[196] Eileen Roberts: *The Hill of the Martyr*, p. 218.
[197] Peter Ferriday: *Lord Grimthorpe*.

In 1885, once other work inside the nave was completed – the reconstruction of the north-west wall that had been built after the demolition of St Andrew's Chapel, the insertion of windows in the south-west wall where once the abbots lodging had abutted the nave, and the reconstruction of the decorated nave piers, which showed signs of distress. The nave was reopened with a magnificent service attended by the ecclesiastical and lay great and good.

The transepts

Beckett now turned his attention to the transepts, where he replaced the low-pitched roofs with a high pitch to match that of the nave. He found the west wall of the south transept to be so rotten that he refaced the lower stage, destroying the remnants of the arcading of the former cloister (similar to that which is still visible on the south wall of the nave.) The fronts of both north and south transepts comprised large perpendicular windows of similar design flanked by octagonal turrets and Becket, driven

The south transept windows before and after restoration. Drawings by Steinmetz. (By courtesy of St Albans Cathedral.)

by his distaste for perpendicular, resolved to replace both with windows of his own design. For the south transept he chose a design based on Early English lancet windows, inspired by the Five Sisters window at York (where he was the chancellor and vicar general) supported by 'Norman' turrets.

For the north transept he opted for an oversized circular window, but retained the pair of Norman windows at the bottom stage. Again the perpendicular octagonal turrets were replaced with Victorian Norman square turrets.

The north transept windows before and after restoration. Drawings by Steinmetz. (By courtesy of St Albans Cathedral.)

By now the architectural establishment had grown bored with criticising Beckett's architecture, although Ferriday, in his biography of Lord Grimthorpe, concludes that of all his works 'the worst feature is generally agreed to be the north transept wheel window'. But north or south windows, it's a close-run thing. Eileen Roberts provides a critique of the transept design, which she dismisses as 'another lapse of taste and judgement'.[198]

Sir Edmund Beckett had spent some £150,000 of his own money in the restoration of the abbey and its conversion to a cathedral. For this he was ennobled in 1886, choosing the not-inappropriate title of Lord Grimthorpe. In their report of this, the *Times* described Lord Grimthorpe as a banker and an authority on ecclesiastical architecture. The first epithet was refuted by Grimthorpe himself while the second drew a vitriolic response from the *Builder*: 'Sir Edmund Beckett is not and never was an authority on ecclesiastical architecture. No person who does understand the subject would care a button for his opinion on it. His reputation in this respect rests solely upon the fact that he writes letters to the *Times* asserting that he is an authority, and that a number of dunces are silly enough to believe him'[199].

But Denison/Beckett/Grimthorpe was not done yet: the presbytery roof had to be rebuilt at a steeper pitch so that the ridge level of each of the four arms of the church were consistent. In the course of this work he could not resist inserting tracery into the Early English lancet clerestory windows (appropriately described as 'chaste' by Eileen Roberts), introducing a triangular window into the new gable end and restoring, with a heavy hand, the east presbytery window[200]. But his powers and energy were beginning to wane and the cathedral authorities had begun to weary of the freedom his faculty gave him. His old adversary Archdeacon Blomfield (whom he had previously described as a blockhead) had been created the Suffragan Bishop of Colchester and increasingly took over some of Bishop Claughton's duties in the latter's declining years. Furthermore, another source of wealth emerged, one Henry Hucks Gibbs, later Lord Aldenham. After a career in banking, Gibbs had been a governor of the Bank of England and in retirement worked with Blomfield on the restoration of the high altar screen, which had been deprived of its statuary in the Dissolution. This was carried out at Gibbs' expense under the Beckett faculty, initially with Beckett's agreement. However, a row broke out over the sculpture of Christ on the cross[201]: as a low churchman Beckett was bitterly opposed but eventually lost the argument, but not before a bad-tempered

---

[198] Eileen Roberts: *The Hill of the Martyr*.
[199] Quoted in Peter Ferriday: *Lord Grimthorpe 1816–1905*.
[200] Eileen Roberts: *The Hill of the Martyr*, p. 226.
[201] Sir Nikolaus Pevsner described the sculpture as 'hideously ungenuine'.

correspondence between the two from which Grimthorpe emerged with little credit.

The final works carried out under the Beckett faculty were the modifications to the lady chapel, which included the replacement of the wooden roof vault with one in stone and the provision of blind arcading at the base of the chapel walls.

Grimthorpe retained his loathing of architects, antiquaries, high churchmen and committees until his death in 1905. In his final illness he ordered H Toulmin, the secretary of the Restoration Committee, to burn the committee minutes, accounts and correspondence[202] – an example of his control-freakery.

Conclusion

By the mid-1890s the restoration of the abbey and its conversion to a cathedral was substantially complete. It had taken sixty years since serious work had started, soon after the collapse of a portion of the south wall of the nave in 1832. It had proved a hard and difficult slog, always critically short of money until EB Denison took an active interest, whereupon it became even more difficult. The similarities and contrasts of Scott and Beckett were extraordinary: Beckett – vituperative, arrogant, supremely self-confident and bursting with energy; Scott, a self-made man of integrity, of amiable disposition and widely respected. They both agreed that the alterations made to the abbey in the fifteenth century were regrettable and both wanted to reverse them, but Scott, by this time an old man of seventy-six, lacked the resolve to press for a reversal, being perhaps conditioned by a career of restoring cathedrals with insufficient funds. If only they had been able to cooperate the outcome would have been cheaper and aesthetically vastly superior. But cooperation was impossible: they were just too incompatible. Beckett loathed architects, although grudgingly acknowledged that Scott was the least bad, but even so 'not a man of much genius with a sadly defective eye for proportion, a poor mechanic and often intolerably careless'.[203] For his part Scott referred to him on occasions as his friend, and once as his tormentor. His praise of Beckett was decidedly faint: 'were it not that he has an unpleasant way of doing things I should have far more reason to thank him than to complain.'[204]

---

[202] St Albans Cathedral Archives Fabric I (6).
[203] Grimthorpe: *St Albans Cathedral and Its Restoration*.
[204] Gilbert Scott: *Personal and Professional Recollections*.

The men who saved the abbey and created a cathedral: clockwise from top left
- *Rector Dr Nicholson: passionate conservator who initiated serious restoration.*
- *Sir Gilbert Scott: engineer/architect who saved the abbey from collapse.*
- *Sir Edmund Beckett, aka Lord Grimthorpe: lawyer and amateur architect whose pugnacity and wealth ensured the expeditious completion of the restoration and creation of the cathedral.*
- *Bishop Claughton, first Bishop of St Albans – determined that St Albans should be a cathedral.*
- *2nd Earl of Verulam: who with his father chaired the Restoration Committee with patience and fortitude from 1833 to 1895.*
- *John Chapple: clerk of works from 1874 to 1887, mayor of St Albans from 1879.*

Timeline of relevant events: part three

Year	Event	Monarch
1547	Imposition of Cranmer's Homilies	Edward VI
1549	Richard Boreman buys lady chapel for use as a school	
1553	Mary returned England to Roman Catholicism	Mary I
1553	St Albans receives charter and purchases abbey for £400	
1558	The Elizabethan Settlement	Elizabeth I
1596	Brief to raise funds for repairs authorised by Elizabeth I	
1611	Authorised Version of the Bible translated	
1612	King James visits St Albans Abbey	James I
1613	£2,000 raised from a brief authorised by James I for repairs	
1642	Outbreak of civil war	Charles I
1648	Execution of Charles I: Church of England suspended	Protectorate
1662	Restoration of the monarchy – reintroduction of the BCP	Charles II
1681	Brief to raise funds for repairs authorised by Charles II	
1697	Celia Fiennes visit	James II
1705	Great Storm destroyed the south transept window	Anne I
1725	Brief to raise funds for repairs authorised by George I	George I
1764	Brief to raise funds for repairs authorised by George III	
1797	Severe rainstorm flooded the abbey	
1818	Church Building Commission set up to build new churches etc. restore	George III
1818	Lewis Wyatt inspection of the abbey	
1832	Collapse of the western end of the south wall of the nave	
1832	LN Cottingham surveys the abbey: estimates £14,000 repair costs	George IV
1832	First public meeting called by 1st Earl of Verulam to organise repairs	
1834	Repairs completed – abbey reopened	William IV
1835	Rev Dr Nicholson appointed rector – restoration continued	

1856	Second public meeting – Gilbert Scott appointed architect	
1870	Stabilisation of the tower	
1871	Evacuation of lady chapel by St Albans School	
1872	Shrine of St Alban re-created from fragments of the original	
1877	Creation of the diocese of St Albans – Bishop Claughton enthroned	
1877	Gilbert Scott dies, south-west wall of nave stabilised	Victoria
1878	Nave re-roofed	
1880	Sir Edmund Beckett given faculty to complete restoration	
1880	West front rebuilt to Beckett's design	
????	North and south transept fronts rebuilt to Beckett's design	
????	Restoration of the presbytery and the great screen	
1900	Foundation of the dean and chapter	

Epilogue

At the turn of the century, the main objective of the Victorian era – the creation of the St Albans diocese and the conversion of the old, semi-ruined abbey to a structurally secure cathedral – had been substantially achieved. There were, however, several loose ends: principally the lack of a dean and chapter and the manifestly unsatisfactory diocesan boundaries. The first was corrected by Queen Victoria who, on 26 February 1900, 'has been pleased by Letters Patent under the Great Seal, to found and constitute a Dean and Chapter of the Cathedral Church of Saint Albans'. The rector, Walter Lawrance, was installed as the first dean. The second loose end was resolved by the establishment of a new diocese of Chelmsford and the transfer of the ancient archdeaconry of Bedford from the diocese of Ely to St Albans in 1914, resulting in a geographically more coherent diocese. Of course there remained a great deal to be done, including new choir stalls and the construction of the bishop's throne: these and many other restoration works and improvements continue up to the present day.

It is difficult to overstate the importance of what St Alban means for the city and the county. Just as for the other eleven cathedrals created in the nineteenth century, the 'promotion' of a parish church to cathedral status was a source of great civic pride. But St Albans is fundamentally different from the others in that it is the only English city to be named after its saint: the martyrdom of Alban was the sole reason for the town's existence. It originated as a small settlement that grew up to service the Saxon monastery, which was itself built on or adjacent to the traditional site of Alban's martyrdom, just to the north of the Roman *municipium* of Verulamium. The community that became the city has been familiar and identified with their saint for some 1750 years. This familiarity may have turned into bewilderment when, in 1077, their new masters the Normans replaced their inevitably rather homely abbey with such an enormous new monastery, not perhaps being aware of the fame and prestige of St Alban in continental Europe. As the monastery prospered, bewilderment changed to pride and then to frustration as the freedoms enjoyed by other towns were denied to them. But this was forgotten when 'their' abbey came under attack in the Dissolution – a loyalty which transmuted to pride when they were able to buy the abbey as their parish church. At a stroke they found themselves, as a newly chartered borough, owners of the largest parish church in England. With this ownership, of course, came the responsibility of maintenance and conservation of a building whose roof area could, as remarked by Gilbert Scott, be measured in acres, rather than square feet. Inevitably, despite their best efforts, the condition of their church deteriorated to the point where it faced ruination by the early nineteenth century. But again, it was through the sustained efforts of the town, led by the heroes described in the previous chapter, the abbey was rescued and modified for use as a cathedral, with St Albans achieving city status – another source of great pride.

This singular history has resonance in national and ecclesiastical terms. The Saxon abbey was one of the last to be founded, Hertfordshire being situated in no-man's-land – and thus ignored – at the meeting point of its mighty neighbours, Mercia, Wessex, Essex and London. It was only through King Offa's hero-worship of Charlemagne that he came to grasp the veneration in which St Alban was held in the Holy Roman Empire, which led him to emulate his hero by founding the monastery – for geopolitical reasons as well as ecclesiastical. The Normans too, for different reasons, held St Alban in the highest regard – he predated the Anglo-Saxons whom they despised – creating what became the premier monastery in England.

Although it is full of beauty, St Albans does not compare aesthetically with some cathedrals of a more ancient pedigree – Wells, or Ely, for example. However, in terms of the power conferred by the extraordinary – and unequalled – continuity of veneration that it has witnessed, St Albans is in a league of its own. The rough, crude architecture of the Norman abbey is built of bricks salvaged from Verulamium – quite possibly including the very bricks from Alban's house. This provides a tangible as well as an emotional symbol of continuity of veneration of Alban from the last century of the Roman occupation, when the veneration was accessible to the Celtic British, through the post-imperial chaos, to be embraced by the Saxon inheritors of Verulamium. The thread of continuity can then be traced from the martyrium visited by Germanus in the fifth century, to the 'church of wonderful workmanship' mentioned by Bede in his *Ecclesiastical History*, to Offa's monastery (re-founded by both Archbishop Dunstan in the tenth century and then by Archbishop Lanfranc in the eleventh). The veneration of St Alban then survived the

Dissolution, the turmoil of the sixteenth and seventeenth centuries, the neglect of the long eighteenth century and the energy and zeal of the Victorians. It draws additional strength by virtue of being a parish church as well as a cathedral, and there can be little doubt that it will also survive the materialism and cultural wars of the modern era, as long as Christianity itself survives in these islands.

Index

A
Abingdon, 129
Abbots of St Albans (*in date order*)
  Willegod 69
  Wulsig 69, 70
  Wulnorth 69
  Eadfrith 70
  Wulsin or Ulsinus 70, 128, 155
  Alfric 70
  Ealdred 70, 77
  Alfric II 71, 72, 75
  Leofric 71, 75
  Frederick 80, 81
  Paul de Caen 82, 84,
  Richard d'Essai, 133, 134
  Geoffrey de Gorham, 133, 136, 148, 150
  Robert de Gorham 120,
  Simon, 140
  Warin, 140, 156
  John de Cella 108, 140, 143
  William de Trumpington 97, 140, 151
  John de Hertford, 140, 146
  Roger de Norton 128, 146
  John de Maryns 163
  Hugh de Eversden 127, 129, 130, 146
  Richard of Wallingford 109, 119, 123, 127, 130, 156, 158-16
  Michael de Mentmore 109,
  Thomas de la Mare 109, 111, 119, 131, 141, 148, 149, 156, 1
  John of Wheathampstead 110, 111, 148, 149, 154, 157, 163, 164, 172, 175
  William Albon 172
  William of Wallingford 148, 150, 172, 173, 174, 204
  Thomas Ramridge, 148, 175
  Thomas Wolsey 175
  Robert Catton 175
  Richard Boreman 179, 185, 187, 190
Acts of Parliament
  Supremacy 171, 188, 180
  Tolerance 196
  Uniformity 187, 188
  Churches Building 207
  Municipal Corporations 209
  Bishopric of St Albans 217
Adam the Cellarer, *monk* 69, 140
Aethelbehrt, *Kentish king* 53, 56, 59
Aethelberht, *king of East Anglia* 68
Aethelwold, abbot of Abingdon 70, 71
Aidan 57
Alban
Albanstowe 121,
Albrecht of Brandenburg 169
Alcuin 68
Alderman, *Lord philanthropist* 228
Ambrose, bishop of Milan 22, 42
Ambrosius Aurelianus, *British general* 42
Amphibalus, British priest 27, 38, 39, 151, 152
Amundesham, chronicler, 137
Anglicans 197
Antekil, *monk & metal worker*, 148

236

INDEX

Aquinas, 157
Archbishops of Canterbury (*in date order*)
  Augustine 54, 55, 56, 58
  Mellitus (*also bishop of London*) 56, 58
  Theodore 58
  Jaenbehrt 64
  Dunstan 70, 71
  Aelfric 71
  Stigand 80, 81
  Lanfranc 79, 80, 82, 155
  Thomas Becket 124
  Peckham 106,
  Morton 172, 173, 175, 180
  Cranmer 171, 187, 189, 190, 195
  Pole 189
  Laud 192
  Sumner 211, 216
Aristotle, 157
Army Deed of Remonstrance 193
Arthur *British king* 42, 46
Authorised Version 191

B

Ball, John *radical preacher* 131
Bannockburn, *battle of,* 128
Battle of Badon Hill 47, 49
Beckett, Thomas, *aka* Denison & Grimthorpe 137, 212, 214, 219, 223, 224, 225, 227, 228, 229
Bede 33, 38, 50, 53, 55, 63, 66, 72, 75
Bedcanford *battle of* 47
Beowulf 50, 51
Benedictine Rule, monasteries etc 60, 66, 67, 70, 71, 82, 104, 105, 119, 122, 160, 172, 174, 180
Bertha, Kentish Queen 53,
Biddle, *archaeologist* 73, 77
Birinus, *bishop of Dorchester* 57
Black Death 95, 101, 111, 131
Blomfield, Charles, *bishop of London* 208, 210
Blomfield, Arthur, *bishop of Colchester* 218

Boke of Seynt Albans, 142
Boleyn, Anne queen 171
Boniface, *English missionary* 61
Book of Benefactors, 141
Book of Common Prayer 187, 190, 195
Boudicca 10,
Bradwardine, *theologian*, 159
Breakspear (*see Pope Adrian IV*)
Briefs 203
  Elizabeth I 191
  James I 192
  Charles II 203
  George I 203, 204
  George III 203, 205
Bunyan, *writer* 193
Bury St Edmunds, 129

C

Caen 81
Caesar Constantius 19
Calvinists 193
Cambridge 104,
Camulodunum (*Colchester*) 6, 9, 10
Carpenter, David, *historian* 102
Cassivellaunus 5, 8,
Cathedral and Collegiate Churches Commission 211
Catherine 170
Catholic 197
Catuvellauni 8, 9, 10, 48
Cedd, *bishop of Essex* 57
Ceowulf, *bishop of Lindsey* 65
Chanson de St Alexis, 135
Chapel Royal 164, 165
Chapple, John, *clerk of works*, 213, 223, 224
Charlemagne, *Holy Roman Emperor*, 64, 67
Charles V, *Holy Roman Emperor,* 170, 171, 186, 188
Chaucer, Geoffrey 168
Churches Building Commission 207
Christina of Markyate, 132, 133, 136

237

Chronica Majora, 139, 140
Chronicon Angliae, 140
Claughton.Thomas, *1st bishop of St Albans* 216, 217, 223, 228, 228
Clark, James, *historian* 185
Cole, John, *archdeacon and philanthropist* 204
Columbanus 54
Constantin III
Constantius 23, 25, 44
Council of:
  Arles 19, 57
  Rimini 19
  Constantinople 22,
  Westminster
Conferences
  Hampton Court 191
  Savoy 195
Conventicle Act 195
Cottingham, *architect* 207, 208
Court of Augmentation 184, 185
Cromwell, Oliver, *Lord Protector* 193
Cromwell, Thomas 171, 175, 177, 178, 185
Cunobelin 8

D
Declaration of Breda 194
Domesday Book, 129
Donation of Constantine 98,
Diocese of
  Lincoln 210
  London 199, 211
  Rochester 211,
  Winchester 210
Dissolution 111, 177, 179, 185, 202
Diuma, 1st bishop of Mercia
Dugdale, Sir William, *antiquarian* 201
Dunstaple, *composer* 163, 164, 173

E
Earl of Verulam (1st) 208
Earl of Verulam (2nd) 211
Edict of Milan 19

Edwin, *king of Northumberland* 56
Egbert *Kentish king* 64
Elizabethan Settlement 190, 193, 196
English monarchs
  Offa 60, 64, 65, 68, 76, 120
  Alfred 69
  Aethelred 67, 71, 72
  Edward the Confessor 81
  Harold 81,
  William I 79, 80
  Stephen/Matilda 96
  Henry II 86, 96, 102, 128
  Richard I 96, 123, 145
  John 96, 99138, 145, 166
  Henry III 96, 129, 138, 146, 158
  Edward I 102, 167
  Edward II
  Edward III 109, 167
  Richard II, 140
  Henry IV, 140, 162
  Henry V, 140
  Henry VI 97, 174
  Henry V 140
  Henry VI 97, 174
  Henry VIII 95, 167, 170, 171, 184, 186
  Edward VI 187, 190
  Mary 188, 189
  Elizabeth I 190
  James I 191, 196
  Charles I 193
  Charles II 194
  James II 195
  William and Mary 196, 204
Erasmus 174, 180
Ethelburga, *Edwin's wife* 56

F
Fairfax, army general 193
Fayrfax, Robert, composer 165, 173
First Suppression Act 177
Flambard, Bishop of Durham, 133
Flowers of History, 137, 139

INDEX

Fortunatus 61, 71
Fugger, *Jakob, financier* 169

G
Gape, Henry, 185
Gerbert of Aurillac 103
Germanus, *Bishop of Auxerre* 20, 23, 24, 25, 26, 28, 30, 37 40, 48, 50, 60, 61, 72
Gesta Abbatum, 138, 140, 147
Gibbon, Edward *historian* 44
Gildas, *British monk/chronicler* 31, 32, 36, 38, 39, 42, 44, 45, 53, 53
Girtin, Thomas, artist 202
Gloucester College, 140, 156, 157
Gorhambury 184, 190
Grand Remonstrance 193
Great Famine 101,
Great Schism 166, 168, 170
Great Storm 204
Grimstone, Sir Harbottle, *philanthropist* 204
Grindcobbe, William, *rebel leader* 131

H
Haggar, Mark *historian* 81
Hawkesmoor, Nicholas, *architect* 201
Helena, *mother of Constantine*, 19
Hengist 47
Heptarchy 47, 52
Hildeheim, 136
Humphrey, *Duke of Gloucester* 121, 148, 164, 172
Hus, Jan, *theologian* 168
Hygebehrt, *1st Archbishop of Lichfield* 65

I
Iron Age 3, 13
Isabella, *wife of Edward II,* 128, 129

J
Julius Caesar 5, 8,

Julyan Barnes, *Prioress of Sopwell*

K
King, Thomas *chaplain* 180, 184

L
Lambert, *army general* 194
Langland, *poet* 168, 179
Lateran Council, 4th 106,
Lawrance, Walter, *1st dean of St Albans* 219, 223
Layton, Sir Richard, *commissioner* 177
Lee, Sir Richard, *surveyor* 179, 185, 186
Leigh, Dr Thomas, *commissioner* 177, 178
Levison, Wilhelm, *historian* 21, 28, 73, 75
Lievens, Jan, *artist* 200
Lindisfarne 57
Lollards, Lollardism 167, 168, 180
Louis, French Dauphin 96,
Lupus, Bishop of Troyes 23, 24, 25, 60, 61
Luther, Lutherism 169, 170, 180

M
Magna Carta 96, 130, 166
Mainz 61
Matilda *wife of William I* 79,
Matthew Paris, *monk/chronicler* 66, 69, 137-140, 145, 158, 162
Meyer, *Wilhelm historian* 28,
Mercia 52, 53, 56, 64
Mellitus, *1st bishop of London* 56, 58
Merton Calculators, 159
Methodism & Methodists 198, 206
Monck, *army general* 194
More, Sir Thomas 171
Morris, Dr John 18
Mortimer, Roger, 128

N
Neckham, Alexander, *scholar,* 158, 160

239

Newcombe, Peter *18th century historian* 65
Nicholson, Dr Henry, *rector* 209, 210, 213
Nonconformists 195, 196, 197, 206

O
Old Hall music manuscript, 163, 164
Oosthuizen, *Susan historian* 44
Origen 15, 20
Oswald, King of Northumberland 57
Oswius, *Oswald's brother* 57
Oxford 104,
Oysterfield 13

P
Papal revolution 100, 107, 166
Paris, Matthew, *monk & chronicler* 66, 69, 108, 120, 137-140, 145, 155, 158, 163
Paulinus Ist bishop of York 56, 58
Passio Albani 26, 28, 31, 50
Parliament
Peada, son of Penda
Peasants Revolt 97, 109, 110, 130, 168
Pelagius, Pelagianism 20, 22, 23, 24, 25, 26, 37, 42
Penda, King of Mercia 56
Pepys, Samuel, *diarist* 194
Petre, William, *commissioner* 178
Phillip, *king of Spain* 188
Pilgrimage of Grace 177
Pole, Cardinal 188, 189
Popes (*in date order*)
  Fabian 15
  Sylvester I 98
  Celestine 23
  Gregory I 54, 56, 58
  Hadrian 64, 65
  Leo III 65
  Sylvester II, 157
  Leo IX 98
  Alexander II 80
  Gregory VII 98

  nnocent III 99, 127, 138, 166
  Honorius III 127
  Gregory IX 127
  Adrian IV 108, 120
  Nicolas IV 123
  Boniface VIII 99
  Innocent IV 108
  John XXII 119,
  Benedict VII 12
  Boniface IX 119
  Nicolas V 169
  nnocent VIII 173
  Alexander VI 169
  Leo X 169, 170
  Clement VII 170
  Paul IV 189
  Alexander VII 100,
Power, Leonel, *composer* 164
Procopius, historian 47
Protectorate 203
Pilgrim Fathers 192
Presbyterians 193, 194

R
Reformation 95, 170
Reparation/ Restoration Committee 212, 216, 220, 223
Robert the Mason 84
Roberts, *Eileen historian* 27, 77, 152, 225
Roger Wendover, *chronicler* 137
Roger the hermit, 133
Roman Emperors:
  Claudius 8, 9,
  Nero 16
  Severus 15, 16, 17, 21
  Decius/Valerian 18, 21
  Diocletian 15, 18, 19, 21, 31
  Constantine 19,
  Constantine III 41
  Honorius 42
  Martin V 169
  Nicholas V 169
  Leo X 169

Rowlatt, Ralph 184

S
Severus, bishop of Trier 25
SAHAAS 209
St Albans Abbey – daughter houses 112, 113,
  Wallingford 113,
  Belvoir 113
  Binham 116,
  Hatfield 117
  Hertford 117, 130
  Markyate 118, 134
  Pembroke 118,
  Sopwell 118,
  Beaulieu 118,
  Tynemouth 113,
  Wymondham 117, 140
St Albans Abbey – finances 123 -127
St Albans Abbey – *relations with the town* 127-131
St Albans Archdeaconry 210
St Albans Charter 187, 189
St Albans Psalter, 132, 134, 150
St Albans School 187, 191
St Albans shrine, 148
St Albans Society *see SAHAAS*
St Alexis, 135, 136
St Oswin, 154
St William of York, 152
Salisbury, *Marchioness* 214
Salisbury, *Marquis* 216
Sarum Rite, 162
Scott GG *architect* 68, 145, 212, 214, 215, 219, 220
Stenton, FM *historian* 68
Stephens G.R. 18
Sharpe, Richard *historian* 28
Small, Henty *rector* 207
Society of Antiquaries 201, 221, 222
Stukeley, Sir William, *antiquarian* 201
Synods
  Westminster Assembly of Divines 193
  General 193

T
Tamworth 68
Tankerfield, George, 189
Tasciovanus 6, 8
Tertullian 15,
Thomas, Charles, *historian* 21, 23
Trinovantes 5,

U
Unwona, bishop of Leicester 65

V
Venantius Fortunatus, *poet & bishop* 52
Verlamion 3, 6, 9,
Verulamium 3, 11, 12, 13, 14, 15, 26, 30, 37, 47, 48, 50, 52, 60
Vitricius 20, 22, 28, 30,
Vortigern, *British King* 42

Z
Zosimus *Greek historian* 42

www.ingramcontent.com/pod-product-compliance
Lightning Source LLC
Chambersburg PA
CBHW040309170426
43195CB00020B/2904